POWER

AUTHOR

A QUICK GUIDE TO BUILDING YOUR STORY BIBLE

BEN WOLF

PUBLISHED BY

SPL/CKETY
PUBLISHING GROUP

I0130111

Power Author: A Quick Guide to Building Your Story Bible

Published by
Splickety Publishing Group, Inc.

Print ISBN: 978-1-942462-43-9
Ebook ISBN: 978-1-942462-44-6
Copyright © 2021 by Ben Wolf, Inc. All rights reserved.
www.benwolf.com

Cover design by Jenneth Dyck
jennethd1@gmail.com

Available in print and ebook format on amazon.com.
Contact Ben Wolf directly at ben@benwolf.com for signed copies and to schedule author appearances and speaking events.

All rights reserved. Non-commercial interests may reproduce portions of this book without the express written permission of the author, provided the text does not exceed 500 words. For longer quotations or commercial concerns, please contact the author via email at ben@benwolf.com.

Commercial interests: No part of this publication may be reproduced in any form, stored in a retrieval system, or transmitted in any form by any means—electronic, photocopy, recording, or otherwise—without prior written permission of the author, except as provided by the United States of America copyright law. All book links within this work are Amazon affiliate links.

This is a work of nonfiction, yet given the nature of this book and its content, some parts function as fiction. Names, characters, and incidents are all products of the author's imagination or are used for fictional purposes. Any mentioned brand names, characters, places, and trademarks remain the property of their respective owners, bear no association with the author or the publisher, and are used for fictional purposes only. Any similarities to individuals living or dead is purely coincidental.

Printed in the United States of America.

CONTENTS

INTRODUCTION

I've spent well over three years of my life playing video games.

That is, three years *continuously*; if I had sat down and played all in one shot, with neither food, sleep, bathroom, or any other kind of breaks, the total amount of time amounts to more than three years.

I wish that weren't true, but it is. In fact, that number might be low. It could be twice that much.

It might even be fair to say I'm addicted. Granted, it's a low-level addiction, but it's an addiction nonetheless.

I love the adventures video games take me on, whether it's an RPG (role-playing game), a shooter, or a fighting game. (Notice I left out racing games and sports games—I'm not as big a fan of those.)

One of the main benefits of having played so many video games, especially RPG-type games, is that they routinely inspire me in my writing. The stories and characters are colorful and unique, and they often ignite a desire within me to create something just as good, yet different.

Case in point, the inspiration for my Blood Mercenaries sword and sorcery series came from a video game called Fire Emblem—specifically, from *Fire Emblem: The Blazing Blade*, which launched in the US in 2003 for the Gameboy Advance.

Aside from the original *Oregon Trail* computer game, Fire Emblem was the first true RPG I ever played, and it immediately hooked me.

But the four protagonists in the Blood Mercenaries series aren't based on the main characters of that game. Instead, they're based on four supporting characters, all of whom are optional to play.

The Value of a Good RPG for an Author

Anyone who has ever played an RPG knows that a team of characters who all have the same weapons, skills, and abilities will usually result in catastrophic failure. As such, diversifying your team is important.

Usually, that means you've got a tank character who both deals a lot of damage and can also take a lot of damage, a DPS (damage per second) character who deals a lot of damage from somewhere behind or within range of the tank's protection, and lastly, a healer or support character who keeps everyone else alive.

A wide range of character types, classes, and available weapons to be equipped exist in and among those three basic "roles" within an RPG-type story. Even the idea that those three roles function as the "basics" is not set in stone, but the principle provides a useful framework that authors can utilize when they create characters and stories of their own.

The point is, employing different character types makes for a more interesting (and usually successful) story. When it came to *Fire Emblem: The Blazing Blade*, I loved the main characters, but a group of four supporting characters fascinated me even more.

And as I mentioned above, the Blood Mercenaries as you know them today were born out of these four characters. Aeron and Wafer are based on an eclectic wyvern knight and his mount; Kent is based on a powerful mage with a regal background; Mehta is based on an absolutely brutal assassin; and Garrick is based on a tank-type character from a distant land.

(Note that there's no healer/support character in the group. It wasn't that I specifically neglected to include one; I just never factored one into the group of mercenaries I was creating.)

How Can You Get Started?

When I first set out to write my Blood Mercenaries series, I knew it would be a huge undertaking—by far the biggest project I had ever set out to create. To date, the story bible I've developed for the continent of Aletia (the Blood Mercenaries' homeland) is the biggest story bible I've created.

The method of creating your story bible will be unique to your own preferences. Microsoft Access or other database programs have worked well for some. Some authors use spreadsheets, create separate Word documents, or tape handwritten notes to the walls of their offices.

Steven James, a bestselling author of crime/thriller novels, has a series of whiteboards surrounding him as he writes. He erases and adds and updates as he goes.

Another great option is Scrivener, a high-powered composition program designed specifically for book authors. I tried it, but I couldn't get past the tutorial. It's a dense program, and that's great if you're into that, but I prefer something simpler.

Like I said, the creation of your story bible is a process that will be unique to you in some ways. While I like the idea of a forest of white boards and organizing everything in spreadsheets, I just can't get myself to do all the setup to make it work for me instead of becoming a barrier that keeps me from easily referencing important info, recording new info, and then jumping back into my writing.

For me, it was easier to just write it all into a simple Notes file (that's Apple's name for the basic program I use). It's a no-nonsense, no-frills, easy way to write stuff down, and it got me working quickly, so that's what I used.

The focus of this book is not to tell so much *how* you should create your story bible, but rather it's a breakdown of *what* you may want to include in it. The method you choose should be something that works for you, and while I can offer suggestions (like those above), it's ultimately up to you to decide what medium you want to use to capture this crucial information.

As a bonus, you'll get to see my original outlines for each of the

Blood Mercenaries stories (four novellas and three novels) and see how wildly I strayed from them (I almost always do) along the way.

In other words, everything in this book is a sample that you can repurpose (with your own content) for the stories you want to tell.

Want a breakdown for creating characters? That's in here.

Need to build a pantheon of gods/goddesses or plan religions? I've got you covered.

Have a magic system and need to put some structure to it? Take a look at mine, and see how you can adapt yours.

It's in the pages still to come. And you can skip right to any section just by referencing the Table of Contents page to get you where you need to go.

In other words, think of this book as an examples-based story bible on how to create a story bible. (So *meta*!)

A Two-Pronged Approach

I referenced my story Blood Mercenaries bible hundreds (thousands?) of times while writing the first four books of the series, and it clocks in at somewhere around 30,000-plus words when it's laid out in Microsoft Word.

That's about the length of a mid-range novella, and I expect it'll be novel-length by the time I'm done with all ten (planned) books in the series.

But it's not the *only* story bible I've created, nor is it the only one I've included for you to review.

In the second section of this book, I'll introduce you to the sci-fi universe where I've set my Tech Ghost series. You'll get to see the little nuances between the sprawling story bible I've created for the Blood Mercenaries and the much shorter one I've created for the Tech Ghost universe. If you write in multiple genres (like me), you'll get to compare a fantasy story bible to a sci-fi story bible and make use of the various elements within at your leisure.

Prior to jumping into that, you'll get to read another brief introduction like this that discusses how it came about (it was a very different approach than the Blood Mercenaries story bible). I'm including it for the sake of highlighting several differences between the two that you as the reader (and author of your own work) can choose to utilize, ignore, or simply learn from.

Naturally, if you want to get the most out of this book, I'd recommend that you read both series so you can identify and match the individual elements I included in each universe to their respective story bibles, but even if you don't, the breakdown in this book should still provide a nice framework for you to use when creating your stories.

Get it Down, Fix it Later

One last thing: I originally wrote these story bibles and the rest of the info contained in this book by employing somewhat of a stream-of-consciousness process. As ideas came, I wrote them down and tried to organize them later.

As such, you can expect to see things that don't quite make sense, including seemingly random notes to myself, lots of asterisks and bolding to make sure I noticed those notes later on, and a bunch of other weird stuff. It's kind of raw in places, but just roll with it, okay? It won't seem super well organized at parts, but for me, just getting it onto the page was good enough for the time being.

And that really speaks to my stance on "perfecting" your story bibles: you don't have to make them perfect. You do have to make them *functional*. As long as you get the information on the page and can find it later, you're good to go.

That way, you can write uninhibited and work to perfect your actual manuscript instead. After all, the majority of your readers will want to read your finished product anyway, not your notes.

For now, though, I've prattled on long enough, and you should probably be writing (or reading).

So turn the page, dig into the examples I've laid out, and apply what you can to your own work. Happy writing!

THE BLOOD MERCENARIES STORY BIBLE

As I've already described, and as you can probably imagine, the act of writing a multi-book series is daunting.

With so many characters, character motivations, story threads, objects, locations, economies, relationships, and backstories (and more) to keep track of, I needed a singular place I could reference to see what I had already established for my story world.

Before I wrote even a single word in any of the *Blood Mercenaries Origins* novellas, I began to create this story bible to help me track everything. I already had Fire Emblem archetypes to base my four main characters on, so I started by inputting their character info into the story bible, and then I modified it to make them unique to my world and to how I envisioned my characters.

From there, it grew, and when I finished enough pre-work, I began working on the outlines for each of their stories.

Naturally, I've removed some pertinent details about my story world because I don't want to spoil future books in the series for you.

In this book, I've divided everything up into sections to make it easier for you to digest. Those sections are the following "chapters" in this part of this book. Reference them as you need to, or read through this straight. You get to decide.

I've also included lists of resources for you, plus a useful "tool" in Chapter 20 that I use all the time when writing my own books.

Please note that much of what you'll read in here is *not* how the Blood Mercenaries books ended up... including some of the synopses I've included toward the end. But I left them in there so you could see how much stories can change shape as we authors write them. It never quite goes *exactly* the way we plan.

I'm also including the full outlines (*with spoilers*) for each of the stories, complete with chapter-by-chapter summaries of what happens/what was supposed to happen. They should be instructive in helping you form your own outlines. If nothing else, I figure you'll get a kick out of reading them.

And as a final bonus, you'll get to see some of the original artwork (put together by yours truly) that served to inspire the maps and cover designs for the series. Just goes to show you how a talented artist can transform your crappy drawings into something awesome.

WANT TO DOWNLOAD A BLANK TEMPLATE OF THIS STORY BIBLE FOR FREE? VISIT WWW.BENWOLF.COM/POWER-AUTHOR TO GRAB ONE.

Side note: Learn more about character-building, plot & structure, and writing fiction here:

- *Plot and Structure,* by James Scott Bell - https://amzn.to/2XRH24D
- *Writing Fiction for Dummies,* by Randy Ingermanson - https://amzn.to/2XvCtOa
- *The Snowflake Method,* by Randy Ingermanson - https://amzn.to/2nL7sF8
- *How to Write a Dynamite Scene Using the Snowflake Method,* by Randy Ingermanson - https://amzn.to/2xymAqy
- *The Art of War for Writers,* by James Scott Bell - https://amzn.to/2S0b9kZ
- *Fight Write: How to Write Believable Fight Scenes,* by Carla Hoch - https://amzn.to/2ohyILu

STORY BIBLE PART 1: CHARACTERS

A Brief Introduction

This section includes lists of Blood Mercenaries characters, their attributes, and details about them (including their original prequel story arcs).

As you'll see, not everything remained the same in the books.

I've already mentioned how I created my main characters based on four equivalents from the 2003 Game Boy Advance title, *Fire Emblem: The Blazing Blade*. If you've played it, you may be familiar with them:

- Aeron = Heath
- Kent = Lord Pent
- Mehta = Jaffar
- Garrick = Hawkeye

And if you aren't familiar with them, then just consider that a bit of trivia.

After the main characters descriptions you'll find bite-sized details about supporting and minor characters throughout the whole series.

There's just enough info there to remind me of what I need to know about each of them.

As with all of this book, you can add or subtract content as you see fit. Just make sure you include enough that you don't have to go searching through your book later on to find missing information.

Characters

Aeron Ironglade - Wyvern Rider/Scout

(Wyvern is named Wafer)

• Weapon Proficiencies: Usually uses spears/lances, also a pretty good shot with a crossbow while in the air

• Armor: Lightweight armor useful for defense against some physical attacks and some magic attacks

• Personality Type: easygoing (stoner), chip-on-his-shoulder, and well-prepared, introverted (Aaron Rodgers)

• Age: 32 (just past his prime, but only barely)

• H/W: 5' 11"/175lbs

• Appearance: brown hair, ?green? eyes, white skin

• Weaknesses: he has a bond with Wafer, his Wyvern. If they're separated, they don't function as well in tandem, but together they can anticipate each others' actions and perform incredible things much more easily. Also, he has recurring back pain that can be pretty severe if he doesn't take his magic mushrooms. He also gets a tingling numbness in the fingertips on his right hand from the back injury.

• Backstory:

○ The story he tells is that he abandoned a wyvern army for a neighboring kingdom because he didn't get along with one of the captains and because the war finally came to an end, but really, he got kicked out for being kind of lazy and for doing too many magical mushrooms.

○ He grew up as a blacksmith's kid, so he knows his way around a forge but is by no means a master. The irony is, he has put so many horseshoes on horses that he intentionally got into flying on a wyvern instead because he was so sick of horses.

○ He was conscripted into the country's army at age 16 right as a war was starting. His horse-riding skills got him into the wyvern ranks, and he was trained to ride wyverns, etc. He personally chose and hatched Wafer's egg and grew him from a hatchling to a full-grown wyvern. Bonded with him, etc.

○ During the war (which lasted 16 years), Aeron won some, lost some, etc. Toward the end, he injured his back, and while recovering, he got addicted to magic mushrooms. It's his addiction that ultimately got him kicked out of the army.

○ **Aeron's novella begins with the roost door closing in his face.**

○ When he got kicked out, they didn't initially let him take his wyvern with him, despite them being bonded. The thinking was, they would try to get Wafer to bond with someone else.

○ All Aeron had was his severance package (cut in half because of his dishonorable discharge) and the clothes on his back—no weapons, no goods, no wyvern. So he ends up breaking back into the roost to free Wafer, steal him, and take him with. But he can't afford to buy more magic mushrooms AND break into the roost, so he is forced to choose. He chooses to do the break-in.

○ The plan is successful, but now the army from that country is perpetually after him and routinely interferes with his mercenary work/gigs. (THIS IS THE MAIN CONFLICT HE FACES IN HIS NOVELLA, AND IT WILL COME INTO PLAY THROUGHOUT THE BOOKS AS WELL.)

○ *(Later on in the series, he'll be injured or stressed, etc., and he'll either be encouraged to not rely on the mushrooms for help or he'll try to convince himself that he doesn't need them, but then he'll say "forget it" and take them anyway and then perform admirably in battle or whatever as a result.)*

○ It's noteworthy that by the end of the novella, he decides that between going back to blacksmithing or doing something else, he'd rather do ANYTHING else. Now, with Wafer on his side again and with a single spear and everything he needs to ride, he sets off in search of mercenary work.

• Title ideas:

○ The Great Wafer Caper

○ The Wafer Caper
○ The Great Wafer Escape
○ Wafer Madness
• Wafer descriptions:
○ blue-green, metallic scales
○ golden eyes
○ twenty-foot wingspan (think clydesdale with wings)
○ thirty feet long or so, including the tail
○ longish neck, but the tail is much longer
○ BACKSTORY: Wafer got his name because when he hatched, a piece of the egg clung to the top of his head. It looked like a little wafer, so Aeron went with the name. He also didn't like the other exotic names being thrown out.

Kent Etheridge - Mage/Tactics
• Weapon Proficiencies: Proficient with multiple forms of magic, but mostly anima magic and some light magic, knows very little dark magic
• **LATENT MAGIC ABILITY**
• Armor: enchanted armor resistant to magic attacks, affords minimal physical protection, but can create some physical objects (weapons and shields) with his magic
• Personality Type: rich guy, confident, a bit vain and particular, strategic, extroverted (Lord Pent, Dr. Strange)
• Age: 49, but looks a bit younger (except to Ronin)
• H/W: 6' 3"/210 lbs
• Appearance: greying (dark) hair, bright blue eyes, white skin
• Backstory:
○ Miranda, Kent's wife, died in childbirth many years earlier, as did their son, making Kent a widower. He never remarried.
○ Kent grew up as the son of a prominent Lord, or Marquess, or Baron, or something. He was classically trained in the art of physical warfare/tactics/strategy, economics, literature, sciences, and just about everything else, too. He has also been taught his whole life that magic users are an abomination to the world, as their country's chief rivals are

magic users. But at around age 40, Kent's own magical powers began manifesting—about 30 years later than they should have normally shown up.

o All the while, Kent's jealous, scheming younger brother is furious that control will be passing to Kent and not him.

o He managed to hide his powers successfully for the next ten years, but around age 50, as his father was beginning to ail and was ready to pass the reins to Kent to control the family's assets, businesses, etc., there's a magical mishap.

o **Kent's novella begins with that mishap.**

o The mishap happens (in part thanks to prompting from Kent's younger brother, who sparks Kent into accidentally using magic openly), and Kent's father promptly disowns him and installs the younger brother as his sole heir.

o Kent is cast out, literally, into the street with nothing. In fact, it is considered a mercy, because his father's sworn duty in his role within that city was to kill any magic users found within the city limits, no questions asked.

o Kent resists, of course, but ultimately he cannot control his magic, and he is thrown out. His brother threatens to kill him if he ever returns, and perhaps his brother also kills their father shortly after (or later on in the story) so he can take power sooner.

o Afraid for his life and unsure where to turn, Kent heads across the border into the neighboring country populated with magic users. He sticks out like a sore thumb in a lot of ways, and despite his fine clothes, he is now dirt poor. Kent has to get over his prejudices and humbles himself, begging for food and coin on the street.

o Then he realizes he doesn't have to be miserable. He goes out and finds a job at a shop and dramatically increases their profits by using his knowledge, all the while picking up little magic tips and tricks and gradually learning how to use his magic from whomever will teach him.

o Things are going fine until a visitor (either from the neighboring country where Kent is from, or someone whom he somehow knew or ran across from back then) recognizes him and "outs" him for who he really is. They prove it because of a telltale mark or tattoo or piece of jewelry that gives him away. Maybe a ring with his family's crest on it that he refused to sell or get rid of because it would mean he was fully severing his connection with his family. (A ring that he must take off in order to use magic because the metal inhibits his ability to wield magic?)

o Kent is captured and hauled before the local magistrate, who quickly realizes Kent's importance and sends him directly to the Queen as an accused spy.

o The Queen grills Kent with questions and ultimately pronounces him guilty of being a spy. His punishment is death, and he is to be burned alive.

o As the mages in the throne room hurl fire at him, Kent manages to remove the ring and lets it drop to the floor in order to save himself. He would rather live as a nobody than die as a somebody, and he manages to harden his body to stone, which protects him from the fire long enough that they stop and see that he is one of them.

o The Queen orders him released and marvels at his power, and Kent tells the entire extent of his story at this point (about his powers manifesting really late, likely because the metal in his ring kept it from happening). The Queen knows Kent can't be a spy because Kent's home country kills all mages upon sight.

o The Queen has Kent trained in the basics of magic, and Kent catches on very quickly. Before long, he becomes the Queen's most trusted military advisor because of his intimate knowledge of the tactics of fighting against his own homeland, and they eventually fall in love (she has a grown son who despises Kent for his nationality and doesn't trust him, and her former husband, the King has been deceased for several years).

o But her son puts a stop to that by betraying her on the battlefield and by colluding with Kent's brother, who is not the Lord (or whatever) and who openly admits to having slain their father early, just like the Queen's son is about to do. Their combined armies take a hiatus and instead attack the Queen and her elite guards. Kent tries to fight back and does very well at it (his powers have grown to a level almost as strong as the Queen's), but the Queen uses magic to fling him far away, to safety, sacrificing herself to save Kent.

○ She dies, and Kent is expelled from yet another country. Incidentally, the two countries forge a lasting peace as a result of this happening.

○ Meanwhile, Kent is on his own and poor again, and he is stuck wandering the countryside when he encounters (*one of the other three mercenaries—probably Aeron*), who is also wandering around looking for work. And that's how they get connected at first.

Mehta (Requiem) - Thief/Assassin

• Weapon Proficiencies: Proficient with knives, bows, and swords, prefers knives/daggers

• Armor: Minimal armor allows for speed, stealth, etc.

• Personality Type: quiet, mysterious, cunning, wildly introverted (Jaffar, Dexter), introspective

• Age: 27-ish, but he doesn't know for sure

• H/W: 5' 8"/155lbs

• Appearance: hazel eyes, dark skin

• Alias: Requiem

• Special skills: As a form of dark magic. Mehta can eventually learn to "phase" forward or back or wherever by a few feet, primarily during fights (or figure out a better term for it). In other words, he can phase in and out of the air like he's teleporting short distances. Maybe he gains this ability in the second series?

• Backstory:

○ Mehta grew up in a death cult, basically. He has been trained for one purpose essentially from birth: to kill. He's so good at it, that if he plans it out, he can kill without being seen, heard, or even sensed. He employs very little magic (if any, ever), as he is so good that he doesn't need any magical help to do what he does.

○ His parents were slain, and he was taken by Lord Valdis's men a long time ago. Valdis's men sold him to the Xyonates as a slave.

○ But his killing has gotten to the point that he literally MUST kill, or he cannot function. He is essentially a serial killer, and his thirst for blood must be sated often, or he cannot function.

○ **The death cult sends him out on routine missions. Mehta's story begins** as he returns from one of his missions totally unsatisfied, despite having killed his target and going beyond and killing his target's family as well, including the wife, the children, the servants in the house, the pets, the livestock out back, the neighbors, all the neighbors' servants, pets, and livestock, and so on. (Meant to be darkly funny.)

○ The death cult leaders seem unfazed, but Mehta has mastered his skills of reading people, and he catches something physical from them that indicates his future: they mean to kill him next. He has seen it before with his other comrades.

○ They come to cull him that night while he is sleeping—except he's not sleeping. He's waiting for them, and he kills his way out of the situation smoothly and marvelously, and he virtually destroys that entire sect of the death cult that night. That is, until a blade from someone hits him in his gut. He kills the assailant and flees, but he is badly wounded and dying.

○ He stumbles into the nearby town, desperate for help and to hide. He sees a small religious symbol (a triangle, point down, with a line moving up through the center almost as if it's an arrowhead—think "Delta"-something as a possible name for the religion) etched into the doorframe of one house and staggers inside, waking a terrified family. The father is holding a weapon as if to defend himself and his family, but he doesn't try to advance on Mehta. Mehta can see that the father knows what Mehta is. Mehta clutches both his wounded torso and a blade, and a small girl (maybe 9 or so) pulls free from her mother and approaches him, despite her parents' calls to stay back.

○ Mehta is immediately on his guard—he'd killed a girl no older than her back at the target's neighbor's house just hours earlier, and now the familiar bloodlust burbles up within him again, all while his blood continues to pool on the ground beneath him. It's tense, but ultimately Mehta passes out before he can decide whether he should kill her or not.

○ When Mehta awakens, the first thing he sees is the religious triangle symbol again, this time hanging from a necklace around the same girl's neck. She is tending to his wounds.

○ Character development, etc. Think about how Raven adjusted to being with the Zambini family and use that.

○ Ultimately, the father is the head of that religious order in that town (like a priest), and he helps Mehta sate his bloodlust other ways through prayer and meditation.

○ The death cult comes back and kills the whole family when Mehta is about 70% healed, but he and the girl escape (or they aren't there, etc.). The death cult pursues them, but he stashes the girl somewhere safe within her father's church, and he waits.

○ The death cult is sneaky, but Mehta is absolutely the best. Unfortunately, his 70% will have to be better than their 100%, etc.

○ Mehta kills them one by one through a series of wicked, cunning traps. Of course, they get the girl, and he ultimately decides to sacrifice himself for her, because his arrival at her house had been a death sentence for her entire family, yet they'd saved his life.

○ Mehta leaves his guard down, and the remaining assassins come for him, but then the girl gets ahold of a knife and kills her captor, who was preparing to let her go as part of the agreement. Then Mehta kills everyone else and saves the girl. In the end, she rationalizes that while he has learned about their ways from her family, she has learned about his ways also, and they have some practical uses, including saving her own life. If she had died, or if she had let Mehta die for her, then neither of them could continue to live on and use their lives to help others by doing good. There was no chance the assassins were going to do that, so it seemed like a fair trade.

○ Mehta agrees and takes her out of there to somewhere safe (maybe a relative's house). Before they part ways, the girl gives Mehta her necklace with the triangle pendant. She tells him it will be a reminder that his life matters, and so do those of other innocents. It can help guide him and remind him to continue the healing of his sickness, and when he can't control it, it can help him target those who would do evil in the world.

○ Mehta thanks her and heads out. While on the road, he runs into Aeron and Kent. Kent recognizes what Mehta is by a tattoo or something, but he also recognizes the triangle pendant and is thoroughly confused. Whatever the case, Kent invites him to come along because their next gig is a doozy, and someone with the skills of a thief/assassin would come in handy. Mehta initially refuses, but he eventually agrees because Kent discloses how bad a guy this person is.

Garrick Shatterstone - Berserker/Tank

• Weapon Proficiencies: Generally uses an axe or a sword, but proficient with almost every hand-to-hand weapon, and he's stronger than a normal human man because of the troll blood in his background (he's sort of like a viking). He has a big two-handed battle-axe that he prefers to use, and it has two axeheads on it.

• Armor: His troll ancestry thickened his skin against most attacks, so a lot of blows glance right off of him. Heavily armored against physical attacks, affords no magical protection. Wears a leather breastplate to guard against lucky attacks.

• Weaknesses: magic attacks and certain types of metals:

○ Snow Steel (refined metal that is so pure, it looks white like snow)

○ Phantom weapons (weapons forged with dark magic but that have no inherent magical properties or benefits beyond being dangerous to types with low magic resistance)

○ Heat-based weapons can penetrate his skin more easily, but ice does almost nothing to him

○ Water weapons don't really hurt, but he can drown/be drowned

○ He can be choked, too

○ can be pierced with conventional weapons, but it's rare that that could happen. Arrows can pierce his skin, but they usually don't go very deep because they don't carry enough force with them.

• Personality Type: Arrogant, brash, loud, extroverted, loyal (Soren)

• Values: nothing is more important to Garrick than loyalty

• Age: 74-ish, but he looks 40-ish. (He's got some troll blood in him, which lengthens his life and makes him tougher, keeps him younger and stronger, also.)

• H/W: 6' 10"/400+lbs

• Appearance: slightly greenish skin, dark blue eyes, dark blue hair

- Backstory:
  - Garrick was born to a berserker and his wife. The wife (Garrick's mom) was found to have some troll blood in her, and that knowledge led to the berserker treating her poorly—abusing her, etc., when Garrick was considerably younger.
  - As a younger man, Garrick stood up for his mother against his father, who then disowned him for it. His father had trained him to berserk as well, but his father was regarded as one of the better warriors in their village, so when Garrick stands up to him, he is defeated badly. Then his mother stabs the father in the back with something, and he turns on her and kills her. Garrick picks up his father's axe and finishes his father off for it.
  - Garrick's father was a notorious warlord, so when Garrick killed him, it created a huge power vacuum in the islands where Garrick was born (off the western coast of Etrijan).
  - Garrick has spent most of his life as a mercenary. He is by far the most experienced of the four in mercenary practices, tactics, and the like. He has fought in a few dozen different wars for as many employers, oftentimes opposing sides within the same war. He is known as one of the finest mercenaries money can buy.
  - He often has regular customers who use him repeatedly for jobs. One of them is a particular noble named Lord Blaine Valdis, who is hilariously rich and powerful, but who occasionally needs side jobs performed to eliminate or sabotage competition against his shipping company and against his other sources of income.
  - Garrick has lost jobs in the past once people have found out that he has troll blood in him. He is seen somewhat as an abomination, as are pretty much all people whom are mixed with trolls, orcs, or other "nefarious" creatures in this world. However, half-elves are fine and are thought of as superior in some ways to regular humans.
  - GARRICK AND KENT are a main source of ongoing conflict within the group throughout the series. They often disagree about which of them is in charge, and they often have differing views on which path to take in a given situation and why because of their different breadth of experiences. Aeron and Mehta have occasional

feedback to give, but mostly, it's Kent and Garrick trying to outdo each other and lead.

○ **Garrick's story begins with him on a mission with a few other mercs for Lord Valdis.** They've been sent to break into a vault and obtain a map (or something) that will lead Lord Valdis to some sort of legendary item (the dragon egg).

○ Garrick is leading the operation, and together with a team of four other random mercs whom he doesn't know (except for one guy whom Garrick has worked with before and whom he trusts, somewhat), he is supposed to break into the vault. Each member has a distinct role to perform. One guy can be a chemist or alchemist or something, and he can make a concoction that does something (maybe demolitions). Another guy is a mage, and he is useful for something. Another guy is a climber (maybe a tree-dwelling species of people or creatures?) and will need to use his skills at some point. The last guy is a thief/safe-cracker type who can actually get the vault door open. Garrick is there as the muscle/protection against physical threats, while the mage deals with magical threats.

○ Their story will need more development overall as to how they break into the place that has the vault, and then how they break into the vault itself.

○ The one Garrick knows is the climber-guy because they've worked together before. They get along well enough—they sometimes compete with each other for jobs, and sometimes they work together. They're sort of frenemies.

○ At the end, after they recover the map, the mage betrays them and kills the chemist first. The four remaining fight it out, with the thief dying next. It will turn out that the climber and the mage are working together, trying to cut out Garrick and the others and Lord Valdis. But Garrick is loyal and neither wants to die, nor be left to die, nor fail his mission.

○ So Garrick finds a way out/way to overcome them both, using his troll strength and other assets/resources. Or perhaps Lord Valdis gives him a tool or a one-time magic-use item (earlier on) that can help him.

○ Either way, when he gets out, he pursues them, but he can't find them, so he returns to Lord Valdis empty-handed.

○ ^This sets up book 1, because Lord Valdis hires three other mercenaries to help Garrick recover the map. Throughout the book, Garrick remains loyal to Valdis—incredibly, inseparably loyal because Valdis has hired him so many times and because Garrick trusts him, etc. And also because Valdis gave him a second chance after the vault debacle. So when they come to realize what the job actually is for Valdis, it takes Garrick a long time to do the right thing because he doesn't want to fail/be disloyal, even though it will literally mean that he may damn the world in the process.

Antagonist

Lord Blayne Valdis - Archmage
   (A really advanced, powerful mage)
   • Weapon Proficiencies: capable of using virtually any type of magic, but excels in using dark magic.
   • Armor: Heavily armored against magical attacks, can create physical shields and physical weapons with his magic
   • Personality Type: Arrogant, rich, confident, poised, evil, cunning, really intelligent
   • Age: 50-something.
   • His sigil is a three-horned ram.
   • Backstory:
   ○ Essentially, Valdis wants to rule the world. He wants to utterly destroy his rivals and enemies, including a rival shipping company who has started to employ flight-based creatures for deliveries, whereas he has previously only used ground- and sea-travel for delivery.
   ○ As a scholar, he has been fascinated with the mythos of his world since a young age. His fascination with the dark arts has taught him that much can be controlled simply through sheer force of will and manipulation, and most everyone/everything else can be controlled with money and/or fear.

○ Thus, when he discovers an ancient text that suggests a hiding place for a dragon egg, he knows he must find out how to get to it so he can capture the egg, hatch a dragon, master it, and use it to decimate his enemies.

○ The dragon is a means to an end for Valdis: absolutely control over anything and everything he wishes to control—specifically the rival shipping company first, but then he'll begin to take over kingdoms, etc. until everything falls under his dominon.

○ **(Book 2)** Further, he intends to tie his life force to the dragon's, and that means he will live as long as the dragon (thousands of years, potentially) and that he can reign indefinitely. Furthermore, he intends to get the dragon to lay more eggs (it's a girl), and he intends to hatch more dragons over time so he can have new ones when this first one dies.

○ the cliffhanger for book 3 (suggesting that there is more to the story for subsequent books) is that we see another dragon egg get found by someone.

Character Names (by Novella)

Aeron's Novella
• Everlee - a little girl (7-8 years old) with light brown/blonde hair whose cat is stuck in a tree. Aeron helps get her cat (Cracker) down. She's the town apothecary's daughter.
• Commander Larcas Brove - the wyvern rider commander who got Aeron discharged, has an Urthian accent
• Faylen Uridi - an elven female wyvern rider for Govalia; Aeron digs her; her wyvern is named Nilla; was an archer before becoming a wyvern knight
• Porgus Darleton - one of the wyvern riders of Govalia; tried to stop Aeron from stealing Wafer, but he fell asleep thanks to Aeron's magic mushroom.
• Farico Ironglade - Aeron's father
• "Mum" Ironglade - Aeron's mother

• Kallie Ironglade - Aeron's sister

• General Cadimus - A general in the Govalian Army—oversees the Wyvern riders, among others.

• Emperor Taçin Ubardo - the emperor of Govalia

Kent's Novella

• Lord Oswin Etheridge - Kent's father, and chief protector of Muroth's southern border (shared with Inoth)

• Fane Etheridge - Kent's jealous, vindictive little brother who usurps Kent to become the next Lord Etheridge

• Lord Aurelius Frostsong - The lord who controls the province of Muroth to the north of the Etheridge province.

• General Calarook - A general based out of the southeastern fortress in the province of Muroth that the Etheridge family controls/oversees.

• Emperor Elex Bouwen - the Emperor of Muroth

• Sarina Bouwen - Emperor Bouwen's oldest child/daughter; hot-headed, beautiful, intelligent

• Wye Bouwen - Emperor Bouwen's second child and oldest son; subdued, somewhat apathetic

• Graeme Bouwen - Emperor Bouwen's eighth child and sixth son; meets with Kent at the end of his intro novella

• Trag - a big oaf of a man, part orc, whom Kent beats in a fight early in his novella. He's the best fighter the dockmasters have ever seen.

• Kent "Brightmore" - Kent Etheridge's pseudonym

• J. R. Stitcher - a clothier in Goldmoor

• Eusephus - a dark mage who is captured and arrested by the bounty hunter in ch. 4 of Kent's story. He will be executed.

• Ronin Shroud - the bounty hunter who teaches Kent about magic and how to use it.

• General Deoward - the head of the palace guard for Hunera Palace (in Goldmoor, Inoth) and general of the bulk of Inoth's forces in the capital city

• Queen Aveyna Armanix - the queen of Inoth—eventually dies, murdered by her son and Kent's brother Fane.

• Grakios "Grak" Petrakis - The queen's personal guard (born in Caclos), skilled in both magic and physical combat (like Kent). He is sort of in love with the queen, and she constantly rejects him. When he sees Kent getting romancey with the queen, he decides to side with the queen's son, the prince, to overthrow her (out of jealousy and "if I can't have her, no one will"). He and Kent almost fight twice in the novella, but they don't actually fight until much later in the series. Then Kent will kill him.

• Prince Kymil Armanix - Queen Aveyna's son. He's a royal dick.

• General Ruba - the general who is in charge of Inoth's armies on the northern side of the country. Used to be General Deoward's job, but now General Deoward outranks General Ruba.

• Admiral Tagril - the admiral in charge of all of Inoth's navy.

• Sobikal - a long-dead archmage who theorized it might be possible to master all three forms of magic (light, dark, anima) if only a person could live long enough to dedicate a lifetime to the study and mastery of each one.

• King Theldus - Aveyna's deceased husband, and the former King of Inoth.

• Archmage Ivelsted - A now-deceased archmage who doubled as a physician for the Inothian royal family.

Mehta's Novella

• Ghazal - The High Cleric of the Sanctum of Xyon in Sefera

• Lament - One of the clerics. Killed in an alley by Mehta.

• Epitaph - One of the clerics. Killed by Ghazal when Mehta moves out of the way and yanks Epitaph over into his spot during a ritual sacrifice.

• Elegy - the most skilled Xyonate aside from Mehta (and Ghazal). He faces off with Mehta at the end of Mehta's story, but instead of them fighting, Elegy finishes off Ghazal and lets Mehta go free, only to tell Mehta his real name prior to setting him free. He will pop up later in the series.

• Chant, Tribute, Covenant, Canon - Male Xyonates killed by Mehta during his initial escape.

• Myth - one of only a few female Xyonates; killed by Mehta as he is escaping.

• High Priest Rulfran - The high priest of the Temple of Laeri in Sefera. Gets killed by the Xyonates who are pursuing Mehta.

• Ferne - Rulfran's only daughter. Mehta saves her life, even though he can't save the lives of her parents.

• Elanil - Rulfran's wife and priestess of the Temple of Laeri. Gets killed by the Xyonates who are pursuing Mehta.

• Creed - A male Xyonate who finds Mehta at Rulfran's house/parsonage.

• Hymn - A female Xyonate who finds Mehta at Rulfran's house/parsonage.

• Fable and Mantra - two other male Xyonates who find Mehta at Rulfran's house/parsonage.

• Whisper and Hush - male Xyonate twin brothers who come for Mehta in the temple. Whisper has a bow/arrows and daggers, and Hush has a big sword.

• Dictum - another male Xyonate who comes for Mehta in the temple. Wields a spear.

• Idyl - the last female Xyonate in Sefera; she comes for Mehta in the temple as well. Wields a bullwhip.

• Proverb - another male Xyonate who comes for Mehta in the temple. Wields two hand axes—like large-ish hatchets.

• Palomi - Mehta's younger sister; agrees to take Ferne under her care while Mehta sets out to avenge his parents' murders.

• Grandfather - Mehta's super-old grandfather.

Garrick's Novella

• Coburn Tye - a thief-type mercenary who is employed as a part of Garrick's regular team. He's a charming philanderer and a cheat, but he's honest with Garrick enough that Garrick trusts him. He tends to get distracted by shiny objects and beautiful women. He fights using knives because they're easier to throw/carry and because having smaller weapons means he can carry more loot with him when he robs people or places. (Dies at the end of Garrick's Novella.)

• Irwin Tiller - the alchemist who is employed as a part of Garrick's regular team. He's not very socially adept, and he's kind of a yes-man. He is brilliantly talented with manipulating various elements to do his bidding (alchemy), and he bases his skills on science. He also manages the mercs' books/finances because he's that kind of meticulous person.

○ Irwin's Vials

▪ Normal Blue = sleep

▪ Orange = burns skin but doesn't cause irreparable harm or actual burns—just pain

▪ Glowing Yellow = flashbang—abrupt, super-bright light and a loud sound

▪ Green = acid—eats through pretty much anything

▪ Clear = puts out fires/shields against fire-type attacks. It's actually a "suspended solution" and turns into thick, white foam when it reacts

▪ Red = ignites upon contact with the air, causing substantial flames and setting fires

▪ Purple = poison—lethal

▪ Light blue = instant ice/freezing

▪ Black = big explosion—very dangerous, rarely used

▪ Pink = healing salve; doesn't outright heal everything, but it numbs pain and enhances one's natural healing abilities.

• Falna - a busty barkeep who is associated with the Crimson Flame. She turns out to be a powerful mage capable of wielding fire, and she attacks them after they defeat the dudes in the pub in Etrijan and the Crimson Flame members who show up. She survives the initial confrontation and may appear later on in the story/series. (Or maybe she is the final boss they have to fight/defeat within the dungeon?)

• Noraff - The climber type (Onni) who ultimately betrays Garrick and the rest of the crew to steal the map of the Path of Shadows from Garrick

• Phesnos - the mage who sides with Noraff in betraying them

Characters that can/should pop up later on in the actual series

Aeron

- Commander Larcas Brove - the wyvern rider commander who got Aeron discharged, has an Urthian accent
- Porgus Darleton - one of the wyvern riders of Govalia; tried to stop Aeron from stealing Wafer, but he fell asleep thanks to Aeron's magic mushroom. (Lash is the name of his wyvern—he's brown and has a tan underbelly. He is killed early in book 1, and Porgus goes without a wyvern from that point on.
- Faylen Uridi - an elven female wyvern rider for Govalia; Aeron digs her; her Wyvern is named Nilla
- Kallie Ironglade - Aeron's sister
- General Cadimus - A general in the Govalian Army—oversees the Wyvern riders, among others.
- Emperor Taçin Ubardo - the emperor of Govalia

Kent

- Prince Kymil (Kent's enemy)
- Grak Petrakis (Kent's enemy; Prince Kymil's personal bodyguard)
- Inothian Officials
  - General Deoward - the head of the palace guard for Hunera Palace (in Goldmoor, Inoth) and general of the bulk of Inoth's forces in the capital city
  - General Ruba - the general who is in charge of Inoth's armies on the northern side of the country. Used to be General Deoward's job, but now General Deoward outranks General Ruba.
  - Admiral Tagril - the admiral in charge of all of Inoth's navy (possible encounter with his forces and with some Septerran pirates near Caclos?)
- Fane Etheridge (Kent's treacherous younger brother who stole his inheritance)
- Lord Aurelius Frostsong - The lord who controls the province of Muroth to the north of the Etheridge province.

• General Calarook - A general based out of the southeastern fortress in the province of Muroth that the Etheridge family controls/oversees.

• The Bouwens (the ruling family of Muroth)

o Emperor Elex Bouwen - the Emperor of Muroth

o Sarina Bouwen - Emperor Bouwen's oldest child/daughter; hot-headed, beautiful, intelligent

o Wye Bouwen - Emperor Bouwen's second child and oldest son; subdued, somewhat apathetic

o Graeme Bouwen - Emperor Bouwen's eighth child and sixth son; meets with Kent at the end of his intro novella

• Ronin Shroud - the mage bounty hunter who taught Kent how to use magic

Mehta
• Palomi - Mehta's younger sister
• Ferne - the young girl whom Mehta saved
• Grandfather - Mehta's grandfather
• Elegy - the most skilled Xyonate aside from Mehta (and Ghazal). He faces off with Mehta at the end of Mehta's story, but instead of them fighting, Elegy finishes off Ghazal and lets Mehta go free, only to tell Mehta his real name prior to setting him free. He will pop up later in the series.

Garrick
• Noraff - The climber type (Onni) who ultimately betrays Garrick and the rest of the crew to steal the map of the Path of Shadows from Garrick
• Phesnos - the mage who sides with Noraff in betraying them
• Falna - the fire mage barmaid

✿

Novels

• Lord Arasmus Glavan - the dark lord and former admiral of the Govalian fleet. Has the map. Is actually a decent fellow because he wants to keep Valdis from doing bad things with the map.

• Lord Glavan's sons - though not seen in book one, they are mentioned. Mayra paints them as cruel and abusive. They will want vengeance for the death of their father, and they may emerge in the series at some point to try to claim that vengeance for themselves.

• Mayri - a servant girl in Lord Glavan's house. Mehta has the chance to kill her, and because he allows her to live, she helps them access the vault. She survives and leaves Govalia, and she takes a large bag of gold off to Hachéron, a city on Govalia's eastern coast.

• Raqat Ubardo - the younger son of Emperor Taçin Ubardo of Govalia. He is a Steelwing in the Govalian Wyvern Knight Corps. Rides a light-green male wyvern that has splotches of blue scales sporadically on its body, as well as one splotch over its right eye. Young and ambitious, with a good sense of justice. Will come in handy once Commander Brove is killed, because he can and will partner with Aeron when fighting the dragon, whereas Commander Brove would not have. (His wyvern is named Trokos.) Raqat has a spear.

• Darvies - A female wyvern knight. She fights Mehta in book 2 in the caverns but survives. But then Commander Brove sends her into the obstacle course, and it kills her and her wyvern.

• Fjorst - the god of ice/wintery things. He gives them each cool weapons at the end of *Path of Shadows*. For more info, check out the "Pantheon" section.

• Nexus - The ancient Aletian Warrior whom the four mercs awaken to help them fight the dragon. Wields the sword Varaghast, forged by Xyon himself.

  ○ Has tan skin, long burnt-orange hair, and sharp facial features

• Pravix - the head of the Aletian city guard of Boroni, an ancient coastal city in ancient Lower Aletia. Is killed accidentally/in a fit of rage by Nexus.

• The Undying Six/Five - The six/five undead Aletians who sacrificed a part of themselves to imprison the warrior Nexus forever.

• Ghojiv, Shevala, Rapha, and Eviro - a family that is killed by the frost dragon in ch. 1 of Frostbane

• Crayl Barreth - the young soldier whom Mehta spared in PoS. He ends up being instrumental in saving Mehta's life in the aftermath of the final battle of book two (in early book three). Light-skinned, square chin, usually has dark stubble.

• Darvesh - Palomi's boyfriend (suitor) who leads everyone away from the aftermath when the dragon attacks their village.

• The Tribunal - The de facto ruling body of the nation of Xenthan and unquestionable ruling body of the capital city of Xenthan, Tebaryx. They share one mind to some extent and often finish each others' sentences.

○ Chazak - if you're looking at him, he stands on the left of the center guy, is second tallest

○ Hamal - the center guy, is shortest, has a piece of Nexus's essence embedded along with the stone in his chest, goes along on the journey.

○ Mirav - if you're looking at him, he stands on the right of the center guy, is tallest

• Siril - the healer elf-lady that saves Garrick with her light magic. Has emerald green eyes and fiery red hair. Is/was married to a dick of a merchant (Ryland) who abused her. She's really obnoxiously pretty. Wears a golden triangle (symbol of Laeri) necklace. Smells like honeysuckle and roses.

• Ryland - the treacherous, abusive merchant/mage who abuses his wife and captures Garrick. Is eventually killed by Garrick.

• General Northridge - the commanding officer of the Red Helm

• Ruggs - a member of the Inothian Royal Guard who protects King Kymil and who reports directly to Grak; gets subdued by the Blood Mercs when they're capturing Kymil.

Short Stories

• Commander Engstrom - Aeron's commander in the cavalry who recommended Aeron to the Wyvern Knight Corps.

STORY BIBLE PART 2: CHARACTER VALUES

A Brief Introduction

One of the things I've learned about character-building over the years is that my characters need to have a set of core values that govern how they react to other characters, to various situations, and to the story world itself.

This type of foundational character detail is essential to figuring out who they are and what is important to them. For me, it helps to phrase them as "nothing is more important than..." statements. They're succinct and proved helpful while I was writing the books.

They function as a sort of guide for your characters; either your characters always stick to their values or they are forced/find a reason to break their values. It's a fun concept to play with either way.

Out of your characters' values spring their ambitions, and out of their ambitions come their individual story goals.

(For more on this topic, check out
Writing Fiction for Dummies
by Randy Ingermanson - https://amzn.to/2XvCtOa.)

Oftentimes, characters' values can conflict with each other—sometimes two values within the same character.

That's when things get really exciting.

Character values can also change over time, and you might see that some of the four main characters' values shifted throughout the course of the first four books of the series. I've included their original set of values here for you to check out.

Core Character Values

Aeron

• Nothing is more important than my family's wellbeing.

   • Nothing is more important than my bond with Wafer and being with him.

   • Nothing is more important than finding a purpose for my life.

   • Nothing is more important than having a way to deal with my ongoing back pain.

   • Nothing is more important than clearing my name with the Govalian Army.

Kent

   • Nothing is more important than justice.

   • Nothing is more important than killing my brother, Fane, and avenging my father's death.

   • Nothing is more important than killing King Kymil of Inoth and avenging his mother, my fiancée, Queen Aveyna of Inoth.

   • Nothing is more important than obtaining greater mastery and power through magic.

Mehta

• Nothing is more important than ensuring my family's safety (including Ferne).

• Nothing is more important than satisfying my thirst to kill.

• Nothing is more important than overcoming my thirst to kill.

Garrick

• Nothing is more important than having a good reputation as an effective, trustworthy mercenary.

• Nothing is more important than finding and killing Noraff and Phesnos, thus avenging Irwin and Coburn.

• Nothing is more important than not ending up like my father—a drunken, violent brigand who used his strength for the wrong reasons, including harming those weaker than him.

⚙

STORY BIBLE PART 3: PEOPLE GROUPS & CREATURE TYPES

A Brief Introduction

A great fantasy story wouldn't be complete without a wide range of weird and interesting people and creatures in it.

If you've read the Blood Mercenaries series, you've already encountered many of these people groups and creature types. And you also know that some are only mentioned in the stories but haven't shown up yet.

That's okay! Sometimes just knowing a thing exists in your story world is good enough to get you going on the writing portion. You can always make changes and weave new elements in later on.

People Groups & Creature Types

• Humans - pretty self-explanatory. They're the same as actual humans, but some have the capacity to use magic, and some don't.

• Elves - They exist, but they're rarely sighted and few in number. The ones who do exist are the tall kind, not the Santa kind. They're a secluded, inward-focused people who live in small, scattered communes throughout the continent, but their magic helps to conceal them from the outside world. (Faylen Uridi is a rare exception in that she chose to leave and join a larger society in Govalia.) They're stronger and faster than humans, have a stronger proclivity toward the use of magic, and are generally more beautiful and better at everything than humans.

• Dwarves - Like the elves, they're not seen very often anymore. They're basically LOTR dwarves in that they live underground, and do mining, working with stone, and are fantastic builders. They also can forge god-forged weapons if they've been trained by a god to do so.

• Wyverns - there are entire groups who have wyverns as mounts, and wild wyverns exist on Aletia as well. The mounts are bonded with their riders in a unique way; as such that the rider can communicate almost telepathically with the wyvern both during flight and not during flight (within a modest range). The wild wyverns are hard (if not impossible) to tame, but it can be done if a wyvern is young enough to bond with a rider. They can also be tamed by force or by "breaking" the wyvern like a rider would a horse, but the results aren't nearly as spectacular as when bonding occurs. There are lots of wild wyverns in Xenthan, and they're part of why it's such a dangerous place for travelers—a full-grown wyvern (huge) can easily devour a whole human man, and juvenile wyverns can easily kill a human man if he is not a capable fighter.

• Orcs - these are dark, fell creatures with generally nothing good within them. They are murderous, rapey, and cruel. They steal, loot, pillage, etc. Structurally, they're like a bulky version of elves, only stronger and slower and less intelligent. They're not dumb, but the average of their IQ is considerably lower than the average of the elves', and it's even lower than that of the average human. They know how to fight, though. Every orc, whether male or female, knows how to fight and fight well.

• Trolls - Much larger and much stronger than orcs, trolls are typically cave-or-dark-place-dwelling creatures that don't often emerge from the bowels of the continent. When they do, they tend to wreak havoc for a little while, sometimes in small groups, sometimes alone, and then they leave once they find what they need (food). They're ridiculously hard to kill because of their durable, resilient skin, but they're really, really dumb. Garrick is part-troll because of some treachery in his ancestral past that he doesn't fully understand, but he is likely the only troll/human hybrid on the continent.

• Goblins - small, quick, mischievous creatures. They tend to err on the side of mass attacks because their strength is in numbers rather than one-on-one. They're smarter than orcs, but not by much.

• Onni - a race of hair-covered humanoids (kind of sloth-like in appearance) with exceptionally lanky arms and legs. They're expert climbers and live in rocky places replete with mountains and cliffs and also in forest-y places where they can climb trees. The rock Onni are typically gray to black in color, and the tree Onni range from tan to brown. They make for pretty good fighters, but they're not naturally inclined to violence. They usually keep to themselves unless they feel threatened.

• Dragons - Thus far, there's only one true dragon in the series, and it's an ice dragon. It's large enough to devour a full-grown wyvern and its rider whole, so it's freaking massive. This particular version is an ice dragon that either started as a flame dragon and was converted via magic, or it just always was an ice dragon.

• Half- or Partial-Combinations or Hybrids - Half-orcs, half-elves, half-Onni, etc. exist, but they're hard to come by. Usually this comes from the offspring of two different species mating, and the offspring shares the attributes and weaknesses of both parents, though there's also potential for magic to yield similar results. In Garrick's case, he gained the partial strength of a troll plus some of the increased size, enhanced healing, and resilient skin, but he is still susceptible to his skin being pierced/punctured, to fire, to drowning, and to a handful of other means to harm him.

• Gods & Goddesses - ultra-powerful beings who wield massive control over various aspects of the continent. Their organizational structure is loosely modeled after the Greek/Roman pantheon, so different gods and goddesses have different "roles" and specialties. The water goddess is strong in the water, for example, but she'd be weak in the desert. The goddess of light is strong in the day and weak at night. The god of darkness/the underworld is powerful in dark places like Xenthan and of course in the underworld, but weak in less-oppressive places. They also share the common weakness of being able to be killed by each other through neutral contest or by weapons forged by another god or goddess, regardless of who is wielding the weapon.

• Aletians - This is a race of meta-humanoids who "founded" the continent. They're basically demigods, and there are a lot of them. They were banished to another realm through a gate centuries before along with Laeri, the Goddess of Light, who had convinced them to align with her against most of the rest of the gods/goddesses. The Aletians are an ancient race who know the secrets of crafting excellent weapons, tools, buildings, etc. that have since been lost to normal men and other races. They're stronger and smarter than every other race, but they're only slightly larger than humans. They're durable and bent on reclaiming what they've lost. Regular races/hybrids can kill Aletians using normal weapons, but it takes a LOT to bring one down, so getting ahold of enchanted weapons or high-level magic power is essential to defeating them on a larger scale.

• Frostbloods - A race of ice-bodied humanoids. They are hard to kill without using heat or fire, as steel tends to only chip away at them. They only reside in frigid places, though, so there usually isn't much fire nearby. They pretty much always wield snow steel or ice-based weapons. If they're near a source of something frozen, they can regenerate. They are, essentially, deceased humans whose bodies have melded with ancient ice magic. They are infectious, in that if they bite you or kill you, they can make you into an icewalker as well, and then you're basically an ice zombie for the rest of eternity.

• Spiderbats - Literally what they sound like. They're spiders with bat wings, and they're nasty. They have all the attributes of both species: they can fly, they can build webs, they can jump, they can bite, they are carnivorous. They're big, too. When they hatch, they start around the size of a chihuahua and grow to be about the size of a medium-sized dog. One of those can easily take down a full-grown man or woman. They have a venomous bite that can be fatal as it literally liquifies people's insides. It also inflicts paralysis. Little ones' bites mostly just inflict paralysis and only locally (bit in the leg, leg goes numb/paralyzed, etc).

• Bounders - These are thirty-pound part-rat, part-rabbit, part-mole creatures with long nails clustered at the ends of their forepaws. They have legs like a rabbits and bounce around, trying to knock over their prey before they burrow into it with their nails. They don't have eyes because they live in wooded areas where no light can reach them, so they don't need eyes. They use sonar (like bats) to hunt their prey. They're a swarm-type creature.

• Skulks - Skeleton warriors. They're made of bones and the occasional piece of rotting flesh still hanging from them. They're created via dark magic from the bodies of souls harvested from animals, humans, or any other race. They can wield weapons and even wear armor. They're all but impervious to fire. Ice slows them down but doesn't kill them. Phantom blades are highly effective in slaying them. Crushing their skulls is a good way of killing them, but simply decapitating them won't do the job. Their bodies turn to dust when they are killed.

• Firebloods - Same as Frostbloods, only made of fire. Hard to kill without ice or water. Sometimes rocks can slow them down, but eventually they burn through. Wood-based weapons burn up when they get to close (metal spear head on a wooden shaft just becomes a metal spearhead), and the closer you get to their core, the hotter they burn, so stabbing one with a normal steel weapon means the steel might melt. Like with Ice Walkers, they only live in hot places, like in volcanic regions, etc., so there's usually no water or ice around. They are susceptible to snow steel and magic-forged weapons. If they are near a source of heat, they can use it to regenerate.

• Mermaids - Pretty obvious what these are. They primarily live in saltwater and occasionally venture into rivers, streams, and lakes. They're mischievous, alluring, and dangerous in the water. When out of the water, they can temporarily survive, and their tails can split into legs so they can walk around, but they can only stay onshore for a limited period of time before they dry out. Usually about two hours or so.

• Scorpers - Spider/scorpion hybrids; about the size of a small dog. Big abdomens, hard bug-like shell, big pincers, spider fangs, eight legs.

They screech. They skitter. They're surprisingly durable, but they burn like any other bug.

- Golems - (typically) Rock creatures. Hard to kill except by extreme force (shattering them) or melting them with extreme heat. They can be frozen, but it only slows them down (though it also makes them more brittle). Explosive power is also useful as it helps to shatter them. Garrick typically swings with enough force to shatter them.

- Water Golem - a water-based creature designed to use the brute force of water to kill its enemies/targets. Able to be defeated by ice or by striking at their core (chest or head, usually) with a burst of magic.

- Minotaur - same as the mythological creature. Not very smart, and not a true fell creature, but definitely monstrous all the same.

- Duotaur - an undead Minotaur powered by a source of dark magic, but it has two heads and four arms. (This is what Garrick and crew face in his novella to get one of the two keys.) Wields a hammer or another big, unruly weapon. Can be killed easily with light magic/Laerian steel, but otherwise smashing their heads is necessary to kill them.

- Subux - Slime monster that lives in water. It grabs you, pulls you under, and the last thing you see is its glowing purple tongue before it devours you. Capable of eating almost anything, but the bigger the thing it eats, the more it has to stretch. Thus, the easier it is to cut your way out. They're more dangerous because of the possibility of drowning before being eaten. They just eat and eat and eat without any reason to stop eating. Can't really be killed unless they can be removed from the water. Then they dry out.

- Anguilon - an angler fish-type thing (but more like an eel in appearance) that floats in the air—lures prey with its light into the shadows, then eats it. Nothing magical about it—just a scary thing.

- Screets - smallish spidery bugs that skitter and have horizontal blade-like pincers in front of their teeth. They flay skin and flesh off. One of them would be painful, but manageable, but they usually come by the dozens.

- Hapes - hairless apes who live underground in caves. They have pale skin and are freakishly strong and carnivorous. They can also see really well in the dark. (Think biggish chimps with more muscle and sharper teeth.)

• Flynos - Flying Rhinos with fairy-type wings. They are definitely magical beasts, because there's no way that their pitiful, translucent wings should enable them to fly, but they can fly and even carry passengers nonetheless. (You have a stock image pic of one, so use it well.)

• Reptides - Scale-covered humanoids. Feral but somewhat sentient. Dark green with yellow underbellies. Pointy, narrow teeth (think anglerfish). Gills. They look part reptile, part fish. Their claws are capable of scratching through Garrick's skin, and their teeth can pierce through as well. Webbed hands, venomous (poison) talons. They are tribal-esque, and they have a hierarchy. They usually have a leader of some sort who commands them.

• Pit Beast - a one-off creature (probably) that lives in a pit. It eats whatever falls into the pit. Its mouth glows with faint orange light, and it has rows of sharp teeth curved inward, so once you're in its mouth, you can't get out. It also has tendrils on the sides of its mouth that grab onto potential food/victims and pull it toward the mouth.

• Ice Beast - a one-off creature (probably) that lives in the tunnels/caverns along the way to Fjorst's temple. It is huge and camouflaged like a wall, except for multiple shafts of icy blue light that stream out of several holes in its hide. Whenever something comes across those shafts of light, red tentacles (they look like intestinal tubing) lash out and grab its prey. The tentacles reel them in, and when they get close to the openings, they are frozen and broken into chunks and then devoured through the holes. Can be killed by fire, but that's pretty much it.

✿

STORY BIBLE PART 4: PLACES & LOCATIONS

A Brief Introduction

As with weird and interesting people and creatures, unique, colorful, and dynamic places and locations are a must in great fantasy stories.

If you have map-drawing skills, I recommend creating a sample map that you can refer to, even if it's a super rough version. That'll help you keep places and locations straight in your head. Later on, as your story world develops, you can add more complexity and quantity of places and locations as you see fit.

Places & Locations

- ALETIA - the name of the entire continent
  - Govalia - the nation where Aeron is from/served in the army - known for their booming commerce and wealth, ruled by an emperor
    - Dreynoth - a city just outside the army fortress near Govaliston. The army crowd frequently visits the town for recreational purposes.
    - Govaliston - the capital city of Govalia
    - Osnal - A southern port city located in Govalia

- Hachéron - the largest eastern port city in Govalia, nearly due east from Osnal except a little farther north
  ○ <u>Muroth</u> - the nation where Kent is from—no magic is allowed there; no one upper-class in Muroth speaks with contractions
    ▪ Drion - Muroth's capital—very strong from a martial sense
    ▪ Lowmir Keep - the emperor's castle in Drion
    ▪ Etheridge - the southeastern province of Muroth; named after the Etheridge family, run by Fane Etheridge, Kent's treacherous brother
    ▪ Ranhold Fortress - Located in southern Muroth in Etheridge)
    ▪ Frostsong - the province just to the north of Etheridge; named after the Frostsong family, run by Lord Frostsong
  ○ <u>Inoth</u> - Muroth's chiefest rivals/enemies. They share common ancestry but are now sworn enemies. They are a nation of magic-users.
    ▪ Goldmoor - Inoth's capital city.
    ▪ Hunera Palace - the royal palace/castle in Goldmoor, Inoth.
    ▪ Dewmire Fortress - a fortress in northern Inoth.
    ▪ Boroni - A now-destroyed city from ancient Aletia. Home of Nexus, the legendary warrior.
  ○ <u>Urthia</u> - known for neutrality in conflicts and having a citizen-led army capable of enforcing their neutrality. Keeps Xenthan in check.
    ▪ Stroeton - Urthia's capital
    ▪ Royal Bank of Urthia - the central bank for Urthia, located in Stroeton but with branches across the country. Arguably a more powerful institution than the Urthian monarchy.
  ○ <u>Xenthan</u> - the country where Lord Valdis is from - known for being slightly oppressive, inhospitable, and militant. Lots of orcs and trolls live there. Sometimes known as "the black realm."
    ▪ Tebaryx - the capital of Xenthan
    ▪ Valdis Keep - Lord Valdis's castle
  ○ The Thornback Mountains - a wide mountain range stretching along the border between Xenthan and Etrijan
    ▪ The Cratered Mountain - the unofficial name for an otherwise unnamed mountain within the Thornback Mountains; located right on the border between Etrijan and Xenthan; it's actually a dormant volcano
  ○ <u>Etrijan</u> - another country, mountainous and green

- Sefera - the capital of Etrijan—the third most populous city on the continent, known for their pursuit of wisdom and knowledge.
- The Sanctum of Xyon - the holy place/gathering place of Xyonates, or death cult adherents, specifically located in Sefera in Etrijan.
- Mirstone - a small town in north central Etrijan. It's located relatively near the Temple of the Crimson Flame (in Etrijan).
- Obaris - a port town on the northern edge of Etrijan—one of the only cities of any size that far north.
- The Temple of the Crimson Flame (Etrijan) - the "home base" of the Etrijan chapter of the Crimson Flame cult. There's a big dungeon underneath it and plenty of secrets.
  - Caclos - a sparsely populated island nation south of Govalia with an incredible navy/army - great vacation nation
- Pashatan - the capital of Caclos
- The Central Bank of Caclos - the name says it all. The island isn't that big, so there's just the one bank in Pashatan.
  - Zinehx Ocean - the major ocean to the west of the continent
  - Kuhnleas Ocean - the major ocean to the north the continent
  - Tahn Sea - the sea separating Caclos from Inoth and Govalia—pirates are known to frequent the area and raid, etc.
  - Bonan Ocean - the ocean south of Caclos and east of the continent
  - Liparulo River - runs down through Govalia
  - Tosca River - runs down along Urthia's and Govalia's western border; essentially divides the continent in half (east/west)

Places - Other Forms of Place Names/Citizen Names

- *Aletia* - Aletian; Aletians
  - Govalia - Govalian; Govalians
  - Muroth - Murothian; Murothians
  - Inoth - Inothian; Inothians
  - Urthia - Urthian; Urthians
  - Xenthan - Xenthanian; Xenthanians
  - Etrijan - Etrijani; Etrijanis
  - Caclos - Caclosian; Caclosians

STORY BIBLE PART 5: SOLDIERS, COLORS, & NATIONAL ARMY INFO

A Brief Introduction

Many genres of fantasy often include some sort of medieval military element, and unless you know who's wearing what uniforms, you don't know where to aim the catapult. Make sure you record those little details for the sake of consistency and continuity.

Note how I added emphasis by way of underlining or capitalization below whenever I felt I needed to remember something especially crucial to the story/story world.

I also included some relevant continental history since it often involved soldiers from different nations clashing in battle.

Soldiers/Colors/National Army Info

• Murothian Elite Soldiers/Officers wear BRONZE-colored armor, but it is actually a unique alloy that is somewhat magic-resistant.

• Murothian Regulars wear WHITE IRON armor which is somewhat magic resistant.

• Muroth's colors are White and Bronze and Black—that's what is on their flag. Their state "animal" is the lion.

○ Etheridge House Crest- a green and bold-red flame with a bronze gryphon in the center.

○ Frostsong House Crest - Blue and silver with a snow leopard in the middle.

• Inothian Elite Soldiers/Officers wear WHITE LEATHER armor/greaves (in the throne room).

• Inothian Regulars wear BROWN leather armor on their chests/greaves.

• Inothian Royal Emissaries/Servants wear DARK BLUE cloaks accented with GOLD DIAMOND SHAPES

• Inothian ranking system:

○ One diamond = Captain

○ Two diamonds = Major

○ Three diamonds = Lieutenant General

○ Four diamonds = General of the Army

• Govalian Army Elite Soldiers/Officers wear GRAY armor

• Govalian Army Regulars and Wyvern Knights wear FOREST GREEN armor

○ Ranks for Wyvern Knights:

▪ Featherwing - New recruits who have not yet bonded/paired with a wyvern - normal forest green armor

▪ Leatherwing - established soldiers who are fully initiated into the ranks of the wyvern knights - normal forest green armor

▪ Steelwing - soldiers who command small groups of knights on patrol (Porgus Darleton has just been promoted to this rank) - normal forest green armor with a steel wyvern wing stamped on the left shoulder.

▪ Silverwing - commanding officers of the wyvern knights (this is what Commander Brove is) - dark gray armor with a silver wing stamped on his left shoulder

▪ Goldwing - Generals of the Wyvern knights (this is what General Cadimus is) - dark gray armor

• Xenthan Army Elite Soldiers/Officers wear VIVID RED armor

• Xenthan Army Regulars wear BURGUNDY armor

• Xenthan Lords/Nobility wear BLACK armor (like obsidian)

- Etrijani Army Regulars wear BLUE armor
- Etrijani Army Elite Soldiers/Officers wear COBALT BLUE armor
- Etrijani Lords/Nobility wear VIBRANT BLUE armor
- Urthian Army has armor colored in the spectrum of PURPLE
- The Septerran, high seas pirates, have black sails decorated with red Snake Eyes
- Xyonates are a death cult, and they typically have shaved heads. The High Cleric wears deep purple robes marked with runic symbols, and the Clerics wear red robes marked with runic symbols. Normal Xyonates wear dark clothes, usually strips of fabric wrapped tightly around their bodies.
- Lord Valdis's men wear the sigil of the three-horned ram—charcoal armor with a silver three-horned ram sigil (matching shields)
- Aletians' symbol is a four-pointed star with an eye in the center. The iris is like a cat's eye, only it is horizontal rather than vertical.
  - Ancient Aletians' armor is MAGE STEEL and glints with ALL THE COLORS OF THE RAINBOW in sunlight.
- Ryland the Merchant wears royal blue robes. His ship's sails are also royal blue and have a swan emblem on them, but it sort of looks like a duck instead.

Relevant Continental/Story World History

- Muroth vs. Inoth - Once these two nations were one large country, but Inoth (southern Muroth) seceded over the treatment of mages and over the use of magic. Most magic users headed south and sided with Inoth in the war, and Muroth expelled or killed any mages found in the country. Muroth lost the war, but Muroth has grown incredibly powerful in military strength since then, and now a war with Inoth could definitely go either way as they know how to better deal with mages. The secession and the war happened about 100 years prior to the start of the story. This war is known as the Mage War.
- The Aletian race founded the continent several thousand years earlier. They also left a LOT of really sweet, ancient, cool stuff behind, ranging from treasures to buildings to traps to dead Aletians, etc.

STORY BIBLE PART 6: PANTHEON

A Brief Introduction

F antasy also sometimes relies on a set of deities (or sometimes just one) to help drive the story. It was pretty fun to think through the various deities in this world, even though we don't see all of them in these first few books. Again—know it, even if you never use it.

Pantheon

• <u>Laeri</u> (as in the Temple of Laeri) - the Goddess of Light/Wisdom, one of many deities in this world. (*Major Goddess*)
  ○ Those who serve her and the light are afforded a place in "heaven" - The Aetherworld
  ○ Her symbol is the triangle (upside down).
  ○ Human in form, also has wings and a third eye in the center of her forehead.
• <u>Xyon</u> - the God of Death/Darkness/the Underworld (depending on whom you ask) (*Major God*)
  ○ The underworld is called Hell, but there are at least three hells within Hell (hence the expression "what in the third hell")

○ Upon death, the dead are brought to the Gates of Hell and before Xyon, who judges them.

○ Human in form, but has wings and a third eye in center of forehead.

○ Followers are called Xyonates

• Zovalon - God of Gods (ruler of the gods) *(Supreme Being/God)*

○ Fatherlike figure, has terrible (frightening) powers (think Zeus)

○ probably the most dangerous/powerful god

○ Usually stays neutral in conflicts since most of the other gods are his children/creations and he doesn't want to play favorites

• Senros - the God of Love/Romance/etc. (Has a lasso in his constellation, and the lasso points due south.) *(Major God)*

• Lyrena - the Goddess of War/Battle (Has a sword, and her sword has a constellation.) *(Major Goddess)*

• Kecana - Goddess of the Sun/Sky *(Lesser Goddess, under Tirrus)*

• Gorav - the God of Night/Moon/Stars *(Lesser God, under Laeri/Xyon, but operates alone since Laeri is gone and Xyon is disinterested)*

• Aquina - Goddess of the Sea/Water *(Lesser Goddess, under Tirrus)*

• Tirrus - Goddess of Nature/The "Earth" (Married to Ravzar) *(Major Goddess)*

• Dheveri - Goddess of Fire *(Lesser Goddess, under Tirrus)*

• Fjorst - God of Ice *(Lesser God, under Tirrus)*

• Ravzar - God of Beasts (legendary and normal) (Married to Tirrus) *(Lesser God, under Tirrus)*

○ He gives Wafer the ability to breathe fire.

• (other gods/goddesses)

Prayers

• "Laeri, Goddess of Light," Ferne began and Mehta repeated, "may your blessings be upon us, and may your favor shine upon our steps. Bless us with mercy and justice, and cover us with your protection, both within and without. Help us to control our minds and our bodies. Give us the strength to resist temptation, and let us shine your light into the darkness everywhere. By your grace, we ask these things."

STORY BIBLE PART 7: OBJECTS & WEAPONS

A Brief Introduction

What fantasy story is complete without fancy weapons and objects?

This section is crucial in helping you create and organize the various unique objects and weapons in your story world. Here, you can delineate the rules for how these objects and weapons work, what can counter them or what they can counter, what effects they have, and much more.

Rather than trying to remember all of that, write it down instead.

Objects/Weapons

- Scorallite - a green crystal used to identify mages/magic users. It makes their powers show up, but it doesn't harm them—it simply coaxes magic forth from the one holding the crystal.
- Aeron's spear - it's one blade, but it has three separate points, and it looks beastly.
- Magic mushrooms - they come in a variety of colors and effects but always glow blue if they've been infused with magic:

- ○ Yellow spots = painkiller - tastes earthy and weird
- ○ purple stripes = muscle relaxant/good for quelling anxiety
- ○ pale blue = sleepy time—so potent that even exposure to bare skin will put a person to sleep. It also spits out spores that have comparable effects
- ○ orange-and-black = prevents people from sleeping, even against the pale blue mushrooms and their spores—tastes like honey and dirt mixed
- ○ light green, solid color but with white gills under the cap = adds in some fun color effects when he takes it with the other shrooms
- Mehta's knives - gray iron blades, dark brown wooden handles wrapped in black fabric. There's nothing special about them, but they're wildly sharp.
- Garrick's Battle-Axe - It's a big, hulking thing with two steel blades. Weighs probably 50-60 lbs, but Garrick is strong enough to use it with no problem. Has a steel shaft.
- Snow Steel - Weapons forged in ice instead of fire through a special process involving ice magic. It is white in its appearance instead of gray. Snow Steel is effective against fire-type enemies (including fire-type dragons) and is stronger than normal, fire-forged steel. In fact, Snow Steel can cut through normal steel with enough force (by making it brittle and shattering it), but it is weak against Arcane Steel. It also tends to be strong against water-type enemies because it freezes them, but in water itself, it has no power. It reverts back to being a normal steel weapon, basically. Can generate ice on its own if magic is pushed into the weapon, and that ice can be used/manipulated like normal ice by a mage.
- Ice-Forged Steel - Weapons forged in ice by the god Fjorst. Incredibly rare, incredibly powerful. More powerful than snow steel by a factor of at least ten. These weapons are always cold, always capable of freezing anything and cutting through pretty much anything as well. Blades are blue and translucent, like ice. When wielded by someone with magic, they can do all sorts of cool ice-themed things. They can form entire bridges across rivers or chasms, they can shoot ice at things to freeze things. They can freeze lakes and even dam up rivers (tem-

porarily, of course). (And so on.) Because they are god-forged, they can cut through magical barriers as well as physical ones. Some limitations exist, but that is where they become the most useful. They are forged using a mix of Dheveri's arcane fire and Fjorst's god/ice magic.

• Mage Steel - Weapons forged with non-specific magic. They are effective against enemy types with low magic resistance and occasionally have other attributes applied to them (extra durability, extra sharp, good against water or fire or ice-type foes, can function like a boomerang when thrown (comes back to wielder), etc.). These weapons are to be used by non-magic users, typically against other non-magic users as it gives them a slight advantage.

• Phantom Steel - Actual, physical weapons forged with dark magic that can absorb power for their wielder, but not as much as full-on magic weapons (like those used by dark magic practitioners Kymil, Eusephus, and (maybe) Valdis). A Phantom Steel weapon takes the power of the souls slain with it and uses that added power to increase the wielder's speed, to enable them to move through shadows in an instant, to phase through walls (sometimes), to become more durable (shielded with darkness). The blades are dark gray/black, and if one is broken, it releases all the souls entrapped inside it. These weapons are to be used by non-magic users, typically against other non-magic users as it gives them a slight advantage. Weak against Laerian Steel.

• Laerian Steel - Weapons forged by powers of light magic, named for the Goddess Laeri. They're actual steel weapons but they glow with a white or pink aura. They're not subtle at all. They are designed specifically to counter and break Phantom Steel, but they are also especially effective against fell beasts (orcs, ogres, goblins, skeletons, and basically everything you'd find in a dungeon). These weapons are to be used by non-magic users, typically against other non-magic users as it gives them a slight advantage. This metal is incredibly rare, and most of Aletia doesn't even know it exists. Laerian Steel is weak against everything except basic steel (or lesser metals) and Phantom Steel.

• Arcane Steel - Weapons forged in fire through a special process involving fire magic. It is red in its appearance instead of gray, and it is essentially always red-hot (when being wielded) but without the propensity to bend like actual red hot steel would upon impact. The only time is isn't burning something is when it is sheathed (in a special sheath). As such, it sears when it cuts, sort of like a lightsaber. Arcane Steel is effective against ice-type enemies (including ice-type dragons) and is stronger than normal, fire-forged steel. In fact, Arcane Steel can cut through normal steel with enough force. It is very strong against Snow Steel, but it's weak against anything in the water/water-type enemies. If exposed to water, it becomes basic steel again (temporarily) until it is again exposed to a super hot heat source (like fire or lava, etc.) Can generate fire on its own if magic is pushed into the weapon, and that fire can be used/manipulated like normal fire by a mage.

• Dragonfire Steel - Weapons forged in dragonfire through a special process involving magic. The steel is a brilliant, mirror-bright silver in its appearance instead of gray or steel-colored. It is effective against pretty much everything because it's ridiculously sharp, and it can even cut through rock-type and metal-type foes. It does not wear down nor lose its sharpness. It is a sword that will exist until it is destroyed, and it can only be destroyed by more dragonfire.

• Varaghast - Nexus's sword. Forged by Xyon himself, it has the power to harness different types of magic without requiring much of anything for fuel except magic from its wielder. It is a god-tier-level weapon, which puts it above anything shown in the story to this point—including Fjorst's weapons. It can slay dragons with ease.

• Aeron's Dragonfire Lance - Unique only to Aeron, this lance was physically burned onto his back by Ravzar using Wafer's dragonfire. Only he can call it forth and wield it. As a result of the process, he is now essentially immune to fire.

Magic Weapons Notes

• Weapons like snow steel, arcane steel, etc. that are forged with magic can be wielded by anyone, but in the hands of a mage with the proper training (or even worse, in the hands of an Aletian) they can have other powers (including shooting out elemental blasts—ice, fire, wind, water, crystal, stone, etc.).

• But they can also have significant kickback/recoil depending on how the magic is used: snow steel freezes hands and forearms, arcane steel burns, etc.

Forgotten/Hidden Objects and Places

• The two Crimson Flame temples and their corresponding dungeons
• Lord Valdis's phantom steel weapons—one sword in Valdis Keep and the battle-axe and flail in the Aletian tower
• Aeron's ice-forged naginata and Garrick's ice-forged hammer are buried under the collapsed tower from Lord Valdis's ritual.

⚙

STORY BIBLE PART 8: MAGIC

A Brief Introduction

Another hallmark of fantasy is the inclusion (and sometimes abundance) of magic in the story world.

If science and technology are the engine that drives sci-fi, then magic is the engine that drives fantasy.

My magic system is broken down into three main categories, as you'll see below (four, if you include basic/raw magic). They all have their benefits and drawbacks, but super powerful mages can bend or even break some of those rules, depending on the situation.

And if you've read the Blood Mercenaries books, you know that sometimes happens.

When creating your own magic system, make sure you establish rules and stick to them. You *can* break those rules if need be, but you need to establish *how* and *why* it is possible to break them so your readers don't end up feeling cheated via "author intrusion."

There are plenty of great resources out there for creating magic systems. This breakdown is to show you how I created mine, not to explain to you how you should create yours. Enjoy!

Magic

• Four types of Magic: Dark, Light, Anima, and Basic

   ○ <u>Basic Magic</u> - This is the standard blue energy contained within a mage. It is the root of all magic uses, but on its own it can achieve very little. It requires the addition of outside influences to be effective.

   ○ <u>Anima Magic</u> - This is the most common form of magic because it is the easiest to use and master efficiently, and it requires little sacrifice on the part of the user. The user holds a natural object in his hands (or in some cases only touches the natural object) and then his magic makes use of the object's essence to multiply it, command other comparable objects nearby, and manipulate the element to his will.

     ▪ Manifestations - This typically involves the use of plants, rocks/ground, water, fire, animal attributes (to an extent—a la feathers from a bird or fur from a furry animal), air, ice/snow, crystals, and other natural elements.

     ▪ Deeper Mastery - includes turning one's body into that element temporarily, creating armor out of the elements, bending large amounts of the element to the mage's will (think earthquakes, typhoons, tornados, tsunamis, volcanic eruptions, and other cataclysms)

   ○ <u>Light Magic</u> - the hardest type of magic to master, Light Magic requires the user to sacrifice himself on some level in order to obtain true power. That sacrifice typically comes in the form of extensive study and time investment, as well as a dedication to living a holy life focused on doing good and helping others.

     ▪ Manifestations - limited healing powers, small light shields/barriers, light weapons, flashes of blinding light, the ability to use light to move physical objects

     ▪ Deeper Mastery - enhanced healing powers, light shields/barriers capable of protecting entire groups of people (not just the wielder), stronger weapons, the ability to teleport through light.

     ▪ Blinding Flash affects anyone not using Light Magic, but the attack can be directed, and if the Light Mage touches someone, they can keep the flash from hitting them or cut its effects off early.

     ▪ Monks, scribes, saints, holy folks, priests (employ/consider the battery concept)

- Misuse of light magic yields what consequences?
- Obtaining holy relics? More about the journey than the relic?
- ***NOTE: **Healing magic is the most draining for a Light Magic wielder**.*** Healing manifests as WHITE LIGHT.

  ○ Dark Magic - Dark Magic is not as difficult as Light Magic to master, but it comes at a high cost—particularly through the lives of living beings, whose lives, souls, and essences fuel the dark mage's powers. As with Light Magic, sacrifice is necessary, but it is the sacrifice of others rather than of one's self. Dark magic is typically associated with evil mages, but not all mages need to be evil to practice dark magic. Essences can be stored within the dark mage for short periods of time unless a containment spell of some sort is cast to help them hold more.

  - Manifestations - runic magic, blood magic, reanimation, divination, manipulative magic, dark weapons (spikes/arrows, including coming up from the ground and from the bones of deceased foes), dark shields/barriers, shadow magic (multiple uses)

  - Deeper Mastery - enhanced runic magic, vampiric weaponry, more powerful dark weapons/barriers/shields, the ability to travel/teleport through shadows, magic stripping (of magical creatures) for otherworldly powers, necromancy, advanced magical manipulation and distortion

  - As a form of dark (shadow) magic, Mehta can eventually learn to "phase" forward or back or wherever by a few feet, primarily during fights (or figure out a better term for it). In other words, he can phase in and out of the air like he's teleporting short distances. Maybe he gains this ability in the second series?

Specific Dark Magic Notes/Uses

- Vampiric magic has a purple light associated with it, whether it is runic in nature (like Eusephus's vampiric weapons that drain essence) or direct (like Lord Glavan absorbing the life of his guard to preserve his own life).
- Eusephus uses pale green fire to create a border around himself.

- Red light means it's a type of blood magic.
- Kymil uses a venomous snake to create a poison arrow—still blood magic, but the venom gets added to the arrow as a bonus.
- Eusephus uses something with swirling red light that looks like a bunch of snakes. it can be defensive or offensive (so this has something to do with blood magic—maybe just a different manifestation instead of an arrow). Ronin's crystal shield diffuses it.
- Lord Glavan's hands glow red when he rips the bones out of his guards to use them as projectile weapons. This is a type of higher-level blood magic (which also applies to the ability to manipulate bones).
- Lord Valdis has his pressure power which is disabling to nearby foes. Using his blessing from Fjorst, Kent's ice shield resists the pressure long enough that the Blood Mercs can reengage in the battle.
- Lord Valdis rips his own chest open, and three dark-purple forms plop out and writhe in the blood. They suck up the blood and form into three copies of Lord Valdis, each independent, but they have a pinkish gray pallor and dark coal for eyes. Essentially they're copies of Lord Valdis and have a sizable fraction of his power. This is a type of blood magic. They're blood clones.
- Shadow magic allows for a lot of things, including transportation between shadows, using shadows as weapons and armor, and more.
- Kallie and the dragon are suspended in orange light for the ritual.
- The Tribunal shares dark magic powers. When the three lords are together, their magic is greater than the sum of their parts. They formed a bond years ago in order to gain this profound power. Together, they are about half as powerful as Lord Valdis was before he was killed (which is still wildly powerful). Their eyes glow red like the gems in their black crowns when they're united in thought and deed, and they often speak either in unison or in broken sentences which the others not talking will finish (their eyes do NOT glow red when they are finishing each other's sentences). Their minds are fully melded together.

Other Dark Magic Notes

There's a whole practice of dark magic dedicated to harvesting essences from magical creatures, which dark mages use to empower themselves. Unicorns and dragons are the main ones.

- Creatures like centaurs, dwarves, and elves are just other races, but fairies are pretty common targets for having their essences stolen.

- Dragons (mostly extinct and hidden), Unicorns (same as dragons), Pegasi, Gryphons, and other mythical creatures with inherent magical properties are prime targets for such dark practices.

- By comparison, stealing the essence of another mage is better than stealing the essence of a non-mage person (regardless of race), and it does imbue the dark mage with a lot of extra power as compared to just taking the essence of a non-mage.

Total Magic Mastery

To gain godlike magical powers, some mages have aspired to master all three types of magic.

○ The Archmage Sobikal was the most famous of these, and he wrote the definitive work on the subject, but he didn't get very far because he was so old when he figured it out.

○ The secret is to master Dark Magic, basically. At high levels of Dark Magic mastery, users can take essence from living creatures to give them unique attributes and abilities, and by taking enough essence from humans, they can steal fractions of lifespans and add them to their own. Typically, younger and healthier targets yield the best results. Twenties, teens. Harvesting children is not unheard of, but the magic works better with targets who have stabilized physically.

○ The capability to live longer via Dark Magic makes it more likely that someone can achieve mastery of all three forms of magic.

○ The trick is that when a Dark Magic user wants to use Light Magic, they have to fuel their own bodies with enough essence to keep the light magic from consuming their pitiful souls. So as they are personally drained by the use of Light Magic, they must harvest essence via Dark Magic, or they need a reserve stored up.

○ Everyone only has so much "fuel," so by taking the "fuel" of others, a mage can use all three types of magic at will.

STORY BIBLE PART 9: ASSORTED STORY WORLD INFO

A Brief Introduction

T his section covers a variety of topics, ranging from info about the Crimson Flame cult, dragons, and creative naming systems I came up with. Some of it may prove useful to you in creating your own story bible, so I included it just in case.

Crimson Flame Cult Info

• Dragon parts: Fang, claw, scale, spike, slither, bellow, roar, fire, flame, ember, tongue, tooth, snout
• Structure: One overarching leader to whom the Seven Talons (high priest warriors) report.
• There's a Talon in each of the countries where dragons have historically lived, and they are responsible for safeguarding any and all dragon secrets/artifacts, etc. in their territories.
• The Crimson Flame believes they're waiting for a prophesy to come true before the dragon can be released. The prophesy is essentially that one among them will be born with a mark signifying his or her

birthright to hatch the dragon. As part of the prophesy, that person must be sacrificed as part of the hatching ritual.

• The dragon cult is guarding the following items/secrets needed to get to the egg:

   ○ a map to the egg

   ○ a key to get inside the dungeon where the egg is housed

   ○ the fossilized/hibernating/dormant egg itself

   ○ a scroll/book containing a ritual/spell to awaken the dragon within the egg and another ritual/spell to hatch the egg

   ○ the Crimson Flame's chosen one (probably a teenage girl) to be sacrificed as part of the ritual to get the dragon to hatch

• Once the 4 mercs defeat the Talon in Xenthan (probably in book one, and in doing so they retrieve the egg), the remaining Talons converge on them with their respective forces to try to wrest control of the dragon back to themselves. So there are three factions who have different goals:

   ○ Valdis wants to hatch the egg so he can harvest the dragon's essence (once it is full-grown) and become godlike in his power

   ○ The Crimson Flame wants the dragon loosed upon the continent to cleanse it of the unfaithful with dragonfire

   ○ The four Mercs want to stop both of those things from happening, so they want to kill Valdis and the dragon, even though the dragon may be the last of its kind.

• Ultimately, Valdis has an operative inside the Crimson Flame as well, and that operative will take the girl with the mark hostage and deliver her to Valdis.

• High-ranking mages become masters of fire-type magic, and all they need is a spark to create brilliant displays of (literal) firepower. When they work their magic, their eyes turn fiery red, and the skin around their eyes actually burns and chars black, giving them a frightening appearance.

• Maybe once the Crimson Flame finds out it's an ice dragon, they want to kill it as well because they were hoping for a fire-type? Or maybe Valdis does something that converts it to an ice-type instead?

Dragon Info

• The dragon in this series doesn't breathe fire. It's an ice dragon. It is weak against heat.

• Being an ice dragon, it can breathe ice. It turns rivers and lakes to solid ice with its breath,

• That's why getting it to land on the volcano will work—it would literally blow the dragon apart.

• Maybe once the Crimson Flame finds out it's an ice dragon, they want to kill it as well because they were hoping for a fire-type? Or maybe Valdis does something that converts it to an ice-type instead?

Naming System Ideas

• vocalizations (voice, whisper, hush, shout, screech, cry)

• weapons (blade, dagger, knife, spear, staff, bow, arrow, axe)

• negative emotions (strife, fear, shame, disdain, hate, rage, despair, suffer, pride, weep, envy, contempt)

• insects (ant, beetle, spider, fly, wasp, hornet, bee, scorpion, moth)

• natural objects (tree, bush, mountain, hill, ravine, cave, valley, river, stream, brook, island)

• rocks (shale, coal, slate, quartz, crystal, ash, obsidian, gabbro, granite, marble, breccia, flint, scoria, onyx)

• gemstones (diamond, emerald, ruby, sapphire, topaz, etc.)

• metals (gold, silver, bronze, copper, iron, steel, brass, alloy, lead, tarnish, cobalt)

• colors (black, white, blue, red, green, etc.)

• exotic colors (cobalt, verdant, rouge, crimson, tricorn, umber, vermilion, cerulean, indigo, teal)

• poetry (lament, requiem, elegy, litany, epitaph, ghazal, ode, idyl, lyric, verse, cinquain, soliloquy, liturgy, canon, legend, myth, fable, epic, saga, chronicle, chant, creed, covenant, eulogy, tribute, hymn, mantra, axiom, proverb, adage, dictum, sonnet)

• royalty/ruler (king, emperor, governor, mayor, duke, count, baron, marquess, lord, prince, earl

Setting/Weather Info

• Kent's story begins in early spring. As it draws to a close, winter begins to set in.

• Assuming Aeron's story happens right before Kent's and he is doing other things in the meantime, Aeron's story happens in early spring as well.

• Mehta's story happens in Etrijan near the start of winter.

• During the first trilogy, they are in the first third of winter as they are traveling. About when they arrive in Xenthan at the end of Book 1, that's when the second third of winter starts. By the time they get to the end of book 2, winter is halfway over, so they're fighting an ice dragon in the dead of winter, basically.

Internal Group Conflict

• Garrick was once attacked by a Xyonate who was trying to assassinate him, but he survived and killed the Xyonate. Thus, he inherently distrusts Mehta because of his past.

• Garrick also distrusts Kent because of the mage who'd betrayed him, because on some level he thinks all mages are dishonest and crafty now. This is ironic because Kent is super honorable and generally honest and direct.

• Kent and Garrick argue a lot about what the right course is because they both want to be in charge, and they both think they're more qualified to lead than the other.

• Aeron is the comic relief, but he's also the screw-up in the group. He's a good guy but is totally self-serving when it comes to his back pain and Wafer.

• Kent is power-hungry to some degree and feels pressure because he is so far behind where he should be when it comes to magic, so sometimes his drive to get more power can be detrimental to the group.

• Garrick is overly headstrong and durable, so he tends to charge into situations rather than thinking things through.

• Aeron is not enthusiastic about doing much of anything, so when situations arise, he is inclined to sit back and let things blow over. He's pretty chill, except when it comes to Wafer and to his need for magic mushrooms.

• Mehta can certainly handle himself in an open fight, but he tends toward stealth and secrecy. His quietness makes the rest of the group leery of him.

• Mehta also wants to kill Valdis, so his driving force for the first book is directly at-odds with the rest of the mercs.

• Mehta is meticulous in his planning and is cautious, and that can really get on Garrick's nerves because he likes to just jump in. He will get along with Aeron in the sense that they won't move fast when it comes to the planning, but they won't get along when it comes to actually taking time to plan.

• Something about Mehta's character: he tends to be okay with following commands. It's a part of his upbringing. You can sow confusion when he is forced to choose between two leader-types (Garrick and Kent) because he isn't sure whom to follow.

• When Mehta reveals his true intentions (that he wants to kill Valdis), Garrick goes nuts and loses it. He is still scarred from being betrayed by the previous merc team, so when Mehta does it again, he tries to take out all his aggression on Mehta.

   ○ Mehta and Garrick fight, with Kent and Aeron trying to intervene to stop them, but to no avail.

   ○ Ultimately, Mehta agrees to leave, because neither of them can deal any significant damage to each other. Mehta is far faster, but Garrick is so durable that Mehta can't really deal much damage to him. So Mehta leaves.

   ○ Later, when they learn that Valdis is evil, they have to go find Mehta so they can recruit him to help them stop Valdis. Either that, or they run across Mehta while making their way to Valdis's castle.

   ○ They reluctantly join up since their end goal is now the same, but Garrick still doesn't trust Mehta until Mehta somehow saves his life.

⚙

STORY BIBLE PART 10: TITLE IDEAS

A Brief Introduction

Coming up with good titles is *hard*. Coming up with titles no one else has used before is even *harder*. Coming up with enough titles for an entire series is (for me) the *hardest*.

Here's a list of all the titles I thought through while trying to decide on what to call this series. Most of them are incredibly lame, if I'm being honest, but this was a process I had to go through to better define the feel of the series.

Too comedic-sounding, and I'd need to write the series accordingly. Too kiddish, and the series might not sell because the titles don't appeal to adults. Too serious-sounding, and I'd have to adjust the writing style.

All in all, I'm pretty happy with the end result. I wanted to split the middle between "too serious" and "too comedic," but still lean more toward the "serious" side of the conversation. The books definitely contain some great humor, but the focus is on the sword & sorcery elements and the adventures the character go on.

(Prospective titles from future Blood Mercenaries books have been removed so as not to hint at spoilers.)

Title Ideas

"Quest" Ideas

- Quest for the Dragon's Egg
- Egg Quest: The Search for the Dragon's Egg
- Shell Quest: The Search for the Dragon's Egg
- A Quest for Dragons
- The Dragon Egg Quest

One-Word Trilogy Ideas

- Shells
- Scales
- Skies

"Dragon" Trilogy Ideas

- Dragon's Gate
- Dragon Mercs
- Dragon Raid
- Dragon Heist
- Dragon Runes
- Dragon Blaze
- Dragon Crypt
- The Dragon Map
- Dragon Heist
- Dragon Reaper
- Dragon Breaker

"4 Mercs" Ideas

- 4 Mercs and a Dragon Quest
- 4 Mercs and a Dragon Lord
- 4 Mercs and a Dragon

- 4 Mercs vs. A Dragon Quest
- 4 Mercs vs. a Dragon Lord
- 4 Mercs vs. a Dragon

Series Title Names

Mercenary Lords
4 Mercs
The Dragon Mercenaries/Mercs

Subtitles

A Four Mercs Adventure
A Four Mercs Quest

Final Titles

0. Blood Mercenaries Origins
1. The Crimson Flame
2. Path of Shadows
3. Frostbane

Final Series Title

Blood Mercenaries

STORY BIBLE PART 11: MARKETING COPY

A Brief Introduction

Once you've written the book, you're not done. You still have to publish it and figure out how to get it into readers' hands.

To do that well, you will probably need to write (or hire someone to write) marketing copy for the story (or stories).

The book I'd recommend on this one is Brian Meeks's book on copywriting (disclosure: I edited this book for him):

Mastering Amazon Descriptions
by Brian D. Meeks - https://amzn.to/2XvwQiJ

What follows are my various attempts at writing copy for my books.

You'll see that some attempts turned out better than others. Though I'm satisfied with the end results that are currently present in the respective stories' Amazon descriptions, occasionally rewrite or re-envision the descriptions for the books to optimize reader interaction and experience.

After all, if you've got a solid cover and a solid book, the only thing keeping readers from buying might be your marketing copy.

Marketing Copy

IRONGLADE:

When Aeron Ironglade gets kicked out of the army for his addiction to painkilling magic mushrooms, he is forced to leave Wafer, his battle-mount wyvern, behind.

They've shared a bond since Wafer hatched, and Aeron vows to get him back someday. Without Wafer, Aeron will never truly be complete.

But Aeron's former commander, Larcas Brove, is holding a grudge, and he also controls Wafer's fate. Brove works to stop Aeron and Wafer from reuniting at every turn.

With no money, a dead-end job, and a hopeless future, Aeron decides to rescue Wafer from Brove's clutches—even if it means risking his life.

Will Aeron succeed in rescuing his best friend? Or will disaster befall them both and destroy their futile hope to be reunited for good?

ETHERIDGE:

Kent Etheridge has a secret.

He is the son of a prominent lord in Muroth, a country that has outlawed the use of magic and puts mages to death. Yet Kent's own magic abilities have just awakened.

On the day of Kent's ascension to his father's seat as Lord of House Etheridge, Kent's treacherous brother, Fane, exposes Kent's magical abilities, brands him as a traitor, and murders their father, forcing Kent to flee the country.

Kent takes refuge in the country of Inoth, a land known for its acceptance of mages and magic, and the bitter rival of Muroth. But after he arrives, his past identity catches up with him, endangering his life.

Can Kent convince the beautiful Inothian queen to trust him despite his previous life?

Or will she execute him as an enemy of the state?

REQUIEM:

An unquenchable thirst is threatening to overtake Mehta. Taken as a child and raised by a death cult of assassins, Mehta has grown in a lethal weapon with an appetite for death.

Upon completing a mission to assassinate a lord, Mehta also kills his entire family, his servants, and even his livestock, but none of it satisfies his urge to kill. He craves more death.

When Mehta returns to the cult's sanctuary, the clerics realize they can no longer control Mehta and they try to have him killed. Mehta manages to escape, wounded, and finds refuge with the local priest dedicated to another deity and his family. But the cultists find him, slay the priest and his wife, and Mehta barely escapes with the priest's eight-year-old daughter, Ferne, in tow.

Realizing he can't run forever, Mehta decides to make a final stand against the remaining cultists. Will Mehta be able to protect Ferne and destroy the remainder of the cult, or will they sever his thirst once and for all?

SHATTERSTONE:

Garrick Shatterstone is one of the best mercenaries money can buy. He's huge, a talented fighter, and ridiculously strong and durable thanks to a hint of troll blood running through his otherwise human veins. But when a dark lord named Valdis employs him to find a secret treasure hidden beneath a cult's temple, he realizes he will need additional help to recover it.

Along with the alchemist and the thief who already travel in his mercenary crew, Garrick recruits a climber and a mage to assist in recovering the treasure. But as soon as Garrick and his team descend into the depths below the temple, they encounter an ancient dungeon riddled with traps, fell beasts, and even a river of lava.

Will they overcome overwhelming danger and recover the lost treasure, or will they succumb to the dungeon's perils?

Newsletter:

After failing to deliver on a job to his wealthy and dangerous employer, a berserker forges a shaky partnership with a wyvern knight, a mage, and an assassin to find and retrieve a fabled dragon egg.

But when their employer tries to use the dragon egg in a ritual that will grant him god-like power, the four mercs realize they're the only ones who can stop him. Will they join forces to save the continent from his reign of terror, or will their own motivations keep them--and the world--shrouded in darkness?

The Blood Mercenaries Series is an epic saga of full-length novels set on the continent of Aletia, a mythical land of magic and mayhem.

I already have four prequel novellas written (one for each mercenary) and nearly ready for publication. Watch your inboxes for the first novella, *Ironglade*, coming soon to you, my subscribers, for FREE.

Blood Mercenaries Origins

Four dangerous mercenaries.

Four exciting missions.

Four page-turning novellas.

Blood Mercenaries Origins shares the origin stories of the four legendary heroes in the epic Blood Mercenaries sword & sorcery series.

The author advises that readers read this prequel book **BEFORE** reading *The Crimson Flame*.

IRONGLADE

When Aeron Ironglade gets kicked out of the army for his addiction to painkilling magic mushrooms, he is forced to leave Wafer, his battle wyvern, behind. As he leaves, he swears to get Wafer back someday.

But Aeron's former commander is holding a grudge, and he works to stop Aeron and Wafer from reuniting at every turn.

With no money, a dead-end job, and a hopeless future, Aeron

decides to rescue Wafer from Brove's clutches—even if it means risking his life.

ETHERIDGE

When his forbidden magic powers are exposed, Kent Etheridge is forced to flee his home country, leaving behind his title of nobility, his wealth, his murdered father, and his traitorous brother.

Kent takes refuge in the neighboring rival country of Inoth and soon finds himself face-to-face with its beautiful queen—who wants him dead.

Can Kent convince the queen to trust him despite his previous life?

Or will she execute him as an enemy of the state?

REQUIEM

Mehta, once the best assassin in the Xyonate cult, is running for his life.

Upon realizing they can no longer control Mehta, the Xyonate clerics try to have him killed, but Mehta escapes, wounded, and finds refuge with a local priest.

But the cultists catch up, slay the priest and his wife, and Mehta barely escapes with the priest's eight-year-old daughter, Ferne, in tow.

Realizing he can't run forever, Mehta decides to make a final stand against the remaining cultists—and he'll have to if he and Ferne want to survive.

SHATTERSTONE

A secret treasure resides beneath a cult temple, and only Garrick Shatterstone and his mercenary crew can retrieve it.

Along with an alchemist and a thief, Garrick recruits a climber and a mage to help.

But once Garrick and his team descend into the depths below the temple, they encounter an ancient dungeon riddled with a river of lava, traps, and hideous fell beasts.

Can they overcome the dungeon's overwhelming dangers and recover the lost treasure?

Or will they succumb to the dungeon's perils?

Dive into this prequel collection of unique fantasy stories full of twists and mayhem today. Get it now.

REVIEWS

"In every story he tells, Ben Wolf has a way of drawing you into the world he's created. The Crimson Flame is no exception. It's a perfect blend of peril, death, and humor, and the cast of unique and interesting characters keep you turning pages till the end. A must read!"

- Daniel Kuhnley, Author of The Dark Heart Chronicles

"These stories took me back to the days of the Forgotten Realms and Dragonlance novels, which I still regard very highly. I MUST know what happens next. Each story leaves you hanging like a season finale. I am certainly looking forward to the rest of this series!"

- Chris Hall, Reader

"Not only is Ben Wolf handsome, but he's a damn good writer as well!"

- Kirk DouPonce, Reader & Cover Designer

"Mama Mia! This series is fantastic! Great writing, plot, characters, imagination, and world-building. I'm looking forward to seeing where this story goes. Ben Wolf has a winner here!"

- Peter Younghusband, www.PerspectiveByPeter.com

CRIMSON FLAME BACK COVER - BLURB ONE:

Aeron's sister has been kidnapped. A menacing cult known as the Crimson Flame has taken her, but Aeron vows to get her back—while laying waste to the cult in the process.

When the trail runs cold, Aeron and his mage friend Kent join up with Garrick, a part-troll berserker, to do a mercenary job for a dark lord—a job that will put them directly in the Crimson Flame's path.

Together with an assassin named Mehta, they travel the continent in search of Aeron's sister and in search of Garrick's quarry—a legendary dragon egg, supposedly in the possession of the Crimson Flame.

But success comes at a high cost, and saving Aeron's sister may interfere with finding Garrick's egg.

Through dangerous encounters and excursions into the dark places of the world, Aeron risks everything in order to save his sister...

...but will his everything be enough?

The Crimson Flame is the first in an epic sword and sorcery series sure to thrill you with magic, action, and adventure. Get your copy today and dive into this unique fantasy world full of twists and mayhem.

BLURB TWO:

One dragon egg remains...

...but who is bold enough to claim it?

Aeron's sister has been kidnapped. A menacing cult known as the Crimson Flame took her, but Aeron vows to get her back—while laying waste to the cult in the process.

When the trail runs cold, Aeron and his mage friend join up with a part-troll mercenary to work for a dark lord. Their task: to find a legendary dragon egg—currently believed to be in the possession of the Crimson Flame.

It seems like the perfect gig...

...until the cult's interference threatens to ruin their plans.

Faced with a deadly choice, Aeron must stare death in its eyes and risk everything to save his sister—even if it costs him and his fellow mercenaries their lives...

...but even that may not be enough.

The Crimson Flame is the first in an epic sword and sorcery series sure to thrill you with magic, action, and adventure. Get your copy today and dive into this unique fantasy world full of twists and mayhem.

BLURB THREE:

A strange mark on her neck...

...a mysterious connection to fire...

...an ancient secret soon to be revealed.

Aeron failed to stop the cult of the Crimson Flame from kidnapping his sister. But as a former wyvern knight, he's determined to find and rescue her—and to lay waste to the cult in the process.

When the trail grows cold, Aeron and his mage companion join forces with a half-troll mercenary and an assassin.

Together, they embark on a job for a dark lord that will put them squarely in the Crimson Flame's line of fire.

And that's exactly where Aeron wants to be.

The more cultists he can find, the closer he gets to locating his stolen sister...

...and the more of them he can kill.

Though the job seems like the perfect gig, the cult thwarts Aeron's efforts at every turn.

And all the while, Aeron and his comrades gradually unravel the ancient secret of the Crimson Flame and its ties to his sister.

Faced with a series of deadly choices, Aeron must confront his fate and risk everything to rescue his sister...

...even if it costs him and his fellow mercenaries their lives...

...and even that may not be enough.

The Crimson Flame is the first novel in an epic sword-and-sorcery series sure to thrill you with magic, action, and adventure. Dive into this unique fantasy world full of twists and mayhem today.

Get it Now.

PATH OF SHADOWS

The dragon egg has hatched...

...and a dark lord needs his sacrifice back...

...so he can become a god.

By some miracle, Aeron managed to rescue his sister from Lord Valdis's clutches. Together, they escape to the western mountains and hide out.

But their solace doesn't last long...

...because Lord Valdis's reach extends farther than they know.

And Aeron's sister is soon recaptured by Crimson Flame cultists in the service of Lord Valdis.

Now Aeron's only hope is to gather enough strength--in the form of legendary, god-forged weapons--to kill Lord Valdis and save his sister once and for all. But time is running out. If Aeron doesn't save her by the next new moon, his sister will be sacrificed as part of Lord Valdis's ritual.

Will Aeron manage to get ahold of the legendary weapons in time? And even if he does, will it be enough to snatch his sister from the claws of death yet again?

Path of Shadows is the second novel in an epic sword-and-sorcery series sure to thrill you with magic, action, and adventure. Dive into this unique fantasy world full of twists and mayhem, written by award-winning author Ben Wolf.

Get it now.

FROSTBANE

A dragon corrupted by frost...

...an entire continent at risk...

...and only the Blood Mercenaries can prevent an apocalypse.

The battle with Lord Valdis has awakened a new evil, one that threatens the entire continent of Aletia with icy destruction. And it has wings.

With no one left to turn to, the land of Aletia looks to the Blood Mercenaries to defeat this mammoth, rampaging monster once and for all. In order to do it, they'll need help from an ancient source of power, something sealed away for ages.

But sometimes power is locked away for good reason.

Frostbane is the third novel in the epic Blood Mercenaries sword-and-sorcery series, sure to thrill you with magic, action, and adventure. Dive into this unique fantasy world full of twists and mayhem, written by award-winning author Ben Wolf.

Get it now.

⚙

STORY BIBLE PART 12: WRITING MUSIC

A Brief Introduction

N ot everyone can (or should) write with music, but I definitely do. When I wrote the prequel novellas, I discovered a treasure trove of music on YouTube. These playlists fueled my writing and helped to make the Blood Mercenaries who they are today.

Two Hours of Epic Music:
https://www.youtube.com/watch?v=gFeZh36136E
More Epic Music:
https://www.youtube.com/watch?v=FJpV0920OOM
Undefeated Epic Music:
https://www.youtube.com/watch?v=HFjaEc9aGxs
Superhuman Epic Music:
https://www.youtube.com/watch?v=-rzaSPs__-A
10 Hours of Two Steps from Hell:
https://www.youtube.com/watch?v=DIiWoxBnyJg
Two Steps from Hell Soundtracks: https://www.youtube.com/watch?v=UmUVXOXiLeM&feature=youtu.be

STORY BIBLE PART 13: ORIGINAL BOOK ONE SYNOPSIS

A Brief Introduction

As I mentioned earlier, when I sit down to write a book, it never goes exactly the way I initially envisioned it in my head.

Usually that's a really good thing. It most often means I've created something bigger and better than what I had planned, and so adjustments need to be made.

In the case of *The Crimson Flame*, I actually published and printed about 100 copies of a very early version of the book. This synopsis is closer to that version, but the current version (now published on Amazon) is a better version from a storytelling perspective.

The way I write these first synopses is to dump everything I have in my head onto a page and then try to organize it later. Then, as I develop the concept further, I'll add to it (hence all the random notes and whatnot that you'll see below) and make changes.

So this is not the exact *first* version, but it's the oldest version I have, and it sort of blends my newer ideas with my old ones. Hopefully the synopsis is still helpful to you.

Note that all synopses and outlines contain spoilers for the Blood Mercenaries series. Read with discretion!

NOVEL 1

Beginning of the novel is when Garrick returns to Lord Valdis and begs for a chance to make up for his failure. Lord Valdis already knows of his failure thanks to a gloating message he received from an anonymous rival, but he thought Garrick was dead. When Garrick shows up, Valdis considers having him killed because he thinks he was in on the betrayal, but in fact, Garrick wasn't.

He tries to explain that by showing Valdis his scar from Noraff's wound, but Valdis waves his hand, stating that he hasn't memorized Garrick's scar, and it could be from anything. Garrick reasons with him, saying that he came back to prove his loyalty and to ask for a second chance. Eventually Valdis agrees, and Garrick's first task is to recruit mercs to help him find the map, which was brought to another dark lord in Govalia. Garrick is hoping to find Noraff and Phesnos as well, but he won't. (Maybe by the end of the third book in the series he manages to find them and bring them to justice for killing Coburn and Irwin).

Garrick has heard there was a wyvern knight roaming around Xenthan looking for mercenary work, so he seeks him out and finds Aeron and Kent in a pub. They start chatting about the job. Meanwhile, Mehta has surveyed the castle's defenses, and while he is making a plan in that same pub, and could probably get inside, when he overhears what they're discussing, he offers to join them, thinking that upon their return, he might be taken to Lord Valdis himself. He can either kill Valdis on the spot, or he can at least scope out the castle's interior and look for weaknesses in their defenses, etc., so he can come back and kill Valdis later.

(Make a mention that Aeron and Kent were doing some merc work in Urthia but they headed north after hearing that there were opportunities up in Xenthan.)

Initially, they're all tense around each other, and they're all looking to prove their worth to each other. Garrick makes them "test" the next day to get into the group (or whatever). They pass his tests and prove they're capable, and then they set out for Govalia.

(Sidebar: Aeron is reluctant to return to Govalia after how he left, with stealing Wafer and all, but when Garrick mentions the wyverns, the knights' armor, and Faylen's features, Aeron can't resist. He likes Faylen and doesn't want her mixed up in any of this, so he agrees to the job.)

They head to Govaliston. Aeron often plays the scout role for the group since he and Wafer can fly, but with wyverns patrolling the skies, he has to keep a lower profile. As they advance, a patrol of wyvern knights shows up. Aeron and Wafer aren't around, but if they return, bad things will happen since he's a known defector/traitor (basically), so Kent is trying to get the Govalians to get moving before Aeron returns from scouting.

The knights are about to leave, but then their wyverns start acting up and chirping or whatever, and they search the skies. They see Aeron and realize he's not one of theirs. They realize he was the scout Kent had mentioned, and then they surround the mercs and attack.

Fight scene, etc. The mercs all show their prowess in real time this time, including Aeron who battles with the leader of the group one-on-one in the air. (Maybe it's Porgus?) Anyway, some of them escape, and some are killed. Most of the wyverns fly away, but a couple of them are killed also.

An argument about whether or not their cover is blown ensues, and the group almost fractures apart. They all want to stick it out, but they all have concerns. Mehta, surprisingly, unites them. He wants to make sure the mission succeeds mostly because he needs to kill Valdis, and Garrick needs it to succeed for the same reason, even though he's worried about Aeron/Wafer going forward.

They make it to Govaliston. Garrick wears a cloak and hood because of course he does (easy to identify with greenish skin and blue hair), but Kent and Mehta walk freely among the crowd. Aeron stashes Wafer somewhere safe but within range of calling him with a Wafer Whistle he has developed and that he wears around his neck. It's a hollowed-out wyvern tooth or something cool. When he blows in it, Wafer can hear it, even if no one else can (think dog whistle).

As they progress through the city, Aeron stops by his father's shop.

He finds Pa, who gives him his usual cold reception, but who is kind enough about it all. He asks about his sister, Kallie, and Pa says he doesn't really know what she's up to, but that she has moved out and doesn't come around much anymore, except maybe once every couple of weeks for a family meal. Aeron doesn't think much of it, but he gets info on where to find her.

The mercs make a plan to corner Faylen since Aeron knows she was involved in helping Noraff and Phesnos. They want to see what she knows. Aeron agrees to be the first face she sees because questions from a familiar, friendly face, even if it is the face of someone who has committed crimes against Govalia, is better than a stranger inquiring after her.

They set it up, and that night, Aeron sort of ambushes her in an alleyway when she is on leave without her wyvern. She is not pleased, and she tries to leave, but then Garrick shows up at the other end of the alley, blocking her way. Now she's really pissed, and she's ready to fight. She might even fight Aeron a bit, but ultimately, Mehta comes in and renders her unconscious.

When she wakes up, she's in a room. Kent is sitting across from her because he's the only one she hasn't yet met, and he no longer trusts that Aeron will be able to get them anywhere with her. They have a calm conversation, but they don't get anywhere either. Against Garrick's wishes, Aeron bursts in, and he talks it out with Faylen. She agrees that he was wrongfully accused and that it was horrible what Commander Larcas Brove did to him, but he still shouldn't have stolen Wafer back. When Aeron reveals that Brove had intended to turn Wafer into wyvern chow for the other wyverns, Faylen's attitude shifts a bit. She wouldn't have wanted her wyvern subjected to that, especially when it was perfectly healthy like Wafer.

It breaks through to her, and she reveals what she knows. She took Phesnos on her wyvern (and she hated him, btw; he kept staring at her with cold, piercing eyes and was generally creepy) and another knight had Noraff, and they dropped them at the manse of some lord just outside the city of Govalia. She shows them where on a map, and Aeron invites her to join them. She declines and says that the Govalian Army knows Aeron is around, and they also know a group of mercs have come to town after fighting and killing a few of their own, so they're watching for the mercs now.

She tells them that if she's discovered to have talked with them, then she'll be branded a traitor and cast out as well. Aeron suggests that the surest way to make sure that doesn't happen is to have her report what happened tonight immediately once she returns. Faylen suggests they give her a few smacks to make it look realistic. None of them wants to strike a woman, though—least of all, Aeron, who adores Faylen, so Mehta agrees to do it since he has sifted plenty of women in his day. He doesn't relish the idea of striking Faylen, but he knows he's doing it to help protect her. So he does. Her lip splits open on the side, and her mouth is bruised as a result, because Mehta doesn't hold back.

Aeron is low-key mad at Mehta for awhile, but ultimately he resolves not to stay mad because it was Faylen's idea/request. Faylen tells Aeron straight up that things between them cannot change; she is still a member of the royal army, and as such, pride, honor, and loyalty dictate that if she encounters Aeron again, she will have to fight him, even if she doesn't want to. Aeron understands. That goes for the other mercs as well, but Faylen doesn't voice that concept aloud. They let her go, and they immediately head to the manse outside the city.

They break inside and steal the map, and they have to face the dark lord (who is a rival of Lord Valdis). They defeat him, and he says something cryptic about how trusting Lord Valdis is a bad idea because he intends to rain destruction down on all of Aletia. They ignore him (except for Mehta, who mostly believes it and who adds it to his scales of judgment against Valdis). Garrick is hoping to find Noraff and Phesnos and he asks about them, but the dark lord dies before he can reveal anything. Garrick searches through his papers and finds a payment receipt to Noraff with a mention to send further payment to an address on the island of Caclos. He commits it to memory and takes the paper as well.

They are rushed to get out of there because Aeron alerts them that the Govalian army has come to support the dark lord (albeit too late), and they are led by Larcas Brove and his wyvern knights. Aeron is both dismayed, relieved, and worried to see Faylen is not among them. He wonders if she has been found out and branded as a traitor even after their measures to protect her.

They attack, but a kind-hearted servant/slave girl whom the dark lord had routinely abused shows them a secret tunnel out in thanks for freeing her from his grasp. Aeron manages to escape via the skies with Wafer, and they rendezvous back in Govaliston.

With the map in hand, they plan to flee Govaliston the next morning. But Aeron's Pa shows up and calls him to the house. Kallie is there, and she's in bad shape.

Aeron rushes over with Kent, but Mehta and Garrick stay back to guard the map. (Possibly include a scene where Garrick is prying for information from Mehta. Maybe Mehta has made him suspicious somehow?) At Pa's house, Aeron finds Kallie there, dazed and confused. Aeron fields comments from his pa about her being drugged like he was, so obviously he should know what's wrong with her. But Aeron doesn't know, so he just tries to help take care of her. Kent stands watch and is a good friend.

Aeron notices a strange mark on the back of Kallie's neck—it's not quite a tattoo, but it's not a birthmark, either. It's something else, and he can't tell what it is. At one point in the night, Kallie gets up and stumbles into the fireplace headfirst as if mesmerized by it. Kent notices and tries to pull her back, but is too late. He manages to pull her out with Aeron's help, but Kent burns his hand in the process. They frantically check Kallie for signs that she is harmed but find none. Stranger still, Aeron notices the mark on her neck is glowing now, and it's in the shape of fire. Mum Ironglade and Pa are awake by this point, and Mum tends to Kent's burned hand.

No one has any explanations. In the morning, Kallie is safe and cogent, but she can't remember the night before or much of anything about where she's been, so they keep her home and keep her safe. Aeron is hesitant to go, but he knows he has to, and he trusts his parents with Kallie's wellbeing. (The Kallie thread is all setup for book 2, when they learn that she is a vital piece in Lord Valdis's plan to steal the dragon's essence; Kallie is the Crimson Flame's sacrifice that will hatch the dragon egg. Kallie was supposed to have already been sacrificed, but because of the delay with the map, she managed to escape and wandered off because of some reason, but if Garrick had brought the map back in time, she probably would've been sacrificed. Make that work somehow if it fits.)

A couple weeks later, back at Lord Valdis's palace, only Garrick is permitted inside because Valdis neither knows, trusts, nor cares about the other mercs. Mehta is frustrated at this, but he resolves to remain patient. He will get his chance eventually.

Pleased that Garrick has returned the map to him, Valdis gives Garrick the full payment he is owed, despite Garrick's past failure. Garrick is honored and tries to refuse the full payment, but Valdis is rich and doesn't care. Garrick plans to use it immediately to go find and kill Noraff and Phesnos, but Valdis wants him to follow the map (he translates it on the spot because he's a genius scholar dark sorcerer) to retrieve several things along the way. Ultimately, Garrick accepts because it will help cement his good relationship with Valdis to do so. Noraff and Phesnos will have to wait.

Details on the Path of Shadows (the concept in the book, not the book itself):

• The mercs have to gather the following items from various locations around Aletia (aka they must walk the "Path of Shadows," a term and a path they receive from a guy whom Lord Valdis is torturing when they get their assignment):

    ○ a map to the egg (retrieved by Garrick in his novella from a vault in **Etrijan** but stolen by traitors and taken to Govalia)

    ○ a key to get inside the dungeon where the egg is housed (it's a dragon sword, and it's hidden in **Inoth**)

    ○ a scroll/book containing a ritual/spell to awaken the dragon within the egg and another ritual/spell to hatch the egg (hidden in **Muroth** because it's ironic that a magical item would be hidden there)

○ the Crimson Flame's chosen one (probably a teenage girl) to be sacrificed as part of the ritual to get the dragon to hatch (**Govalia**—it's Kallie, Aeron's sister)

○ the fossilized/hibernating/dormant egg itself (hidden in **Xenthan**)

He takes the news to the mercs and pays them their shares. Aeron is thinking he should get back to Govalia to check on Kallie, but Kent reminds him that Govalia is not a good place for him right now, so he goes for it. Mehta is on board as well because it means he's another step closer to killing Valdis. They all sign on and keep going; together they follow the path of shadows as the map says. The have to retrieve several items from around the continent that will enable them to reach the final item, and that is what Valdis wants, but he doesn't tell them what it is.

All of the items, however, can be found on the map. It will turn out that they're all contained within temples of the Crimson Flame. They go for the key first, in Inoth. Kent has reservations about going there, but the temple is far from the capital city of Goldmoor (where Kymil is, whom he would love to kill in revenge for Aveyna, among others), so he's okay with it. They visit the temple and find a dungeon beneath it, and they work through it together. They retrieve the key, and it's a dragon sword, which Kent wields in addition to his magic.

*** <u>At some point</u>, Mehta mentions that he left a small girl with light skin in his home near the cratered mountain, and Garrick overhears it and remembers seeing Ferne in that town as he was passing through after his novella. He notes it but doesn't say anything at the time.

Then they head north to Muroth. This venture is problematic because after the fiasco in Kent's novella, the borders are tight, so they have to sneak into the country. They succeed, but it comes at some sort of cost. Maybe they bribe someone, or maybe they kill someone. Either way, Kent is not recognized. Muroth continues to be problematic because the temple is housed in the province of Lord Frostsong, a long-time family friend who almost certainly wants Kent dead because of how Fane made it seem like Kent had murdered their father.

(By the way, it is definitely winter time now, so they're trudging through the snow at this point.) They reach the temple and get inside. The dungeon in here is more of a labyrinth than a dungeon, and it's more about evading traps than it is fighting enemies. They succeed and collect a ritual book for magic. Kent can understand some of it, and he finds it ironic that a book describing a magic ritual would be hidden in Muroth, the most anti-magic country on the continent.

When they emerge, they encounter Lord Frostsong and a bunch of his men. Fane is not there. Lord Frostsong "knows his land and thus knows they came into it" or whatever, but he is unexpectedly kind toward Kent. They have a parlay, just Kent and Frostsong, while the others wait outside. He asks Kent to demonstrate his power. Kent shows him some casual magic (his fingers sparking blue, or whatever), and Lord Frostsong nods. Then Lord Frostsong admits that he does not agree with Muroth's oppression of mages and of Inoth. He hasn't ever since he was a child, even though Muroth and Inoth have been separate countries for about a century.

Fane comes up in the conversation, and Frostsong has only grief about Fane. He has been aggressive in renegotiating trade between their provinces, and Frostsong is weary of it. Kent warns him not to trust anything Fane says, and he explains how Fane killed their father. Frostsong is saddened but not surprised. He knew it was not within Kent's character to do such a thing, but Fane has always been treacherous.

Ultimately, Frostsong is bound by his commands to resist magic, but he is also the lord of his province, so he lets Kent and his friends go. He announces to his men that he put a piece of scorallite in Kent's hand himself and saw no sign of magic, so he is allowing Kent to go free. The mercs leave, and they head back to Govalia next.

Upon arrival, Aeron stops to see his parents and Kallie in secret. Mehta helps get him there quietly and in the dark, but Kallie isn't there. Mum and Pa are kind of leery of Mehta because he's creepy and exudes killer vibes, but they tell Aeron that they found out Kallie was involved with the Crimson Flame. Then some men in armor with the crest of a ram with three horns took her one night. Aeron puts it together that whatever the map wants them to get in Govalia (give it a cool, ominous term that suggests a blood sacrifice) is actually his sister. He convinces the others that he's correct (and he is), and they return to Xenthan to try to get his sister back.

In Xenthan, they quest for the final item, knowing that Valdis won't give Kallie back unless they have something worth trading. The dragon sword/key and the ritual are useless without the final item, and Garrick is confident Valdis would not trade Kallie for those. (Garrick is also much more driven to complete the mission, though he does have some conflict about what will happen when they reach Valdis/Kallie.) So they go get the final thing. It ends up being a dragon egg. Garrick secretly finds a second one, and he takes it with him, using his shield to sort of cover the bulge in his pack as they travel back to Valdis's castle.

Back in Valdis Keep, they are all allowed to enter this time. Garrick starts doing the talking, but Valdis refuses to give up the girl. Aeron breaks rank and tells him Kallie is his sister, and he begs for him to release her. Valdis explains Kallie's importance (she's the chosen sacrifice necessary for him to perform a ritual to steal the dragon's essence) and refuses, so Aeron holds the egg up and threatens to smash it if Valdis doesn't bring Kallie out. To further complicate things, Kallie is dazed and thinks it's an honor for her to be the chosen sacrifice.

The situation is tense. Mehta is constantly looking for an opening and wonders if Aeron has given him one. Kent is trying to mediate. Garrick is considering whether or not he should fight Aeron. Ultimately, Valdis brings Kallie to him. They negotiate hard, but Aeron is smart enough to know he shouldn't release the egg until he's outside the castle with Kallie already on Wafer's back. They start to leave, and one of Valdis's men (probably a recurring character of some sort—a recognizable guard or official) tries to kill Aeron, but Mehta intervenes and royally kills the guy.

All hell breaks loose, and Aeron lets the egg smash onto the floor, turning it to dust and ash. Mehta considers attacking Valdis, but he decides it's still not the right opportunity and that helping Aeron and Kallie escape is more important. In the commotion, Aeron and Kallie manage to escape (with Mehta's help), but Garrick and Kent remain there, unable/unwilling to fight back. Valdis's men capture them, but Garrick produces a second egg and leverages it to free Kent and himself with the understanding that they will go back to get Kallie from Aeron because Valdis needs her.

As a side note, Valdis's men don't let Garrick keep his snow steel sword and shield because they are obviously going to be effective against a fire-type dragon, so Valdis makes Garrick give them up as a sign of faith. Nor does he allow Kent to keep the dragon sword/key. Instead, he outfits Garrick with a phantom steel axe that has been used many times to kill people and steal souls, so it's a beastly weapon. Valdis breaks it out of his vault and everything specifically for that reason. He gives Kent some cool weapon as well, even though Kent is a mage.

Garrick doesn't feel good about it, but he is willing to do it for the sake of his reputation and future. Plus, Valdis is about ready to kill him based on one failure already and the potential that he's been betraying Valdis this whole time. Kent goes along with it as well in part to save his own life but also in part because he realizes that Valdis taking a dragon's essence is a terrible idea, and he must be stopped. (End of Book One)

STORY BIBLE PART 14: ORIGINAL BOOK TWO SYNOPSIS

A Brief Introduction

This is pretty much the same breakdown as the previous book's synopsis, so I won't re-explain everything.

What I will add, though, is that planning Book Two (and Book Three, for that matter) before writing Book One proved to be both necessary and perilous. I can't imagine how I ever would've completed the first trilogy if I hadn't planned most of it out in advance.

And on that same note, I can't imagine how I ever would've finished it if I hadn't sat down and made sure I wrote all three books within the course of a year. Including the prequel novellas, it took me two years to write it all (also including this story bible).

NOVEL 2

Lord Valdis hatches the egg using more knowledge from the dragon-worshipping cult, and a dragon is born. Once it is full-grown enough, he intends to steal its essence, but he is counting on Garrick and Kent to face off against Mehta and Aeron to get Kallie back for the sacrifice as part of the ritual. Garrick isn't feeling good about this, and as they travel, Kent's conversations with him make him feel even worse. Falna shows up at the beginning of book 2, and she accompanies Garrick and Kent into the mountains to enforce Lord Valdis's will.

Kallie is barefoot and wearing a Crimson Flame robe. The farther away from Valdis Keep she gets, the more of her cognition returns, and the less she feels inclined to go back. This will be an important character thing for her throughout because when she finally decides she needs to go back (if that ends up happening), she will be doing so while fully aware and awake, and that will make her sacrifice all the more powerful.

They eventually find Mehta and Aeron hiding in the mountains where Mehta's hometown is located because Garrick remembers that's where Mehta had said he'd left Ferne, and Garrick actually saw her while trekking back from Etrijan after failing to get the map. Aeron obviously can't take Kallie back to Govalia for a number of reasons, but Mehta thinks no one knows where he calls home. So Kent and Garrick set out for that town.

When Kent and Garrick arrive, Mehta wants to kill them both before they realize Mehta is watching them, but Aeron won't let him kill Kent. Maybe Garrick is untrustworthy, but Kent has been a true friend to Aeron thus far.

Instead, they confront Garrick and Kent. This is the door leading from Act 1 to Act 2 (probably) because instead of choosing to bring Kallie back, Garrick decides to side with Mehta and Aeron and Kent in trying to stop Valdis/dragon, etc. They make a blood pact, joining themselves together as the Blood Mercenaries, that they will stop Valdis at all costs, even their lives. Now unified, they can move forward.

(They also have to fight off a bunch of Lord Valdis's men, led by Falna, who are sent as a contingency to bring Kallie back, in case the mercs should fail. The mercs kick their asses, but the townspeople are pissed due to damage and due to their history, knowing that the soldiers will return, and it will be worse next time. But the mercs assure them that they're going to take care of Lord Valdis once and for all. The townsfolk are still very dubious, though.)

Mehta's grandfather tells them about a legendary temple in northern Etrijan (an arctic region that is super cold) dedicated to the God Fjorst...

They quest to a temple of Fjorst, the God of Ice (and cold places), to try to get get ahold of some more snow steel weapons that are capable of killing the dragon and, hopefully, Lord Valdis. How they will deal with Valdis, they aren't entirely sure, but based on Kent's experiences with three other dark lords (Eusephus, Kymil, and the dark lord they all fought in Govalia), he's confident that if they can GET to Lord Valdis, they can take him down with physical attacks (that's how they took down the other dark lord, and that's how he took down Eusephus as well).

No one knows Kallie is with them, but Aeron is unwilling to leave her behind, so they bring her along. Meanwhile, they quest for the weapons. The Crimson Flame cultists bother them as they quest for the weapons, and the cultists manage to hypnotize Kallie and get her to come out of the tent or whatever. They abduct her and take her away, and the mercs can't stop them/catch them... etc.

They chase the cultists, but the cultists cause an avalanche that temporarily slows the mercs down. They only survive thanks to help from, of all people, a group of Govalian soldiers led by Commander Larcas Brove who were pursuing them based on a tip from someone somewhere (figure it out). The knights are not friendly, and they take the mercs prisoner, but Faylen has a crisis of conscience and realizes she loves Aeron, and she secures his release because he was kind enough to let her go once, and also because she doesn't agree with the Govalian Army anymore—particularly not Brove.

She doesn't go with them and instead heads due south. (She may turn up later in the first trilogy when everyone is fighting the dragon, but she might not show up until sometime later in the series.) Before she leaves, she gives Aeron a kiss that he will never forget.

Now free from their delay, they return to Mehta's hometown, then they head on to Valdis Keep.

When they get there, they fight their way through what seems like only a handful of guards/soldiers, comparatively, only to find that Valdis isn't there. They learn (somehow) that he has gone to an ancient

Aletian tower somewhere in the distance in Xenthan to perform the ritual (at sunset, or whatever). They retrieve the snow steel sword and shield Garrick had, as well as the dragon key/sword and then, naturally, they head out to the tower to stop Valdis and save Kallie.

They fight their way through the tower's various levels (think the PS2 LOTR game fighting Saruman), including Crimson Flame warriors (possibly this is where Falna comes back into play), Lord Valdis's men, some fell beasts and stuff that just occupy the tower thanks to Lord Valdis being a dark mage, and then they finally reach the top (interior) level and face Lord Valdis.

Lord Valdis is unstoppable—in LitRPG terms, he's too high-level for the 4 Mercs to do any real damage to him, but they change their tactics and manage to succeed in knocking his harvest ritual off-kilter. In the process, they're able to save Kallie, but it results in the dragon flipping out and eating Lord Valdis (a la the T-Rex in Jurassic Park). Unfortunately for the 4 Mercs, the ritual finishes and merges Lord Valdis's essence with the dragon's instead (because the ritual malfunctions), and since Valdis is killed, the dragon absorbs Valdis's essence. Mehta is disappointed, but ultimately justice is done in Valdis's death, so he can dig it.

Fearing the worst, the 4 Mercs stab the dragon with their snow steel weapons to try to kill it before the ritual concludes. Instead of killing the dragon, they only wound it, and it absorbs the power of the snow steel blade, and transforms into an ice dragon instead of a fire dragon.

As such, it gains a new degree of sentience and becomes more powerful somehow. It immediately tries to kill the 4 Mercs by leveling the tower from the sky, but Aeron and Wafer escape, and the others are buried (but protected) thanks to Kent's magic creating a wedge between them and falling rubble.

✾

STORY BIBLE PART 15: ORIGINAL BOOK THREE SYNOPSIS

A Brief Introduction

This is pretty much the same breakdown as the previous books' synopses, so I won't re-explain everything.

Of the three synopses, this is the shortest one. For me, the farther away a story is from me writing it, the less defined it is in my head, but it's not like that for everyone.

As I said before, write as much as you can to "dump" it out of your head. It'll at least give you a trajectory to aim for when you're writing the first book in the series.

NOVEL 3

The mercs must defeat a fully-grown, rampaging dragon. But first they must quest to find a series of legendary weapons capable of getting the job done (including ancient knowledge of magic that can enable Kent to erupt a volcano). Meanwhile, the dragon is literally ravaging the land around them, and a cult of dragon worshippers is trying to prevent them from succeeding so as to enable the dragon to bring about the world's apocalypse. In the end, they trap the dragon over the mouth of an exposed volcano (The Cratered Mountain from Mehta's novella) and make the volcano erupt, and that kills the dragon, because the dragon cult destroys the legendary dragon-slaying weapon.

***NOTE:** the reason why Lord Valdis's men kept raiding the towns and villages around Mehta's village was because they were mining scorallite nearby and needed resources periodically for their men. So at some point in Book 3, the Blood Mercs can visit one of those mines.

IMPORTANT:** Perhaps the dragon starts forming an icy nest in the cratered mountain because of its shape, and it starts laying eggs. If those eggs hatch, the continent will be turned to ice before very long because the ice dragons will freeze everything over.

The mercs don't realize the cratered mountain is a volcano until Mehta's grandfather tells him/them that it is. At first, none of them believe him because they've never seen a volcano, except for Garrick, who has the one time he visited Caclos (the whole island was born of a volcano). But he's convinced they only belch out smoke and a bit of molten rock. Grandfather assures him that when the cratered mountain blew, it was considerably worse. His own grandfather was alive to see it, and the skies were filled with ash and smoke for days. Take it from there (research why some volcanoes are worse than others, like Mt. St. Helens).

Kent will learn magic techniques that allow him to manipulate weather and cataclysmic happenings. So he will be the one who makes the volcano erupt, though initially he isn't sure he can make it happen. Maybe there is something (a breastplate or a set of armor) he can acquire that will give him a surge of magic big enough to make it happen? Scorallite? Perhaps if it is handled properly, it can hold additional magic/act as a battery? Maybe he finds some magic gauntlets that still allow him to do magic and that actually enhance his magic abilities further?

They go get some scorallite from near Mehta's village (Lord Valdis's mine) because they anticipate Kent needing it for the final battle. Kent is granted permission from Lord Frostsong to try to harvest nearby scorallite from his land. By now, the dragon has wrought havoc on much of the continent, so Lord Frostsong doesn't care that Kent is a mage. He just wants to try to help stop it. So Kent holds a piece of scorallite and tries to manipulate the scorallite buried in the ground. Kent has never used scorallite to bolster essence for his magic, so he doesn't know if it'll even work, but he tries anyway.

As he is doing it, he can feel the scorallite messing with his power, but ultimately, it works, and a vein of scorallite erupts from the ground. (This is a plant for the payoff of Kent harnessing the volcano's power when the time comes.) They then dig a hole in the center of the volcano crater, plant the scorallite deep within the volcano, and Kent touches the scorallite (which is still glowing) and the volcano floor at the same time to make it erupt.

Faced with no other options, he elects to try. But he doesn't have to control it—he just has to make it happen. The act almost kills Kent in the process, both because a volcano is erupting and because it's messing with his magic so hard. (btw, at the end of the series, he develops a larger pool of magic to draw from, thanks to the scorallite expanding his capacity, basically.)

***NOTE: With the scorallite feeding/drawing out Kent's magic, his mind nearly shatters from the strain of having to focus on so many things at once. In later books, he will gain more control over this phenomenon (being able to focus on multiple magical things at once). In essence, the more magical uses and processes that are going on that the wielder can still control, the more powerful they are. Examples would be homing multiple points of magic in on multiple enemies and doing damage and being able to manage all of that in his head at once.

Meanwhile Aeron and Wafer will be distracting the dragon, while Mehta and Garrick will be taking on minions (dragon cult?).

When the volcano erupts, it will bury Kent. They will think he's dead, but he will survive thanks to magic.

Aeron lures the dragon on top of the volcano via some crafty flying, but he'll be knocked away at some point, and that will fix his back.

***NOTE: Whenever the time has come for Garrick to find Noraff and Phesnos, Kent mentions he knows a fine bounty hunter who can help locate them. (It's Ronin Shroud.) Ronin will then lead Garrick (and probably Kent) to their hideout (in exchange for fair pay, of course). Take it from there.

✿

STORY BIBLE PART 16: ORIGINAL PREQUEL OUTLINES

A Brief Introduction

For a thorough explanation of how I make my synopsis into an outline, jump to the next chapter where I explain in a lot of detail.

If you've already read the synopses for these novellas and the novels, this outline chapter and the upcoming outline chapters will probably feel redundant for you, especially in the earlier books and the novellas.

If it gets too redundant, maybe skip ahead to the later books in the series, and you'll be able to see more of how those outlines evolved as I got more of the story written.

Even so, compared to my novel outlines, which don't spell out the three-act structure as blatantly, these novella outlines show more "parts" of that structure, so this should still be instructive for you.

I actually don't have an outline for Aeron's novella. For whatever reason, when I wrote the novella, the outline ceased to exist after that.

Sorry about that, but there's a super basic outline of his story under the "Characters" section in the first chapter of this story bible guide.

(As a bonus, you'll see Mehta's original name before I changed it.)

✿

Kent's Novella

Backstory

Kent grew up as the son of a prominent Lord, or Marquess, or Baron, or something. He was classically trained in the art of physical warfare/tactics/strategy, economics, literature, sciences, and just about everything else, too. He has also been taught his whole life that magic users are an abomination to the world, as their country's chief rivals are magic users.

- But at around age 40, Kent's own magical powers began manifesting—about 30 years later than they should have normally shown up.

- All the while, Kent's jealous, scheming younger brother is furious that control will be passing to Kent and not him.

- He managed to hide his powers successfully for the next ten years, but around age 50, as his father was beginning to ail and was ready to pass the reins to Kent to control the family's assets, businesses, etc., there's a magical mishap.

Act I

Inciting Incident

A magical mishap happens (in part thanks to prompting from Kent's younger brother, who sparks Kent into accidentally using magic openly), and Kent's father promptly disowns him and installs the younger brother as his sole heir.

Kent is cast out, literally, into the street with nothing. In fact, it is considered a mercy, because his father's sworn duty in his role within that city was to kill any magic users found within the city limits, no questions asked.

Kent resists, of course, but ultimately he cannot control his magic, and he is thrown out. His brother threatens to kill him if he ever returns, and perhaps his brother also kills their father shortly after (or later on in the story) so he can take power sooner.

Afraid for his life and unsure where to turn, Kent heads across the border into the neighboring country populated with magic users.

First Disaster/Door of No Return (DNR)

Now banished from his family and on the run from his own people because of his magic abilities, Kent chooses to venture into the neighboring kingdom of magic users to try to build a new life there.

ACT II

Kent sticks out like a sore thumb in a lot of ways, and despite his fine clothes, he is now dirt poor. Kent has to get over his prejudices and humbles himself, begging for food and coin on the street.

Then he realizes he doesn't have to be miserable. He goes out and finds a job at a shop and dramatically increases their profits by using his knowledge, all the while picking up little magic tips and tricks and gradually learning how to use his magic from whomever will teach him.

Things are going fine until a visitor (either from the neighboring country where Kent is from, or someone whom he somehow knew or ran across from back then) recognizes him and "outs" him for who he really is.

They prove it because of a telltale mark or tattoo or piece of jewelry that gives him away. Maybe a ring with his family's crest on it that he refused to sell or get rid of because it would mean he was fully severing his connection with his family. (A ring that he must take off in order to use magic because the metal inhibits his ability to wield magic?)

Second DNR

Kent is forced to choose to either kill the person who recognized him in order to stay safe or let the person go. He lets the person go and makes preparations to leave/flee, but...

Kent is captured and hauled before the local magistrate, who quickly realizes Kent's importance and sends him directly to the Queen as an accused spy.

The Queen grills Kent with questions and ultimately pronounces him guilty of being a spy. His punishment is death, and he is to be burned alive.

As the mages in the throne room hurl fire at him, Kent manages to remove the ring and lets it drop to the floor in order to save himself. He would rather live as a nobody than die as a somebody, and he manages to harden his body to stone, which protects him from the fire long enough that they stop and see that he is one of them.

The Queen orders him released and marvels at his power, and Kent tells the entire extent of his story at this point (about his powers manifesting really late, likely because the metal in his ring kept it from happening). The Queen knows Kent can't be a spy because Kent's home country kills all mages upon sight.

The Queen has Kent trained in the basics of magic, and Kent catches on very quickly. Before long, he becomes the Queen's most trusted military advisor because of his intimate knowledge of the tactics of fighting against his own homeland, and they eventually fall in love (she has a grown son who despises Kent for his nationality and doesn't trust him, and her former husband, the King has been deceased for several years).

At some point, they hire Aeron as private security for the Queen for this particular battle. She rationalizes it, suggesting that by hiring random mercenaries at times, she can be assured that someone is always available to be a failsafe in case something wonky happens.

Third DNR

Kent agrees to go into battle along with the Queen and her son to fend off an encroaching force of his former countrymen. He doesn't want to fight his own people, but they've disowned him, so he rationalizes that he is among his new people now.

Fighting against his own people with the Queen will also cement her and her son's approval of him as a full member of their citizenry.

Act III

Climax

The Queen's son betrays her on the battlefield.

Grey Moment

The son admits to colluding with Kent's brother (who shows up on the scene). Kent's brother is now the Lord in their father's place, and he openly admits to having slain their father.

Black Moment

Their combined armies take a hiatus and instead attack the Queen and her elite guards. Kent tries to fight back and does very well at it (his powers have grown to a level almost as strong as the Queen's)...

The Turnaround

...but the Queen uses magic to fling him far away, to safety, sacrificing herself to save Kent. He sees her die as he is transported away (maybe Aeron gets hired as a mercenary for them, and he follows her orders instead of Kent's and saves him instead of her? That way, Kent can hold this against Aeron into book 1 of the series).

Denouement/Resolution

She dies, and Kent is expelled from yet another country. Incidentally, the two countries forge a lasting peace as a result of this happening.

Falling Action

Aeron and Kent set out on their own as mercenaries who work together, since their skills complement each other.

JAFAR'S NOVELLA

Backstory

Jafar basically grew up in a death cult.

- He has been trained for one purpose essentially from birth: to kill.

- He's so good at it, that if he plans it out, he can kill without being seen, heard, or even sensed.

- He employs very little magic (if any ever), as he is so good that he doesn't need any magical help to do what he does.

- But his killing has gotten to the point that he literally MUST kill, or he cannot function.

- He is essentially a serial killer, and his thirst for blood must be sated often, or he cannot function.

ACT I

Inciting Incident

Jafar returns from one of his missions totally unsatisfied, despite having killed his target and going beyond.

He has also killed his target's family, including the wife, the children, the servants in the house, the pets, the livestock out back, the neighbors, all the neighbors' servants, pets, and livestock, and so on. (Meant to be darkly funny.)

- The death cult leaders seem unfazed, but Jafar has mastered his skills of reading people, and he catches something physical from them that indicates his future: they mean to kill him next. He has seen it before with his other comrades.

- They come to cull him that night while he is sleeping—except he's not sleeping. He's waiting for them, and he kills his way out of the situation smoothly and marvelously.

- He virtually destroys that entire sect of the death cult that night. That is, until a blade from someone hits him in his gut.

- He kills the assailant and flees, but he is badly wounded and dying.

- He stumbles into the nearby town, desperate for help and to hide.

He sees a small religious symbol (a triangle, point down, with a line moving up through the center almost as if it's an arrowhead—think "Delta"-something as a possible name for the religion) etched into the doorframe of one house and staggers inside, waking a terrified family.

- The father is holding a weapon as if to defend himself and his family, but he doesn't try to advance on Jafar.

- Jafar realizes that the father knows what he is.

- Jafar clutches both his wounded torso and a blade, and a small girl (maybe 9 or so) pulls free from her mother and approaches him, despite her parents' calls to stay back.

First Disaster/Door of No Return (DNR)

Jafar is immediately on his guard—he'd killed a girl no older than her back at the target's neighbor's house just hours earlier, and now the familiar bloodlust burbles up within him again, all while his blood continues to pool on the ground beneath him.

It's tense, but ultimately Jafar decides not to kill her and passes out.

Act II

- When Jafar awakens, the first thing he sees is the religious triangle symbol again, this time hanging from a necklace around the same girl's neck. She is tending to his wounds.

- Character development, etc.

- Ultimately, the father is the head of that religious order in that town (like a priest), and he helps Jafar sate his bloodlust other ways through prayer and meditation.

Second DNR

The death cult returns and takes the family hostage. Jafar is offered the chance to return to the death cult and be forgiven and put back into immediate service, but he instead chooses to help her escape.

- The death cult kills the family, but Jafar manages to stop them from killing the girl.

- They flee to relative/temporary safety.

- Jafar knows they won't be safe until/unless he can kill off these remaining members of this sect of the death cult.

- Against the girl's urgings (she just wants them to run away and be safe somewhere else, living different lives), he sets up an ambush in the delta church.

Third DNR

Jafar is about 70% healed, but he decides to fight anyway.

The death cult pursues them, but he stashes the girl somewhere safe within her father's church, and he waits.

Act III

Climax

The death cult is sneaky, but Jafar is absolutely the best.

Unfortunately, his 70% will have to be better than their 100%, etc.

Jafar kills them one by one through a series of wicked, cunning traps.

Grey Moment

The girl is found by the death cult leader and his remaining assassins, and he has her at knifepoint. He makes Jafar surrender.

Black Moment

Jafar ultimately decides to sacrifice himself for her, because his arrival at her house had been a death sentence for her entire family, yet they'd saved his life.

The Turnaround

The girl gets ahold of a knife and kills her captor, who was preparing to let her go as part of the agreement.

Then Jafar kills everyone else and saves the girl.

In the end, she rationalizes that while he has learned about their ways from her family, she has learned about his ways also, and they have some practical uses, including saving her own life.

If she had died, or if she had let Jafar die for her, then neither of them could continue to live on and use their lives to help others by doing good.

There was no chance the assassins were going to do that, so it seemed like a fair trade.

Denouement/Resolution

Jafar agrees and takes her somewhere safe (maybe a relative's house).

Before they part ways, the girl gives Jafar her necklace with the triangle pendant.

She tells him it will be a reminder that his life matters, and so do those of other innocents.

It can help guide him and remind him to continue the healing of his sickness, and when he can't control it, it can help him target those who would do evil in the world.

Falling Action

Jafar thanks her and heads out.

While on the road, he runs into Aeron and Kent.

Kent recognizes what Jafar is by a tattoo or something, but he also recognizes the triangle pendant and is thoroughly confused.

Whatever the case, Kent invites him to come along because their next gig is a doozy, and someone with the skills of a thief/assassin would majorly come in handy.

Jafar initially refuses, but he eventually agrees because ...?

Garrick's Novella

Backstory

Garrick was born to a berserker and his wife. The wife (Garrick's mom) was found to have some troll blood in her, and that knowledge led to the berserker treating her poorly—abusing her, etc., when Garrick was considerably younger.

- As a younger man, Garrick stood up for his mother against his father, who then disowned him for it. His father had trained him to berserk as well, but his father was regarded as one of the better warriors in their village, so when Garrick stands up to him, he is defeated badly.

- Then his mother stabs the father in the back with something, and he turns on her and kills her. Garrick picks up his father's axe and finishes his father off for it.

- Garrick has spent most of his life as a mercenary. He is by far the most experienced of the four in mercenary practices, tactics, and the like. He has fought in a few dozen different wars for as many employers, oftentimes opposing sides within the same war. He is known as one of the finest mercenaries money can buy.

- He often has regular customers who use him repeatedly for jobs. One of them is a particular noble named Lord Blaine Valdis, who is hilariously rich and powerful, but who occasionally needs side jobs performed to eliminate or sabotage competition against his shipping company and against his other sources of income.

Act I

- Garrick arrives at the place (with four other mercs) where he is going to break into a vault and obtain a map (or something) that will lead Lord Valdis to some sort of legendary item (the dragon egg), and they find a way inside.

- Garrick is leading the operation, and together with a team of a four other random mercs whom he doesn't know (except for one guy whom

Garrick has worked with before and whom he trusts, somewhat), he is supposed to break into the vault.

Each member has a distinct role to perform:

o One guy can be a chemist or alchemist or something, and he can make a concoction that does something (maybe demolitions).

o Another guy is a mage, and he is useful for something.

o Another guy is a climber (maybe a tree-dwelling species of people or creatures?) and will need to use his skills at some point.

o The last guy is a thief/safe-cracker type who can actually get the vault door open.

o Garrick is there as the muscle/protection against physical threats, while the mage deals with magical threats.

- Their story will need more development overall as to how they break into the place that has the vault, and then how they break into the vault itself.

- The one Garrick knows is the climber-guy because they've worked together before. They get along well enough—they sometimes compete with each other for jobs, and sometimes they work together. They're sort of frenemies.

Inciting Incident

- They start in a bar, and Garrick's co-mercs are trying to buy information about the dungeon, but a group of dudes doesn't want the information found. (This can be a few low-level members of the dragon cult.)

- The dragon cult guys (whom we don't specifically know are part of the dragon cult—they're just dressed distinctly)

- The place they're breaking into is a temple controlled by the dragon cult, and so the mercs are trying to gather info about what they'll be up against. The thief is doing the talking because he's smooth and charming.

- Garrick is sitting off to the side, clothed in an oversized cloak and hunched over, disguised as a large nobody nursing a beer. He's listening to how everything is going and he's keeping watch on the scene along with the alchemist, who is a nervous sort.

- The thief, for as smooth as he thinks he is, isn't that smooth. In the process of prying for information, he alarms someone (the bartender, or maybe just a patron), and a ruckus stirs up.

- The thief defends himself well at first, while Garrick waits and watches. The nervous alchemist is worried for the thief's wellbeing, but Garrick refuses to join the fracas right away. He wants to see how the thief handles himself in a tight spot.

- The alchemist gives in and joins the fight, using some of his alchemy skills as well as some hand-to-hand.

- One of the bad guys escapes the fight and scrambles toward the back room/kitchen. He comes back with five (or more?) more guys, all of whom are bearing swords and other weapons, which escalates the fight to a new level.

- As they start approaching the thief and the alchemist, Garrick finally stands to his massive full height, casts his cloak aside, and enters the fray.

- The newcomers stop short at the sight of his huge 7-foot frame, and they hesitate. Then he thrashes them. We also see weapons glancing off of his hardened skin.

- They fight, and Garrick rolls through them like a boss until one of them comes at him with a torch. That can actually hurt him, so he reacts differently to it—maybe the alchemist douses it with something, knowing that he's protecting Garrick in the process.

- They win the fight and obtain the info they need to move forward (it's safeguarded in a Crimson Flame temple in Etrijan; be sure to include quips from Garrick about what a stupid name Crimson Flame is for a cult).

- Garrick, the alchemist, and the thief report back to Lord Valdis, and he sends them to retrieve the map.

- Garrick asks for funds/permission to recruit another merc for the quest. Valdis agrees and grants him both.

- Garrick recruits an old friend of his (the climber), and the climber recommends a reliable mage they can bring along as well.

- Garrick is hesitant to bring along the mage at first because he's not certain they'll need one, but the climber insists that they're a package deal.

- Garrick agrees, and they get together and head out to the temple in Etrijan.

First Disaster/Door of No Return (DNR)

This is a literal door. They enter the temple disguised as travelers. Ultimately, they find the hidden room with a staircase that descends into the depths beneath the temple, and they go inside. It shuts behind them, locking them inside.

ACT II

- They progress through a variety of levels and dangerous situations and encounter various fell beasts and monsters as they descend toward the map.

- As they advance, they also encounter Crimson Flame cult members who mean to impede their progress.

Second DNR

At some point, they reach a crossroads; they can take either one path or the other. But there is a key to unlock access to the vault in both directions, and they need both keys to unlock them.

One of them involves a lot of climbing over lava pits, so the climber and the mage go that way. The other involves dark caves and paths, so Garrick and the alchemist (who can create light) and the thief (who can see pretty well in the dark) go that direction.

- They face additional bad guys/monsters and Crimson Flame members who attack further.

- They run into a "dungeon boss" type whom they must defeat before they can claim the key.

- They defeat the boss and claim the key, and they rendezvous with the climber and the mage at the vault entrance.

Third DNR

Garrick inserts his key into one vault door along with the climber who inserts his key into the other, and they turn them in unison. The vault doors open, releasing the magic seal on the vault door.

Act III

Climax

They get into the vault and find a bunch of cool treasures as well as the thing they came for: the map.

Grey Moment

Before Garrick can recover the map and tuck it into the enchanted map holder Lord Valdis gave him, the mage betrays them and attacks the alchemist, seemingly killing him. Shocked, Garrick turns toward him to fight him, but the climber stabs Garrick in his side with a knife made of snow steel, one of the only weapons that can cause Garrick actual harm. The thief is not part of their plan, and he manages to wound the mage with a quick knife throw or something, but the mage blows him away right after.

Black Moment

It will turn out that the climber and the mage are working together, trying to cut out Garrick and the others and Lord Valdis because they have another buyer. They succeed and trap Garrick in the vault with the dead thief and the alchemist.

The Turnaround

The alchemist is not dead, just gravely injured. He won't survive, but he gives Garrick a rare magic mushroom from his bag that helps heal

Garrick's wound somewhat. Garrick keeps the snow steel blade (it was lodged in his side), and he vows to use it to kill the climber with it someday. Then the alchemist tells Garrick which of his ingredients to mix to blow the vault doors open (which is possible now that the keys have removed the magic seal). Garrick hates science because he feels like he isn't intelligent enough to do it, but he follows the alchemist's instructions and creates the concoction. It works, and it blows the vault's doors open.

Denouement/Resolution

When Garrick gets out of the vault, he is forced to take the climbing/lava path to get out of the dungeon because the mage somehow sealed off the cave path. It is a trying, nerve-wracking escape, and Garrick almost falls into the lava, but he survives. He can't find or catch up with the climber/mage, so he returns to Lord Valdis empty-handed and begs for a second chance. Lord Valdis begrudgingly grants him one more chance.

Falling Action

This sets up book 1, because Garrick has to recruit three other mercenaries to help recover the map from the rival lord who now has it in his possession. Or, somehow, Lord Valdis finds and hires the three mercenaries instead.

✿

STORY BIBLE PART 17: ORIGINAL BOOK ONE OUTLINE

A Brief Introduction

M y outlining process is pretty straightforward. Once I have a synopsis (like the ones in the preceding "chapters"), I start breaking it into chunks and putting it under different chapter headings.

Along the way, I look specifically for points where chapters can end at cliffhangers, revelations, or other moments that can make the reader ask a compelling question that forces them to turn the page to find out the answer.

As an author, you don't want to give your readers any reason to put your books down, so... don't. Do the opposite. End your chapters (and your books, sometimes) on cliffhangers and revelations so your readers *have* to turn the page and keep reading.

Anywho, once I have the outline more or less done, then I start writing based on the notes I've created for myself for that chapter. Sometimes I'll go through once more and add more notes if I feel I need to, but usually that happens as I'm writing the actual story instead.

Most of the time, I end up adding a *lot* more than was initially included, and as such, my chapter count tends to increase as I go through the book. That's why this outline has eighteen chapters, but the published version of *The Crimson Flame* has twenty-seven.

Also, the story won't necessarily follow the outline to a tee, but by now, since I've expressed multiple times how much my work tends to change as I'm working on it, that shouldn't surprise you.

You'll also notice that I have "Act I/II/II" and "Midpoint," "Climax," and other aspects of the three-act structure marked in the outline. That's to help me keep the story's structure and framework in mind when I'm writing it.

Wherever you see the Power Author gear (from the cover) in the center, that's to denote a planned scene break in the chapter.

There's probably other good stuff in here as well, so have fun hunting for treasure.

The Crimson Flame Outline

ACT I

Chapter 1

(Garrick's POV) Garrick returns to Lord Valdis and begs for a chance to make up for his failure. Lord Valdis already knows of his failure thanks to a gloating message he received from an anonymous rival, but he thought Garrick was dead. When Garrick shows up, Valdis considers having him killed because he thinks he was in on the betrayal, but in fact, Garrick wasn't.

He tries to explain that by showing Valdis his scar from Noraff's wound, but Valdis waves his hand, stating that he hasn't memorized Garrick's scar, and it could be from anything. Garrick reasons with him, saying that he came back to prove his loyalty and to ask for a second chance.

Eventually Valdis agrees, and Garrick's first task is to recruit mercs to help him find the map, which was brought to another dark lord in Govalia. Thinking Garrick was dead, Valdis had put out a call for new mercenaries to come assist him with regard to the stolen map. They are to gather at a pub in the adjacent town (whatever it's called) and await his instructions.

Valdis tells Garrick that he was intending to send a messenger with instructions, but instead, Garrick is going to go and lead the excursion. Garrick gladly agrees.

Garrick is hoping to find Noraff and Phesnos as well, but he won't. (Maybe by the end of the third book in the series he manages to find them and bring them to justice for killing Coburn and Irwin). As Garrick leaves Valdis Keep, it is snowing big white flakes around him.

✿

(Mehta's POV) Mehta is watching Garrick from behind the rocks. He is doing recon on Valdis Keep, he sees Garrick exit, notices he isn't wearing the same armor or garb as the soldiers guarding the keep, and he wonders how Garrick is allowed in and out. Rather than following continuing to recon the Keep, looking for a way to sneak in and kill Valdis, he elects to follow Garrick instead to see if he can glean any information from him. And, if need be, he'll just have to sift Garrick if anything goes wrong.

Chapter 2

(Kent's POV) Garrick finds Aeron and Kent in the pub. (Kent notices Mehta come in shortly after Garrick does, and Mehta sits in a corner facing them, but not near them.) Kent notices him because he's a shady-looking character.

Aeron, Garrick, and Kent start chatting about the job and about their qualifications. It's tense, because Kent and Garrick aren't getting along, and Aeron, who wants the job, is trying to mediate. Kent and Aeron are the only mercenaries who showed up.

✿

(Mehta's POV) Mehta is seated in the corner, and he overhears what they're discussing. Kent catches him watching them and approaches. Mehta feels threatened, and he has to fight off his urge (the thirst) to sift Kent (who has left Aeron and Garrick at the table to discuss terms). Instead, he challenges Kent verbally, stating that the job they're about to go perform will require more than just a pretty face.

Kent isn't moved or intimidated. He doesn't flare his magic or anything. He just stands his ground, and Mehta keeps sitting there until Garrick comes over and breaks it up. He asks Mehta what he wants, and Mehta says he wants to join the group and help with the commission.

Garrick looks him up and down and asks what his skills are. Mehta considers how honest he ought to be, and he opts to tell almost the entire truth (withholding the part about killing Valdis and anything about Ferne or his family near the cratered mountain). He explains his history as a Xyonate and explains that there are no more Xyonates in Sefera because of him. When pressed why, he either does not elaborate, and they all realize why; or he does elaborate, but only briefly.

Kent is immediately on his guard, because he has heard of Xyonates before, and he now trusts Mehta even less. Mehta assures him that if he had come to kill any of them, they'd already be dead, and they would never have seen Mehta coming. (Play off of that thread some more with some disagreements from Kent, etc.)

Mehta's thought process is that upon their return from the job, he might be taken to Lord Valdis himself. He can then either kill Valdis on the spot, or he can at least scope out the castle's interior and look for weaknesses in their defenses, etc., and then he can come back and kill Valdis later. Plus, he'll make a little money in the process, and he's out of funds after having give everything he'd taken from the Temple of Laeri in Sefera to his family.

Despite Kent's objections, Garrick agrees to bring Mehta along mostly because of his skill set. Kent is a mage, and Aeron is a wyvern knight, and Garrick isn't exactly stealthy given his size, so having someone on the team whom they can entrust to handle those elements of any given job is a good decision. Garrick welcomes Mehta to the team and extends his large hand.

Mehta hesitates before shaking it, knowing he may have to betray these people at some point, and wondering what it would be like to fight and try to sift a person Garrick's size. His thirst rises up, but he pushes it back down and shakes Garrick's hand.

(Normally Garrick prefers to see the mercs he hires/partners with in action before hiring them, but in this case, he decides against it in the interest of time. If they get killed in the process, then he'll just have to find new partners.) Play with this idea as well.

Garrick pays for their drinks, and then they start heading out of the pub. When Aeron asks where they're going for the mission, Garrick replies, "Govalia."

Aeron's eyes widen. (Make this a cliffhanger ending somehow.)

Chapter 3

(Aeron's POV) Now outside the pub, standing amid the snow, Aeron is reluctant to return to Govalia after how he left, having stolen Wafer and all. He expresses as much to Garrick and Kent. He senses Wafer flying around somewhere nearby and sends him the impression to stay put for now.

Garrick tells him about how Noraff and Phesnos escaped, including about the wyverns, the knights' armor, and Faylen's features. He states that he was hoping (expecting) Aeron to be of even more use because he was familiar with the Govalian Army and the Wyvern Knights. He even notes that the job kind of hinges on his knowledge and information about the army and what they might be getting themselves into.

Ultimately, Aeron can't resist. He likes Faylen and doesn't want her mixed up in any of this. Plus he has a chance to get back home and see his family, even if it is risky to do so, so he agrees to the job.

Garrick asks about this supposed wyvern and where it is, and Aeron calls Wafer down with a new Wafer Whistle he has developed. It hangs around his neck, and it's a hollowed-out wyvern tooth. Only Wafer (or other wyverns) can hear it.

Wafer lands in front of Garrick and the others, and they are impressed—particularly Mehta, who as a sheltered Xyonate in Etrijan (which is generally too far north for wyverns to roam freely) has never seen anything like it before. Kent is less impressed since he has been traveling with Wafer.

Aeron takes pride in their reactions, but as he climbs onto Wafer's saddle, his back messes with him. He takes a mushroom in front of all of them, figuring that hiding it isn't going to end well, and he'd rather they know now. Garrick doesn't have a problem with it as long as it doesn't affect Aeron's performance. With that out of the way, the others find horses, and they all head to Govalia.

✦

(Kent's POV; maybe interspersed with Aeron's POV as well) They head to Govaliston. Aeron often plays the scout role for the group since he and Wafer can fly, but with wyverns patrolling the skies, he has to keep a lower profile and keeps more of a distance.

As they approach the city (maybe a couple miles out, still in the countryside to the north of the fortress), a patrol of wyvern knights lands before them. Aeron and Wafer aren't around, but if they return, bad things will happen since he's a known defector/traitor (basically), so Kent is talking and trying to get the Govalians to get moving before Aeron returns from scouting. He's using one of his skills, which is his charm, tact and intelligence.

The knights are about to leave, but then their wyverns start acting up and chirping or whatever, and the leader commands some of his knights to search the skies. They see Aeron and realize he's not one of theirs. They realize he was the scout Kent had mentioned, and then they surround the mercs and attack.

Act II

Chapter 4

(Multiple POVs and scene breaks) Fight scene, etc. The mercs each show their prowess. They all impress each other, but they're working primarily as individuals and not as a team. At least one of the horses gets killed, but Kent is actually doing a lot of fighting on horseback.

※

(Kent's POV) Kent notes Mehta's speed and clean precision, and he notes Garrick's durability and incredible strength.

※

(Mehta's POV) Mehta notes Kent's overwhelming skill with magic—and he wonders how Kent compares to Lord Valdis. Mehta also notes Garrick's strength and durability, particularly how steel weapons are hitting him and just bouncing off. So if the time comes when he has to sift either of these people, he is taking those elements into account.

※

(Garrick's POV) Garrick is wary of Kent more than Mehta, mostly due to Phesnos's betrayal, and because he doesn't think Mehta is capable of bringing him down, even though he views Mehta's skills as incredibly effective. Kent, on the other hand, with the breadth of his magical abilities could prove a huge problem.

(Aeron's POV) Meanwhile, Aeron battles elsewhere with the leader of the group one-on-one in the air. (It's Porgus Darleton, and Aeron is surprised that he's earned a promotion in light of Aeron putting him to sleep along with the rest of the knights in his novella.)

Some of the wyvern riders escape, and some are killed. Most of the wyverns fly away, but a couple of them are killed also. Porgus's wyvern is killed, in part thanks to Kent's magic knocking it from the sky, but Porgus stays alive. (This is the first indication that the mercs can potentially work as a team.)

Porgus is heartbroken, but he becomes a cautionary tale (mostly for the reader) of how important the bond between wyvern and rider are. At the beginning of the fight, he is cocky and arrogant. At the end, when his wyvern is dead, Porgus is deadened and becomes a husk, a shell of his former self.

Aeron empathizes with him, but at the same time, Porgus had sided with Brove when Aeron got kicked out, so he doesn't feel that bad. Even so, Aeron won't let Garrick, Mehta, or Kent kill Porgus. (Kent wouldn't, but the other two have no qualms about it.) They leave Porgus behind, mourning over his dead wyvern (who needs a name, btw).

✿

(Mehta's POV) Once they leave the site, an argument about whether or not their cover is blown ensues, and the group almost fractures apart. They all want to stick it out, but they all have concerns.

Mehta, surprisingly, unites them. He wants to make sure the mission succeeds mostly because he needs to kill Valdis, and Garrick needs it to succeed for the same reason, even though he's worried about Aeron/Wafer going forward. They make it to Govaliston. (Cliffhanger)

Chapter 5

(Garrick's POV) Garrick wears a cloak and hood because of course he does (easy to identify with greenish skin and blue hair), but Kent and Mehta walk freely among the crowd. Aeron stashes Wafer somewhere safe but within range of calling him with the Wafer Whistle.

As they progress through the city, Aeron leads them to his father's shop. He finds Pa, who gives him his usual cold reception. Pa mentions how the Govalian Army canceled a bunch of blacksmithing contracts with him, and how funds are tight in light of Aeron's actions (an unintended consequence). Aeron is dismayed at it, but Pa assures him that while he's pissed, he still has some savings left, and they're getting by. He's also fighting it in the courts because, after all, "A contract is a contract." He doesn't really expect to win, but it's the principle of the thing.

Aeron asks about his sister, Kallie, and Pa says he doesn't really know what she's up to, but that she has moved out and doesn't come around much anymore, except maybe once every couple of weeks for a family meal. Aeron doesn't think much of it, but he gets info on where to find her. (This is all from Garrick's POV.)

The mercs make a plan to corner Faylen since Aeron knows she was involved in helping Noraff and Phesnos. They want to see what she knows. Aeron agrees to be the first face she sees because questions from a familiar, friendly face, even if it is the face of someone who has committed crimes against Govalia, is better than a stranger inquiring after her.

✿

(Aeron's POV) They set it up, and that night, Aeron sort of ambushes her in an alleyway (in the town halfway between the fortress and Govaliston) when she is on leave for the weekend without her wyvern. She is not pleased, and she tries to leave, but then Garrick shows up at the other end of the alley, blocking her way. Now she's really pissed, and she's ready to fight. She might even fight Aeron a bit, but ultimately, Mehta comes in and renders her unconscious.

Chapter 6

(Kent's POV) When Faylen wakes up, she's in a room, like at an inn. Kent is sitting across from her because he's the only one she hasn't yet met, and he no longer trusts that Aeron will be able to get them anywhere with her. They have a calm conversation, but they don't get anywhere either.

✿

(Aeron's POV) Against Garrick's wishes, Aeron bursts in, and he talks it out with Faylen. She agrees that he was wrongfully accused and that it was horrible what Commander Larcas Brove did to him, but he still shouldn't have stolen Wafer back.

When Aeron reveals that Brove had intended to turn Wafer into wyvern chow for the other wyverns, Faylen's attitude shifts a bit. She wouldn't have wanted her wyvern subjected to that, especially when it was perfectly healthy like Wafer

It breaks through to her, and she reveals what she knows. She took Phesnos on her wyvern (and she hated him, btw; he kept staring at her with cold, piercing eyes and was generally creepy) and another knight had Noraff, and they dropped them at the manse of a well-known lord and former naval commander in the city of Osnal, in the south of Govalia. She mentions that she saw the lord take the map into his study, and he mentioned some sort of vault.

Garrick asks about Noraff and Phesnos, and she says she doesn't know if they're still there or not because she left before they did.

She shows them where on a map, and without consulting the others in the group, Aeron invites her to join them. She declines anyway and says that the Govalian Army knows Aeron is around, and they also know a group of mercs have come to town after fighting and killing a few of their own, so they're watching for the mercs now. She also agrees that she will wait to give them a head start, but ultimately she has to tell her superior officers about what is going on.

She tells them that if she's discovered to have talked with them, then she'll be branded a traitor and cast out as well. Aeron suggests that the surest way to make sure that doesn't happen is to have her report what happened tonight immediately once she returns.

Faylen suggests they give her a few smacks to make it look realistic. None of them wants to strike a woman, though—least of all, Aeron, who adores Faylen, but Mehta agrees to do it since he has sifted plenty of women in his day. He doesn't relish the idea of striking Faylen, but he knows he's doing it to help protect her. So he does.

Her lip splits open on one side, and her mouth is bruised as a result, because Mehta doesn't hold back.

Aeron is low-key mad at Mehta for awhile over it, but ultimately he resolves not to stay mad because it was Faylen's idea/request.

Faylen tells Aeron straight up that things between them cannot change; she is still a member of the royal army, and as such, pride, honor, and loyalty dictate that if she encounters Aeron again, she will have to fight him, even if she doesn't want to. Aeron understands. That goes for the other mercs as well, but Faylen doesn't voice that concept aloud. They let her go, and they immediately head to the manse in Osnal, near the southern coast. Their approach to the manse is a cliffhanger.

Chapter 7

NOTE:** For this sequence, there is a ticking time bomb in that Faylen is notifying her superiors of what is happening because she has to. So they're in a time crunch to get to the manse, break in, get what they need, and get out before Govalia's army catches up to them.

(Kent's POV) They plan their infiltration of the manse, which is fortress-like in its defenses. The lord who lives there is a former admiral for Govalia's navy, most of which is based in Osnal. The city reminds Kent of Goldmoor, which reminds him of Aveyna, and of all that happened. Roll with that train of thought, and maybe have Aeron talk with him about it since Aeron was there for some of it.

Then Garrick can walk over to them, and Kent will be reminded of Trag, the half-orc guy with gray skin whom Kent beat in a small fight in the Temple of Laeri in Goldmoor. Then he can think about how after what he'd already seen Garrick do, he was certain Garrick could've torn Trag apart. He muses about inviting Garrick to come along to help him kill the king of Inoth sometime (thinking he can deal with Grak while Kent deals with Kymil), but he doesn't bring it up.

They discuss the plans to break inside. (The plan is not described because we see it play out, but they do discuss their escape plans.) Part of the escape plan is to hijack the lord's personal skiff and boat away from the estate (since it's right on the Tahn Sea). Garrick has some legit seamanship skills from having grown up with a Viking-like family that raided along the western coast of Etrijan from their island homes to the west of the country, so he's confident he can get them to safety.

○

(Mehta's POV) Mehta is to be sent in before everyone else to "clear a path" and get the others inside. Wafer can't go inside, but Aeron uses him to fly Mehta to the manse's roof and drop him off there at night.

Mehta sneaks around inside, being stealthy, hiding in shadows, seeing in the dark with his enchanted vision (first opportunity in the story where he really gets to use it), and sifting a few guards. He has opportunities to sift the servants as well, in particular a slave girl who notices him. But she reminds him of an older version of Ferne, and he can't bring himself to do it, even though by that point his thirst is raging out of control. So he lets her go. (This is a plant that will pay off later).

Mehta lets the others inside, and they all get in (except for Aeron and Wafer, who are patrolling while the others do stuff inside). They sneak to the lord's study, where they discover a hidden vault. They can't get inside it. As they're in the study, it fills with bad guys, including the dark lord. (Cliffhanger)

Chapter 8

(Multiple POVs/Fight Scene)

(Kent's POV) Kent believes he is the only one capable of taking on the dark lord because he's had experience with it before (Eusephus), but Mehta insists he is capable (and he needs the practice so he knows what to expect with Valdis, though he doesn't say that aloud).

✪

(Mehta's POV) They fight the soldiers and defeat the dark lord, and he says something cryptic about how trusting Lord Valdis is a bad idea because he intends to rain destruction down on all of Aletia. They ignore him (except for Mehta, who mostly believes it and who adds it to his scales of judgment against Valdis). And the dark lord refuses to open the vault.

✪

(Garrick's POV) They threaten him and try to get him to open the vault (Mehta is willing and able to torture him), but he still won't do it. He says he would rather die, and he means it, as he is already mortally injured thanks to a blow by Mehta.

Garrick is hoping to find Noraff and Phesnos and he asks about them, but the dark lord dies before he can reveal anything. Garrick searches through the papers in his desk and finds a payment receipt to Noraff with a mention to send further payment to an address on the island of Caclos. He commits it to memory and takes the paper as well.

✹

(Aeron's POV) Aeron realizes that the army has arrived.

Chapter 9

(Aeron's POV) They are rushed to get out of there because Aeron alerts them (Wafer lands on the edge of a balcony outside the study or something) that the Govalian army has come to support the dark lord (albeit too late). They are led by Larcas Brove and his wyvern knights.

Furthermore, their original plan to escape by sea is thwarted because the navy is aware of them as well and has marshalled a significant force to block them.

Aeron is both dismayed, relieved, and worried to see Faylen is not among the wyvern knights. He wonders if she has been found out and branded as a traitor even after their measures to protect her.

✹

(Mehta's POV) As the soldiers draw nearer and prepare to attack, the slave girl whom Mehta spared both opens the vault for them (even though she's not supposed to know how), and shows them a secret tunnel out.

She tells them the dark lord was not abusive in his old age, but his sons were, and he knew and did nothing, so she has no qualms about screwing them over. She encourages them to take anything they like, so long as they leave something for her afterward. She's planning to escape via the same tunnel as well later on, but first, she's going to tell the soldiers (who are still keeping their distance) that the mercs are holding everyone hostage to buy them extra time.

Aeron manages to escape via the skies with Wafer (flying over the navy, but much higher up so they can't see him among the clouds in the night sky), and they rendezvous back on the road to Govaliston.

With the map in hand, they plan to flee Govalia the next morning. They arrive back in Govalia, and they rendezvous at Pa's blacksmith shop, as planned. But Pa shows up and calls him to the house. Kallie is there, and she's in bad shape.

Chapter 10

(Aeron's POV) Aeron rushes over to his parents' house with Kent, but Mehta and Garrick stay back to guard the map.

At Pa's house, Aeron finds Kallie there, dazed and confused. Aeron fields comments from his pa about her being drugged like he was, so obviously he should know what's wrong with her. But Aeron doesn't know, so he just tries to help take care of her. Kent stands watch and is a good friend.

Aeron notices a strange mark on the back of Kallie's neck—it's not quite a tattoo, but it's not a birthmark, either. It's something else, and he can't tell what it is. At one point in the night, Kallie gets up and stumbles into the fireplace headfirst as if mesmerized by it. Kent notices and tries to pull her back, but is too late.

✿

(Possibly include a scene where Garrick is prying for information from Mehta. Maybe Mehta has made him suspicious somehow?)

✿

(Kent's POV) He manages to pull her out with Aeron's help, but Kent burns his hand in the process. They frantically check Kallie for signs that she is harmed but find none. Stranger still, Aeron notices the mark on her neck is glowing now, and it's in the shape of a dragon's head (or something). Mum Ironglade and Pa are awake by this point, and Mum tends to Kent's burned hand.

No one has any explanations, though Kent asks if she has ever demonstrated any magical abilities. In the morning, Kallie is safe and cogent, but she can't remember the night before or much of anything about where she's been, so they keep her home and keep her safe. Aeron wants them to take her to a physician, but by now, Pa's savings are tapped out between fighting the army in the courts and just paying bills. They can't afford it.

Aeron is hesitant to go, but without any answers, he knows he has to. He has a big payday awaiting him that he can use to get Kallie some real help and to even move his parents out of Govaliston, which is becoming more and more hostile because of Aeron's actions, but he has to get the map to Lord Valdis first. He reluctantly entrusts his parents with Kallie's wellbeing, and he leaves to head back to Xenthan with the others.

Kent offers his share of the spoils from the dark lord's vault, and combined with Aeron's share, it should be enough for them to get by, as well as get Kallie to a physician.

(*The Kallie thread is all setup for book 2, when they learn that she is a vital piece in Lord Valdis's plan to steal the dragon's essence; Kallie is the Crimson Flame's sacrifice that will hatch the dragon egg. Kallie was supposed to have already been sacrificed, but because of the delay with the map, she managed to escape and wandered off because of some reason, but if Garrick had brought the map back in time, she probably would've been sacrificed. Make that work somehow if it fits.*)

Chapter 11

(Mehta's POV) A couple weeks later, back at Lord Valdis's palace, only Garrick is permitted inside because Valdis neither knows, trusts, nor cares about the other mercs. Mehta is frustrated at this, but he resolves to remain patient. He will get his chance to kill eventually.

✿

(Garrick's POV) Pleased that Garrick has returned the map to him, Valdis gives Garrick the full payment he is owed, despite Garrick's past failure. Garrick is honored and tries to refuse the full payment, but Valdis is rich and doesn't care.

Garrick plans to use his share to immediately go find and kill Noraff and Phesnos using the info he found about them being in Caclos, but Valdis wants Garrick to follow the map (he translates most of it on the spot because he's a genius scholar—he only translates enough of it for them to realize what he needs them to find—he's not worried about them finding Kallie because he's already got a line on her for that) to retrieve several things along the way.

Ultimately, Garrick accepts because it will help cement his good relationship with Valdis to do so. Noraff and Phesnos will have to wait.

(MIDDLE OF ACT II/MIDPOINT OF BOOK)

Chapter 12

(Mehta's POV) Garrick takes the news to the mercs and pays them their shares. Aeron is thinking he should get back to Govalia to check on Kallie instead of going along with the others on the Path of Shadows, but Kent reminds him that Govalia is not a good place for him right now, so Aeron agrees to come alone.

Mehta is on board as well because it means he's another step closer to killing Valdis. They all sign on and keep going; together they follow the Path of Shadows as the map says. They have to retrieve several items from around the continent that will enable them to reach the final item, and that is what Valdis wants, but he doesn't tell them what it is.

Details on the Path of Shadows (which the mercs will follow):

The mercs have to gather the following items from various locations around Aletia (aka they must walk the "Path of Shadows," a term and a path they receive from a guy whom Lord Valdis is torturing when they get their assignment):

○ a map to the egg (retrieved by Garrick in his novella from a vault in **Etrijan** but stolen by traitors and taken to Govalia)

○ a key to get inside the dungeon where the egg is housed (it's a dragon sword, and it's hidden in **Inoth**)

○ a scroll/book containing a ritual/spell to awaken the dragon within the egg and another ritual/spell to hatch the egg (hidden in **Muroth** because it's ironic that a magical item would be hidden there)

○ the Crimson Flame's chosen one (probably a teenage girl) to be sacrificed as part of the ritual to get the dragon to hatch (**Govalia**—it's Kallie, Aeron's sister)

○ the fossilized/hibernating/dormant egg itself (hidden back in **Xenthan**)

All of the items, however, can be found on the map. It will turn out that they're all contained within temples of the Crimson Flame (hence the title).

They go for the key first, in Inoth.

○

(Kent's POV) Kent has reservations about going to Inoth, but the temple is far from the capital city of Goldmoor (where Kymil is, whom he would love to kill in revenge for Aveyna, among others), so he's okay with it.

○

(Multiple chapters/POVs) They visit the temple and find a dungeon beneath it, and they work through it together. (Inoth's soldiers may or may not interfere.) They retrieve the key, and it's a dragon sword, which Kent wields in addition to his magic. It has some sort of bonus powers.

***NOTE: As a result of stealing the sword, they are harassed by Crimson Flame members who follow them from Inoth from that point on.

There is some debate amongst the group members about felling remaining Crimson Flame cultists along the way. Garrick is in favor, as is Mehta, but Kent and Aeron are not. Once they realize they can be harassed at any time, (maybe they wake up and their room at the local inn is on fire), they decide to make it a policy to clean out each temple so the cultists can't follow them.

Chapter 13

At some point, as Mehta is opening up, he mentions that he left a small girl with light skin in his home near the cratered mountain, and Garrick overhears it and remembers seeing Ferne in that town as he was passing through after his novella. He notes it but doesn't say anything at the time.

⚙

(Kent's POV) Then they head north to Muroth. This venture is problematic because after the fiasco in Kent's novella, the borders are tight, so they have to sneak into the country. They succeed in sneaking in, but it comes at some sort of cost. Maybe they bribe someone, or maybe they kill someone. Either way, Kent is not recognized.

Muroth continues to be problematic because the temple lies within the province of Lord Frostsong, a longtime family friend who almost certainly wants Kent dead because of how Fane made it seem like Kent had murdered their father.

(By the way, it is definitely wintertime now, so they're trudging through the snow at this point.)

⚙

(Multiple chapters/POVs) They reach the temple and get inside. The dungeon in here is more of a labyrinth than a dungeon, and it's more about evading traps than it is fighting enemies, but there is still a dungeon boss as well.

✿

(Kent's POV) They succeed and collect a ritual book for magic. Kent can understand some of it, and he finds it especially ironic that a book describing a magic ritual would be hidden in Muroth, the most anti-magic country on the continent.

When they emerge, they encounter Lord Frostsong and a bunch of his men.

Chapter 14

(Kent's POV) Fane is not there. Lord Frostsong "knows his land and thus knows they came into it" or whatever, but he is unexpectedly kind toward Kent. They have a parlay, just Kent and Frostsong, while the others wait outside. He asks Kent to demonstrate his power.

Kent shows him some casual magic (his fingers sparking blue, or whatever), and Lord Frostsong nods. Then Lord Frostsong admits that he does not agree with Muroth's oppression of mages and of Inoth. He hasn't ever since he was a child, even though Muroth and Inoth have been separate countries for about a century.

Fane comes up in the conversation, and Frostsong has only grief about Fane. He has been aggressive in renegotiating trade between their provinces, and Frostsong is weary of it. Kent warns him not to trust anything Fane says, and he explains how Fane killed their father. Frostsong is saddened but not surprised. He knew it was not within Kent's character to do such a thing, but Fane has always been treacherous.

Ultimately, Frostsong is bound by his commands to destroy cursed mages whenever he finds them, but he is also the lord of his province, so he lets Kent and his friends go. He announces to his men that he put a piece of scorallite in Kent's hand himself and saw no sign of magic, so he is allowing Kent to go free. Whether or not he killed his father is an issue for the Lord of House Etheridge to deal with himself. The mercs leave, and they head back to Govalia next.

✦

(Aeron's POV) Upon arrival, Aeron stops to see his parents and Kallie in secret (Mehta helps get him there quietly and in the dark), but Kallie isn't there. Mum and Pa are kind of leery of Mehta because he's creepy and exudes killer vibes, but they tell Aeron that they found out Kallie was involved with the Crimson Flame. Then some men in armor with the crest of a ram with three horns took her one night.

Aeron puts it together that whatever the map wants them to get in Govalia (give it a cool, ominous term that suggests a blood sacrifice) is actually his sister.

Chapter 15

(Aeron's POV) He convinces the others that he's correct about Kallie being a sacrifice (and he is), and they return to Xenthan to try to get his sister back.

✦

(Garrick's POV) In Xenthan, they quest for the final item, knowing that Valdis won't give Kallie back unless they have something worth trading. The dragon sword/key and the ritual are useless without the final item, and Garrick is confident Valdis would not trade Kallie for those alone.

(Garrick is also much more driven to complete the mission, though he does have some conflict about what will happen when they reach Valdis/Kallie.)

✦

(Multiple POVs/chapters) So they go get the final thing in another

Crimson Flame temple, which itself is the dungeon rather than being underneath it. It ends up being a dragon egg.

✿

(Garrick's POV) Garrick secretly finds a second one, and he takes it with him, using his shield to sort of cover the bulge in his pack as they travel back to Valdis's castle.

Aст III

Chapter 16

(Mehta's POV) Back in Valdis Keep, they are all allowed to enter this time (Mehta is happy because this could be his chance to fell Valdis). Garrick starts doing the talking, but Valdis refuses to give up the girl.

Aeron breaks rank and tells him Kallie is his sister, and he begs for him to release her. Valdis explains Kallie's importance (she's the chosen sacrifice necessary for him to perform a ritual to steal the dragon's essence) and refuses to release her.

So Aeron holds the egg up and threatens to smash it if Valdis doesn't bring Kallie out.

Chapter 17

(Garrick's POV) Garrick is pissed off big-time at Aeron's hasty actions. To further complicate things, Kallie is dazed and thinks it's an honor for her to be the chosen sacrifice.

✿

(Mehta's POV) The situation is tense. Mehta is constantly looking for an opening and wonders if Aeron has given him one. Kent is trying to mediate. Garrick is considering whether or not he should fight Aeron.

✦

(Aeron's POV) Ultimately, Valdis brings Kallie to him. They negotiate hard, but Aeron is smart enough to know he shouldn't release the egg until he's outside the castle with Kallie already on Wafer's back. They start to leave, and one of Valdis's men (probably a recurring character of some sort—a recognizable guard or official) tries to kill Aeron, but Mehta intervenes and royally kills the guy.

CLIMAX

Chapter 18

(Multiple POVs) All hell breaks loose, and Aeron lets the egg smash onto the floor, turning it to dust and ash. Mehta considers attacking Valdis, but he decides it's still not the right opportunity and that helping Aeron and Kallie escape is more important.

✦

(Kent's POV) In the commotion, Aeron and Kallie manage to escape (with Mehta's help), but Garrick and Kent remain there, unable/unwilling to fight back. Valdis's men capture them, but Garrick produces a second egg and leverages it to free Kent and himself with the understanding that they will go back to get Kallie from Aeron because Valdis needs her.

As a side note, Valdis's men don't let Garrick keep his snow steel sword and shield because they are obviously going to be effective against a fire-type dragon, so Valdis makes Garrick give them up as a sign of faith. Nor does he allow Kent to keep the dragon sword/key because it is needed for the ritual.

Instead, he outfits Garrick with a phantom steel axe that has been used many times to kill people and steal souls, so it's a beastly weapon. Valdis brings it out of his vault specifically for that reason. He gives Kent some cool weapon as well, even though Kent is a mage.

✿

(Garrick's POV) Garrick doesn't feel good about it, but he is willing to do it for the sake of his reputation and future. Plus, Valdis is about ready to kill him based on one failure already and the potential that he's been betraying Valdis this whole time.

✿

(Kent's POV) Kent goes along with it as well in part to save his own life but also in part because he realizes that Valdis taking a dragon's essence is a terrible idea, and he must be stopped.

(End of Book One)

STORY BIBLE PART 18: ORIGINAL BOOK TWO OUTLINE

A Brief Introduction

Here's the outline for Book Two. As I developed Book One, I was developing Book Two and Book Three (and beyond) so I could have a sense of where the story was going the whole time.

I'm glad I did that. It made this daunting task of writing three books in a series (plus the prequels) a lot easier.

Path of Shadows Outline

Act I

Chapter One

Garrick Shatterstone doesn't feel good about agreeing to go retrieve Kallie, but he is willing to do it for the sake of his reputation and future.

Lord Valdis looses the dragon from the egg. It's just a wretched little lizard with four legs, two wings, black scales, and a ravenous appetite. It skitters across the floor, reminding Garrick of the scorpers back in the map dungeon. Then it starts to rip flesh from Lord Valdis's dead guards and eat it.

(By the time Garrick and Kent leave, the dragon has doubled in size, thanks to what it has been eating. Lord Valdis can mention that, as magical creatures, they grow fast so they aren't as vulnerable for as long. Lord Valdis also puts a sleeping spell on it, potentially.)

Once the dragon is full-grown enough, Lord Valdis intends to steal its essence, but he is counting on Garrick and Kent (use his last name, Etheridge, at some point) to face off against Mehta and Aeron to get Kallie back for the sacrifice as part of the ritual (see notes doc in Notes). Garrick isn't feeling good about this, either and as they travel, Kent's conversations with him make him feel even worse.

**As a side note, Valdis's men don't let Garrick keep his snow steel sword and shield because they are obviously going to be effective against a fire-type dragon, so Valdis makes Garrick give them up as a sign of faith. Nor does he allow Kent to keep the dragon sword/key.

Instead, he outfits Garrick with a phantom steel axe that has been used many times to kill people and steal souls, so it's a beastly weapon. Valdis brings it out of his vault specifically for that reason. He gives Kent some cool weapon as well, even though Kent is a mage.**

Then Lord Valdis brings out Falna. (cliffhanger)

Chapter 2

(Garrick's POV) Tense "reunion" with Falna and Garrick. "You left me to die out in the cold." She accompanies Garrick and Kent into the mountains to enforce Lord Valdis's will, as an insurance policy, along with a large group of soldiers. The big soldier at Lord Valdis's side does not come along.

They leave, and Garrick sees the dragon one last time with smoke pouring out of its nostrils. It is double the size of when it hatched.

✿

(Aeron's POV), observing Kallie as they land in Mehta's village. Kallie is barefoot and wearing a Crimson Flame robe. The farther away from Valdis Keep she gets, the more her cognition returns, and the less she feels inclined to go back.

(This will be an important character thing for her throughout because when she finally decides she needs to go back (if that ends up happening), she will be doing so while fully aware and awake, and that will make her sacrifice all the more powerful.)

Throwback to book one—mention that he can't take Kallie back to Govalia because Lord Valdis would expect to find her there, plus he is wanted in Govalia, as is Mehta. (Or maybe Mehta can explain this to Palomi in the next chapter.)

They land in the town, and the townspeople freak out at the sight of Wafer at first, but Aeron makes him fly away, and they chill out. But they still stare at Aeron and Kallie, both of whom are white faces among a sea of brown (reference that Mehta is brown-skinned also, and make sure you don't use the same verbiage as in Shatterstone). They head to Mehta's house, but before they can get inside, the door opens (cliffhanger).

⚙

(Kent's POV) Garrick and Kent are traveling with Falna and the others. (The whole mission is a point of contention between Garrick and Kent early on: "Why did you volunteer if you didn't want to do it?" "To save our lives.")

Kent sows seeds in Garrick's mind about Garrick being a pawn for Valdis, and under his control. Garrick can counter by saying Kent is in the same position, and Kent will agree that he is. And he can challenge Garrick that perhaps they should do something about it.

Get inside Kent's head and explain/remind about his decision that he was going along with this but only so he could find a way to stop Lord Valdis. Garrick doesn't know that yet, but it is very much in the forefront of Kent's mind.

(Maybe throw in some mentions about the Crimson Flame's politics as well.)

Kent very much still wants revenge against Fane and Kymil, respectively, but stopping Lord Valdis is a much bigger priority. Neither Fane nor Kymil can potentially take over the entire continent—they're both too weak. But with Lord Valdis, that's a real threat. Fane and Kymil will still be there when Kent is done with Lord Valdis. (This represents a shift in Kent's values.)

Figure out a cliffhanger/revelation chapter ending.

Chapter 3

(Mehta's POV) Ferne runs out of the house and greets Mehta. He is genuinely happy to see her, and of course, she's elated.

Grandfather is also happy he has returned, but Palomi is not enthused about seeing Mehta bringing MORE white faces into their town, and she's even less enthused about them all staying at her house, but they cram in and stay the night.

(Garrick's POV) Several days later, Garrick and Kent eventually find Mehta's hometown in the mountains. Garrick explains that he remembers that's where Mehta had said he'd left Ferne, and Garrick actually saw her while trekking back from Etrijan after failing to get the map—a white face amid a sea of brown faces (look up the exact wording).

Kent convinces Garrick to let him go in and try to reason with Aeron and Mehta first. Garrick doesn't want him to do it, but he can't deny that the sight of him walking into the town will immediately set Aeron and Mehta on edge. Garrick doesn't see a strategic advantage to allowing Kent to do it, but he trusts Kent's powers of persuasion to a certain point. Maybe he can at least broker some sort of deal.

Falna is also wildly against the deal, and so Garrick is getting pulled in two different directions the whole time because he and Falna hate each other.

Ultimately, Garrick agrees, and Kent leaves. As soon as he gives Kent the chance to go, he regrets it, because he doesn't trust Kent anymore.

Falna gives him hell about it, too, and it makes him want to snap her neck right then and there.

✦

(Mehta's POV) Kent arrives in the village and wants to talk. Mehta wants to kill Kent before he realizes Mehta is watching him. Kent is a mage, so he's dangerous from a distance, and so if Mehta can get in close before Kent notices (and he definitely can), then he won't have to worry about fighting all of Kent's magic in a sort-of wide open space.

But Aeron won't let him. Maybe Garrick is untrustworthy, but Kent has been a true friend to Aeron thus far, and Aeron points out that he didn't fight against them at Lord Valdis's castle. Mehta is not convinced, but he agrees to it as long as Aeron agrees to do the talking while Mehta waits, in hiding, in case something goes wrong.

✦

(Aeron's or Kent's POV) Aeron confronts Kent in the village. This is Kent's door leading from Act 1 to Act 2 because Kent outright says he has no intention of trying to bring Kallie back, and he only said what he said to convince Lord Valdis not to kill him.

They talk about Garrick also, and Kent has to admit that Garrick is probably going to continue to side with Valdis. Worse yet, Garrick has come with a group of soldiers and a fire mage to stand against them.

As they are discussing it, that group of soldiers shows up in the town along with Garrick and Falna. (Cliffhanger)

Chapter 4

(Garrick's POV) Starts fighting his former merc friends, but he doesn't feel good about it. Ultimately, during the battle, he sees Falna trying to fry random villagers as well as the mercs. She is showing no regard for their lives or their property.

Garrick asks himself if that type of behavior is who he is. It reminds him of his drunken, abusive father who'd killed Garrick's mother and generally bullied everyone around him.

He comes to the conclusion that if this is really what Lord Valdis has in mind for anyone who opposes him, innocent or otherwise, Garrick refuses to be a part of it. (This could also be a cliffhanger ending.) Lord Valdis is a sort of father figure for Garrick, but he's an abusive father, yet again, so it's history repeating itself. "Family members can be dicks sometimes."

This represents a <u>shift</u> in Garrick's values, because he stops valuing his reputation as highly and starts valuing his desire to shut down bullies.

Falna is about to torch some children and their mother, or something, and Garrick totally turns on her and tries to cut her down. She sees him coming, though, and manages to avoid the attack, but Garrick saves the family in the process.

Garrick finds something sturdy that he can use as a type of shield (he just has a tortured-looking battle axe that Lord Valdis gave him) or throws heavy things at Falna from afar to get her off of his back.

✿

(Pick a POV) The other mercs notice Garrick has switched sides and is now attacking the soldiers and Falna, so they stop fighting him and start fighting the soldiers together.

Ultimately, they win. Someone kills Falna (possibly Aeron, who finds Falna trying to coax Kallie to go with her, and he impales Falna with his spear). Garrick decides to side with Mehta and Aeron and Kent in trying to stop Valdis/dragon, etc.

✿

(New POV?) Someone proposes that they ought to form a blood pact, which is an unbreakable oath. The oath is that they will cooperate indefinitely until Lord Valdis is brought down once and for all. Make it somewhat open-ended, because Lord Valdis's actions and the mercs' responses trigger a chain reaction that spans 9 books, after all.

"Defeat Lord Valdis and reverse the damage he caused..." or something.

Reactions

Mehta – has already been in a cult. Is dubious.

Aeron – been in the military, which is similar. This is finally a new brotherhood for him, which he likes.

Kent – has not had a true "home" since leaving Muroth. Inoth was temporary, and it went horribly wrong, so he welcomes this idea.

Garrick – pleased that he finally has people around him whom he can trust again.

They make the blood pact, each cutting their forearm deep enough that it will leave a scar as a memento of their pact (the reference to the scars can be something ongoing throughout the series), joining themselves together as the Blood Mercenaries, that they will stop Valdis at all costs, even their lives. Now unified, they can move forward.

Once they finish that, they find themselves facing down an angry mob of townspeople. (Cliffhanger)

ACT II

Chapter 5

The Blood Mercs won, but the townspeople are pissed due to damage and due to their history, knowing that the soldiers will return, and it will be worse next time. But the mercs assure them that they're going to take care of Lord Valdis once and for all. The townsfolk are still very dubious, though.)

⚙

***SUPER CRUCIAL NOTE:** At the beginning of the ritual, Kallie's soul will be tied to the soul of the dragon to some extent. Therefore, when she goes outside to cool down in book one, it's because she's running so hot (like a dragon).

Aeron and Kent eventually recall and realize this when they figure out her connection to the dragon, and they assume (rightfully) that cold is harmful to the dragon.

Thus, they figure they need to gather snow steel weapons and ice magic or whatever to combat it as Lord Valid is doing his ritual at the end of Book 2. If they can kill the dragon, there is no ritual. If they can kill Lord Valdis, there is no ritual. ***

Mehta's grandfather tells them about a legendary temple in northern Etrijan (an arctic region that is super cold) dedicated to the God Fjorst. It is a place of legendary power, including weapons that can be used to fell a fire dragon.

"If it's real."

So they're somewhat dubious until Grandfather says that it is real because he has been there, once. He tells a story of having been trapped in horrible winter weather as a young man while on some sort of adventure, and they stumbled upon it.

Inside they found priceless treasures, mostly in form of weapons crafted by the gods themselves. They also found a huge ice forge (think blacksmith) allegedly used by Fjorst himself to create many of the weapons they discovered. They even made it inside, and it was their shelter for part of the night.

But then things (icewalkers) started attacking their camp. They doused the fire and attacked the men, killing most of them.

Of the original party of nine or so men, only three escaped. One of the others died of hypothermia shortly after escaping, and the other has since died of old age. Grandfather was the third.

When Garrick expressed his doubts about the story, Grandfather pulls a board away from one of the walls and produces a snow steel weapon of some sort. (Cliffhanger)

Chapter 6

It is actually ice-forged steel, which is different. It is light blue in color and the blade is transparent—like blue ice. It freezes faster and more thoroughly than snow steel, which is steel forged with ice but by Aletian craftsmen rather than by the gods themselves.

Now Garrick believes, having seen the weapon, so they quest to the temple of Fjorst, the God of Ice (and cold places), the next morning. Hopefully, the weapons will prove effective against Lord Valdis as well.

How exactly they will deal with Valdis, they aren't entirely sure, but based on Kent's experiences with three other dark lords (Eusephus, Kymil, and the dark lord they all fought in Govalia), he's confident that if they can GET to Lord Valdis, they can take him down with physical attacks (that's how they took down Lord Glavan, and that's how he took down Eusephus as well). Weapons forged by the gods are a good start.

No one knows Kallie is with them, but Aeron is unwilling to leave her behind, so they bring her along.

⚙

(Aeron's POV) Meanwhile, an avalanche buries them within a cave or something.

They only survive thanks to help from, of all people, a group of Govalian soldiers led by Commander Larcas Brove.

Chapter 7

Brove has pursued the mercs into Etrijan based on a tip from the cultists, who have been working together with the Govalian Army (specifically Brove). As soon as the mercs are all released, Commander Brove hands Kallie over to the Crimson Flame cultists.

Aeron is frantic and tries to fight, but they have him restrained. Aeron is essentially reliving what Brove did to him with regard to Wafer, only this time, it's Kallie instead. He calls Brove every foul name he can think of, but none of it fazes Commander Brove.

The cultists leave with Kallie, and the wyvern knights take all of the mercs prisoner at an abandoned fortress in Etrijan (they may have to kick out some squatters first). They have Aeron force Wafer to leave or something, or else they'll kill Aeron, (or Wafer isn't with them, or whatever).

Aeron is pissed because he JUST got Kallie back. He is more incensed at Commander Brove than ever, and he swears to make Brove pay for this. His fellow mercs remind him later that if they can get the weapons in time, then they can get back to stop Valdis before it's too late. Nothing they say comforts Aeron at all since they're locked in the fortress for the night, and they'll be escorted back to Govalia for trial and execution in the morning.

Faylen is also there, and she has a crisis of conscience (having witnessed what Commander Brove just did). She also realizes she loves Aeron, and that night, she knocks out the guard watching the mercs. Then she helps the mercs escape because Aeron has only ever treated her fairly and with love, and also because she doesn't agree with the Govalian Army anymore—particularly not Brove. (There's a cliffhanger in here somewhere.)

NOTE: From this point on, the lunar cycle is the story's ticking time bomb.

Chapter 8

Aeron asks Faylen to join them, but Faylen doesn't go with them and instead heads due south into Muroth. (She may turn up later in the first trilogy when everyone is fighting the dragon, but she might not show up until sometime later in the series.) Before she leaves, she gives Aeron a kiss that he will never forget.

Now free from their delay, they resume their trip north to the temple.

When they finally reach the temple, it is hidden in something ice-like. Perhaps they climb up a tall glacier, trying to reach the equivalent of the aurora borealis, and when they pass through the lights, they actually enter into a temple made of ice. (Cliffhanger)

NOTE: Remember, the lunar cycle is the story's ticking time bomb.

Midpoint

Chapter 9

(Multiple chapters)

The mercs explore the temple. As they progress, they're all wary because they remember what happened in Grandfather's story, and they all remember what he'd said.

Sure enough, they encounter icewalkers, which are basically normal-sized ice golems.

They can defeat them by smashing their frozen cores, but it takes a lot of hits to reach their cores. Mehta has to use a more robust weapon instead of his knives (maybe a hammer or some tomahawks or something?) And maybe Aeron can't rely on his spear anymore, either.

There are enough rocks that Kent can call to, and if they had fire, he could burn through them pretty quickly, but it's so cold, his flint doesn't want to spark, and his kindling won't catch fire, either.

Anyway, they get into some scrapes, maybe fall into some traps, and end up facing a dungeon boss. (Cliffhanger)

NOTE: Though they can't see it from inside the temple, remember that the lunar cycle is the story's ticking time bomb.

Chapter 10

The mercs leave the dungeon and return to Mehta's hometown. Then they head on to Valdis Keep, even though the wyvern knights are chasing after them. (There may be some encounters with the wyvern knights in this time as well).

NOTE: Remember, the lunar cycle is the story's ticking time bomb.

⚙

When they get there, they fight their way through what seems like only a handful of guards/soldiers, comparatively, only to find that Lord Valdis isn't there. They learn (somehow) that he has gone to an ancient Aletian tower somewhere in the distance in Xenthan to perform the ritual that night (at the height of the new moon, or whatever). They head out to the tower to stop Valdis and save Kallie.

You may also want to include the stone gargoyles perched in the halls outside the throne room coming to life and attacking them.

NOTE: Remember, the lunar cycle is the story's ticking time bomb.

Chapter 11

(Multiple chapters)

They fight their way through the tower's various levels (think the PS2 LOTR game fighting Saruman), including Crimson Flame warriors (possibly this is where Falna comes back into play), Lord Valdis's men, some fell beasts and stuff that just occupy the tower thanks to Lord Valdis being a dark mage, and then they finally reach the top (interior) level and face Lord Valdis.

ACT III

Chapter 12

Lord Valdis is unstoppable—in LitRPG terms, he's too high-level for the Blood Mercs to do any real damage to him, but they change their tactics and manage to succeed in knocking his harvest ritual off-kilter.

Chapter 13

In the process, the dragon flips out and eats Lord Valdis (a la the T-Rex in Jurassic Park). Mehta is disappointed, but ultimately justice is done in Valdis's death, so he can dig it.

But with Valdis killed, he has become the sacrifice, and it ends up empowering the dragon more.

Fearing the worst, the Blood Mercs stab the dragon with their snow steel weapons to try to kill it before the ritual concludes. Kallie is sucked into a ball of blue energy along with the dragon, and instead of killing the dragon it absorbs the power of the snow steel blade, and transforms into an ice dragon (never before seen) instead of a fire dragon.

Chapter 14

Aeron is devastated, of course, because he thinks Kallie is dead.

As such, the dragon gains a new degree of sentience and becomes more powerful because it is bonded with Kallie and actually absorbs her. It immediately tries to kill the Blood Mercs by leveling the tower from the sky, but Aeron and Wafer escape, and the others are buried (but protected) thanks to Kent's magic creating a wedge between them and the falling rubble.

Then it flies away, and the Blood Mercs are worried at what they've just done.

(End of Book Two)

STORY BIBLE PART 19: ORIGINAL BOOK THREE OUTLINE

A Brief Introduction

Here's the outline for Book Three. It was especially challenging to figure out how to reconcile the various storylines, and to be honest, I didn't get it right in this outline.

I do think, however, that I got it right in the book itself.

You'll note that I didn't break this outline into POVs as much as I did with the previous ones. That wasn't an intentional choice—I just sort of ran with whatever I felt I needed to run with when it came to POVs in this book.

Frostbane Outline

Prologue

Flashback to ancient times. Nexus is a mighty warrior—one of the mightiest of all of Aletia—and he saves part of Inoth (then known as something else) from a fiery dragon that is attacking.

Once he saves his fellow Inothians from harm, he takes liberties he shouldn't take with the dying dragon: He starts trying to take its essence for himself, to make himself more powerful.

But such an act (dark magic in general is an abomination to the majority of Aletians) is outlawed, and he is caught in the act by other Aletians. (Figure out the structure of the people of the time.)

He denies it at first, then he rationalizes it by saying it is necessary so that he might protect his people. (Protecting the Aletians on the whole is his life's mission and one of his core values.) But since it's still outlawed and an abomination, the other Aletians try to arrest him for punishment.

Nexus is arrogant. He has already succeeded in making himself immortal, he claims. He fights back, killing some of his fellow Aletians (which is the most heinous crime an Aletian can commit—Aletians haven't murdered each other for centuries, so when Nexus resists and kills one of them, it is a HUGE deal), but they manage to subdue him and render him unconscious.

✿

When Nexus awakens, he is restrained by the magic-suppressing blue metal and in some sort of chamber. It's dark except for a shaft of moonlight shining down. Around him are a half-dozen guys in dark robes on platforms. Given how powerful Nexus has become, they each sacrifice a bit of themselves in order to lock him away using dark magic.

Nexus yells at them and calls them hypocrites. But they insist that it is for the greater good. So they siphon his essence, partly into each of the six of them, and they lock his body in a casket made of the same blue metal. The six are there to guard him in perpetuity as undying sentries of days gone by, so as to ensure he can never again go free. But they also cannot kill him because it is against their laws.

The Undying Six each wield a stone on their chests, each of which contains a portion of Nexus's stolen essence. In order to revive him, the stones must be activated with dark magic, and then the stones are to be placed in the palms of his hands, one in the center of his chest, one in his mouth, and one each at the base of his feet.

So he is guarded by the Undying Six, who are essentially undead specters with dark magic powers and great fighting skills. Maybe throw in a prophecy (or an oath sworn by Nexus himself) that he will someday return.

<u>Act I</u>

Chapter 1

We see, from the perspective of someone who is about to die, the ice dragon wreaking havoc on the capital city of Tebaryx. They're trying to flee, possibly with their family (for emotions), and they fail and are encased forever in ice.

Chapter 2

Aeron is having trouble processing what happened to Kallie. She's gone, but when Kent shot the dragon, it seemed like she'd come back to life, albeit briefly and only to suffer. Then when the dragon had become an ice dragon in that blast of blue light, Kallie was just gone—nowhere to be found.

Did she get absorbed into the dragon somehow? Did the dragon eat her? Did the ritual go awry somehow, and that's what created the ice dragon? Did Fjorst set them up by using the cannon? Did he truly intend to help them, or was his aim merely to create a frost dragon?

Now, with the tower razed thanks to the dragon, Aeron knows he'll never find Kallie again, and he has to begin to accept that. Likewise, they don't know where Garrick is, either, but they have to assume he's dead also.

Kent doesn't want to leave Garrick's body behind, but it's buried somewhere in the rubble under the tower, and Mehta is probably going to die if they don't get him some help soon, and Aeron is wounded, too. Aeron gives Mehta a painkilling shroom—his last one—as a way to help keep him alive.

Mehta insists on going back to his village to rescue Ferne and his family. He is adamant that they help him get back there instead, but he is woozy and maybe even passes out, so they overrule him and take him to a nearby village instead where he receives aid from a healer.

Aeron calls Wafer. They head west, away from Tebaryx, and with Wafer's help, they manage to travel fast. It's morning/daytime now as they're traveling along. They resolve to allow the Xenthanian Army handle the dragon.

They get Mehta to a healer, who begins to help him. (Aeron also gets treatment for his shoulder and is expected to make a full recovery. He also buys more shrooms from an apothecary in the village, but they only have a few.)

Once Mehta has recovered, enough to travel, Kent and Aeron take him (atop Wafer) toward Etrijan. They arrive back in Mehta's town a few days later, slower than Wafer and Aeron would've done alone, but still far faster than traveling by foot/horseback. It's a sullen success, though, because it's only possible because Garrick isn't around anymore.

They arrive in Mehta's village in time to find that all is well—except they realize there is a soldier in black armor at Mehta's home. (Cliffhanger)

Chapter 3

Mehta (now more or less recovered) moves to attack the soldier because he's clearly one of Lord Valdis's men, but instead, he realizes it's the soldier he spared from the previous book. Mehta tells him that he warned him what would happen if he ever saw him again, but the soldier begs him to wait and says he's there to help. Ferne rushes out and confirms that he's not a bad person anymore, and that's what gets Mehta to let him go.

Sidebar: Ferne is glad Mehta is back, and they have a joyous reunion, but she also knows what it means that these soldiers are there in the village. It means Mehta has to leave again, and Ferne is pissed about it. She threatens to leave, too, but Mehta insists that she stay put. He doesn't want her getting hurt.

She demands that he train her so she can protect herself. Mehta promises that he will once he returns.

The soldier (whose name we finally get to learn) introduces them to the Tribunal, from Tebaryx, which is now a frozen wasteland thanks to the dragon. The following all comes out in discussions...

The Tribunal is a collection of three of the more powerful lords in all of Xenthan, and they've consolidated their power in a tense alliance in order to exert greater control over what happens in Tebaryx. They have a decent-sized army between the three of them (or at least they did before the dragon got to them), known as the Red Helm (for their red armor, primarily), but they don't often venture out of the city except when escorting their merchant caravans to Urthia. So to see them here, now, is both unprecedented and strange.

The three lords control a network of merchant caravans that run goods primarily from Xenthan down to Urthia. It's lucrative enough that that's pretty much the only trade route they deal with. Anyone in Xenthan who wants something from Tebaryx must come to Tebaryx, generally, to purchase it.

Now that the dragon has destroyed Tebaryx, the Tribunal lords' livelihoods are also all but destroyed. Worse yet, much of the country, which relies heavily on exporting raw materials (iron ore being the main export, but also some lumber and other goods) in exchange for importing grain, rice, and other food is in major peril. Without a functional, centralized hub for distributing resources to the rest of the nation, Xenthanians could die even without coming into direct contact with the dragon.

The Tribunal is especially interested in meeting with them primarily because if Lord Valdis is truly dead, they can take over his fortress and operations in the west and expand their territory and control over a larger portion of the country. In fact, they may need to use it as a base of operations for the time being while they try to deal with the dragon.

The Tribunal members have different personalities and proclivities. (Figure that out as the characters appear.)

Ultimately, the Tribunal asks the Blood Mercs for help in bringing down the dragon.

By now, it's nighttime. The Tribunal insists that anyone else who might've been able to help is already dead, thanks to the dragon, so they're essentially begging the Blood Mercenaries to help and offering crazy fortunes to them as well if they manage to succeed.

The Blood Mercs resist, of course. They believe they're just normal people. And if entire armies couldn't defeat the dragon, what hope do the three of them have? Even with Garrick, they still wouldn't have succeeded. It's impossible.

As they're saying all of this, a reptilian screech splits the sky. The dragon has arrived.

Chapter 4

The Tribunal and their remaining Red Helm soldiers spring into action. They've seen this before. They command everyone to douse fires throughout the village. Every single fire. The dragon is attracted to fire, and all attempts to fight it with fire failed—it just served as a beacon for the dragon to follow before it destroyed the people. Dousing the fires is the only way to survive.

The Blood Mercs scatter throughout the city and fulfill the mandate along with members of the red helm, each of whom use something else that glows to light their way as needed. Maybe scorallite? But Kent refuses to touch it.

The dragon does attack, but only the portion of the city that they were unable to reach in time. Palomi's new boyfriend (whom we meet earlier on in the story, around when they meet the Tribunal) is part of the effort, and as he's trying to get back to his family, he is killed. (Palomi is super sad and furious.)

Once the dragon finally leaves, they watch as it lands within the crater part of the cratered mountain. It's huge now, and fills up half the crater, easily. Now that everything has calmed down, everyone regathers, with Grandpa and Ferne caring for Palomi over her loss. Meanwhile, the Tribunal directs the Red Helm soldiers to go help the villagers.

The Tribunal knows the Blood Mercs killed/defeated Lord Valdis, and they know about the god-forged weapons they managed to obtain, so they figure the Blood Mercenaries are resourceful enough to stop the dragon. There can be talk about Fjorst's involvement in all of this, too.

(Kent's POV) The Tribunal offers them an ancient artifact that is said to unlock the tomb of an ancient Aletian warrior who might be able to help them defeat the dragon.

Legend tells of an ancient warrior known for slaying dragons. His remains were buried under the shrine or near it or whatever, or maybe it's even underwater instead, just off the coast, or in the center of the inlet. That warrior is actually an ancient Aletian. He can either be reborn/revived or he's just hibernating or he's locked away or all of that. The Blood Mercenaries don't realize he's an Aletian at first, but when they wake him up (or whatever) it's clear he's not human.

They explain where it is, too (the peninsula on the west coast of Inoth). They bought it ages ago from Inoth's former king, Theldus, who sold it to them when he was in need of money. They've made a point of collecting interesting oddities throughout the years, and they're pretty superstitious about it all, too, as in they believe most of the lore is rooted in some semblance of truth.

Kent can and should have foul thoughts about Theldus at this point (he's Aveyna's late husband). And then he can think about Kymil as well and about what going to Inoth might mean.

But, naturally, it's dangerous. They've sent dozens of other Red Helm men down there in the past months since the dragon has been wreaking havoc on the land.

They know the Blood Mercs managed to get through Fjorst's temple, through another dungeon, and have defeated not one but two dark lords and essentially crippled the Crimson Flame cult in the process. If anyone can do it, it's them.

The Blood Mercs reluctantly agree because there is no one else who can go. The Tribunal accompanies them (they're heading to Valdis Keep as a home base for now). When they part at the river, they will send some of the Red Helm with the mercs, including Lord Valdis's soldier. One of the members of the Tribunal also comes along to give them diplomatic credibility, too, in case they need it.

⚙

(Aeron's POV) They head east (Kent won't risk traveling through Muroth, even atop Wafer) to take a ship along the river south, but as they go, Aeron and Wafer take Kent and Mehta up to the crater near where the dragon was staying for some recon. When they get up there, they find that it's gone now, but they happen upon a nest of icy eggs—at least a dozen of them (maybe twenty).

Kent wants to torch them right then and there, but the dragon is nearby and will almost certainly realize what's going on. Ultimately, he decides to do it anyway, because this whole crisis could've been averted if he had just stomped the dragon's head when it was little back in Valdis Keep, so he sparks some flames and lights the nest on fire.

As the nest burns, the dragon returns.

Act II

Chapter 6

(Mehta's POV) The Blood Mercs flee, with Aeron and a few of the Red Helm wyvern knights leading the dragon in various directions as a distraction.

The dragon manages to catch one of the wyverns in it mouth, and it starts chomping down on it and its rider. Mehta was riding on that one, and when he realizes he's about to become a snack, he jumps off. Aeron and Wafer catch him.

They manage to escape and then regroup at the river with only the one lost soldier. They part ways with the Tribunal and most of the Red Helm, but one of the three Tribunal lords comes along as a diplomat, and a contingent of Red Helm accompanies him. So does Lord Valdis's soldier.

They book passage on a huge ship heading south along the river, one that is large enough to carry them all and even Wafer at times. (Find a cliffhanger, or do a scene break.)

Chapter 7

Several weeks earlier

Garrick wakes up, and he gasps, clutching at his bare chest where Lord Valdis's shadow spear had pierced through him. He finds only a scar. He feels weak, but it's an improvement over being dead, which is what he should've been.

He looks around to find himself in a room with a beautiful woman. She appears to be elven, or at least part-elf, by the look of her ears. She has brown hair (stick with brown or red because Faylen is blonde) and nice features. She is using an awl and stitching to mend Garrick's leather armor, specifically the spot where Lord Valdis's spear poked into his back.

Run with the scene from there. He's attracted to her, he's unsure where he is, she explains all that and how he survived, etc. (She's a practitioner of light magic, and she healed him, they're at a port in Goldmoor, the capital of Inoth.) They also tell him he's the ONLY survivor of the tower thing, so he operates with the understanding that the other mercs are dead, but he also learns that Lord Valdis is dead, too. He doesn't know about the dragon.

She gives him some food (he's starving). She tells him to eat slowly because he hasn't eaten anything in almost a week. They've barely managed to get water into him.

Garrick notices a bruise on her arm or something, and she covers it with her garment, or whatever. He also realizes he has a metal collar around his neck. As he's starting to pull on it, the man of the house, a merchant, comes in.

They have a conversation, and Garrick asks (or demands) to be released, and even offers to pay them in thanks for saving his life, but they don't believe he has any money. When Garrick gets frustrated, he starts yanking on the collar to try to get it off, but he's not strong enough to do it.

Then he resorts to threatening the man, but the man is a mage and uses his magic to constrict the collar on Garrick's neck until he passes out. (Chapter ends)

Chapter 8

When Garrick wakes up again, he finds himself at some docks in Goldmoor. There is a merchant ship there, and he's tasked with working to load it with stuff. He is very promptly whipped and told to get moving, and he grabs the whip and decks the guy who is whipping him. The merchant lord shows up again, and he constricts Garrick's collar once more, but only enough that Garrick releases the whip and agrees to do what he is told.

Fun note: Garrick is working side-by-side with a big, half-orc man named Trag Gadzag, whose left arm isn't quite as strong as his right, probably due to some old injury, Garrick surmises. Trag is stupid and slow, but he's strong and can get the job done well enough. Trag is also wearing a similar collar, but he doesn't seem to mind. Tells Garrick that he didn't have a choice because some jerk in fine clothes injured his arm, and he had to indenture himself just to make ends meet.

Garrick sees the wife again, and she has a fresh shiner on her eye. It pisses Garrick off, because he KNOWS it's the man doing it.

Garrick works with a handful of other slaves, hauling heavy loads onto the ship, etc. (Figure out what product the merchant is hauling. Booze or wine would be fun. Or maybe it's several products.)

At the end of the day, the ship leaves, and Garrick is locked up for the night. Naturally, he finds a way to escape, but the merchant man is waiting for him. He constricts Garrick's collar again, but yet again, it's only enough to slow Garrick down, not enough to kill him or even put him unconscious. It's a power play more than anything. Perhaps Trag is there also? And Trag fights Garrick to some extent?

When Garrick makes a comment about the merchant's wife, the

merchant snaps and starts constricting the coil around Garrick's neck again.

Chapter 9

Garrick wakes up in the presence of the man's wife again. She is tending to him again, and there is an undeniable attraction there.

He asks her directly about her shiner, and she remains evasive. He tells her his own mother was killed by his abusive father, so he hates seeing this happening to her.

Embarrassed, she leaves, unwilling to discuss it further.

✪

Several weeks pass by, with Garrick keeping his head down, working. He sees an opportunity to try to escape again, this time by attacking the merchant directly. He is ferocious and nearly succeeds, but Trag is there to help protect him, and the merchant also uses other magic to subdue him and then manages to constrict the collar once again. After that point, Garrick is forced to wear restraints/chains that inhibit his movement.

Then one night, the Septerran Pirates attack the docks and try to raid a merchant ship. (Cliffhanger)

Chapter 10

Garrick is restrained and could fight back if he were released, and he tries to get the guy to set him free. In the meantime, he fights the pirates as best he can while still being chained up. (Internally, Garrick's biggest concern is not himself, but the wife.)

Eventually, once the pirates prove too much for Trag, the merchant sets Garrick free from his chains. In doing so, he enables Garrick to fight back. Garrick does and takes out the rest of the pirates alongside Trag and the merchant. Afterward, he demands his freedom as recompense.

The merchant disagrees. His wife agrees with Garrick and says so, to which the merchant responds by smacking her in her mouth. Garrick charges him yet again and is again rendered unconscious.

Chapter 11

Late the next day, the Blood Mercs arrive at the port in Goldmoor (where Garrick is working, but they don't know he's there, obviously, because they think he's dead). It looks decimated and there's a lot of debris everywhere and even some lingering bloodstains that dock-workers are scrubbing.

Also, hanging high above from some of the masts of the ships and from posts and poles are the dead bodies of the Septerran Pirates who didn't survive the raid, as a warning.

But the raid was more or less successful. Several ships had their goods raided, and the pirates got away before the navy could show up to intervene.

It's already late—too late to travel, so the Blood Mercs opt to stay aboard the ship for one more night before heading west, toward Inoth. Kent wonders about how safe they really are—if he is found or recognized, it could be very problematic.

✿

When Garrick wakes up, his only thoughts are for the woman. He finds her (or she finds him, perhaps), and they talk. Emotions run high, Garrick offers to take her away from that place if she'll just set him free, and they kiss (maybe), and then the merchant finds them in the act. (Cliffhanger)

Chapter 12

Garrick roars, yelling for the wife to get back. Trag shows up, and the merchant is choking out Garrick with magic and beating his wife savagely, and Garrick can't do anything about it.

✿

Late that night, Mehta is awakened by a familiar voice nearby. Convinced he wasn't just hearing things, he sets out to look for the source of the sound. He follows the sounds of struggling and of a woman's crying and yelps.

He boards a merchant ship and finds Garrick there as well as the merchant and his wife and Trag. He is stunned to see Garrick alive, but not so much that he prematurely springs into action, though a fight does eventually happen.

The merchant loses the metal object in the ensuing fight, and the wife grabs it and sets Garrick free using her magic.

Now free, Garrick joins Mehta and fights his way through whatever other magic the merchant throws at him and kills the merchant. Reluctantly, Garrick and the wife part ways. They let Trag live, which Mehta doesn't like (thirst) but Garrick insists he's free from his servitude and is now second-in-command of the ship rather than being indentured. Trag doesn't mind the idea of it, and he agrees to keep his mouth shut.

Then Garrick accompanies Mehta back to the other ship where there is a joyous reunion. Everyone feels much better about their odds going forward as a result of their reunion.

The Blood Mercs are back in business.

Chapter 13

Reunited, the Blood Mercs make their way across Inoth and over to the inlet. They find the shrine and get inside. They fight off its various challenges (especially the Undying Six). But when they finally get the vault open, they find only a withered corpse.

But Kent realizes that the stones of the Undying Six probably matter somehow, and he realizes they need dark magic—a lot of it—to activate the stones.

Kent realizes their only hope, the only dark mage he knows of, is King Kymil. So they head to Goldmoor to seek an audience with him. (Cliffhanger)

Chapter 14

Kent and Garrick go visit Kymil with the Tribunal Lord as their diplomatic help to try to get Kymil to aid them in opening/awakening the ancient warrior. Mehta and Aeron stay behind.

Maybe the Tribunal Lord gets killed while they're in there? Or he gets killed later?

Kymil says "no," so later, the Blood Mercs decide to break into the castle and abduct him to force him to help.

The Tribunal leader surprisingly has no problem with it. Even if it causes a war between Inoth and Xenthan, it can't be any worse than what the dragon is already doing to the country. Plus, Xenthan is so far from Inoth, it would be really difficult to get troops there—they'd literally have to march through Govalia and Urthia before even reaching Xenthan, which is unlikely.

And lastly, it might weaken them too much against Muroth, which, though friendlier toward Inoth than ever, still wishes to overtake the entire country at some point.

So they agree they're going to go for it, and they establish a plan.

Chapter 15

This is the break-in/abduction sequence. Kent faces down Grak once again, and this time, he expects it will be an imbalanced fight. But Grak has some sort of magic resistant armor—an upgrade from the last time they faced each other, so they're actually pretty evenly matched overall.

But Kent (and Garrick) are mostly just a distraction.

✿

Meanwhile, Kymil is cowering in his room, guarded by several of his elite guard. Mehta is also inside, and he takes out the guards, then he literally tosses Kymil out the window. (Cliffhanger ending)

Chapter 16

Aeron and Wafer catch Kymil as he is falling out the castle window and fly away with him. Then Wafer lets out a hideous shriek that notifies the others they they're good to leave.

Aeron has a fun "Remember me, asshole?" moment with Kymil.

The other Blood Mercs also escape.

✿

Several days later, they arrive at the inlet again, and they enter into the tomb once more (they had locked it back up previously). They take Kymil inside and force him to do the ritual that activates the stones.

As per the directions on the ritual scroll, they place the stones in the palms of Nexus's hands, one in the center of his chest, one in his mouth, and one each at the base of his feet. Each stone has a different meaning. The one in his heart is for his core, his strength. He can live without it, but he will be weak. So they revive him and keep hold of the final stone so he cannot betray them.

Nothing happens at first, but then Nexus awakens in spectacular fashion. (Cliffhanger)

MIDPOINT

Chapter 17

At first Nexus freaks out and tries to attack, but he feels weak, and the Blood Mercs easily subdue him, even though he's far bigger than they are—even bigger than Garrick.

They update him on what the world has become, and they tell him they need his help to slay a dragon—an ice dragon. Conversation ensues, and all the while Kymil is just watching this, amazed.

To the Blood Mercenaries' disappointment, Nexus doesn't know how to defeat an ice dragon. He brings up Dheveri, and they say they don't know how to reach her outside of petitioning at one of her temples, but they doubt that will work.

Nexus tells them he knows what they must do, and he takes them to the forest north of Goldmoor (Kymil included). Within that forest lies a place of deep darkness and terrible creatures, and Kent knows this from having General Deoward explain it to him. The last time he was there, he was hunting with Kymil, Deoward, and Grak.

They go there and enter the dark forest.

Chapter 18

Together, they navigate the forest, fighting off woodland creatures and terrors. Kymil is still there because he makes for a useful hostage, but Grak and the army are closing in as well.

They keep looking for Ravzar and Tirrus, but they cannot find them.

Then, at one point, Kymil runs off, and he encounters a hair-covered, wolfish man who stares down at him with a wicked smile. (Cliffhanger)

Chapter 19

Kymil stumbles upon Ravzar, and Ravzar contemplates eating him until Garrick shows up. Then he wants to arm-wrestle Garrick (or just normal wrestle him).

Nexus introduces him as Ravzar, and Ravzar is confused and trying to remember Nexus. Eventually, he does remember.

Garrick is confused at first, but Ravzar insists, so he agrees. He thinks he can win because Ravzar looks strong but is far too small comparatively to actually be stronger than Garrick.

Ravzar wins handily, but he remarks that Garrick is pretty strong. "Must be that troll blood in your veins, huh?" he remarks.

Garrick is surprised that Ravzar knows he has troll blood in him, but then again, he's a god, and a beast god, as well.

When Ravzar sees Wafer, he is absolutely enamored with him. Thinks he's handsome and a fine specimen and says as much.

They proceed to ask Ravzar for help, and they describe the situation (ice dragon, rampaging, egg nest, etc., not sure how long it will be until they hatch) and Ravzar tells them the eggs will hatch in a couple weeks. He can feel them (and they're chilly), and he can tell when they're going to hatch.

That's bad news for the mercs. They only have a couple of weeks to destroy the dragon and its eggs.

Ravzar says he's willing to help, but he won't unless they do something for him first.

They ask what it is, and he tells them he wants something outrageous (figure this out later) for an absurd reason.

When the Blood Mercs say they can't do it, he says he can't help. "There must be something else you want. The fate of the entire continent is at stake."

"There is one thing…"

He describes how he's been fighting with Tirrus, his "wife," recently. They aren't even on speaking terms anymore.

Garrick insists that they're not qualified, that they wouldn't even know where to begin. Garrick hasn't had a real romantic relationship in decades, all the women Kent is with end up dead, Aeron is a perpetual virgin (he will openly deny this, but no one will believe him), and Mehta is just as likely to kill a woman as to fall in love with her (and he just sort of shrugs and admits that that's true).

"That's the only other thing I need right now."

The Blood Mercs look at each other, and then they look back at Ravzar.

Chapter 20

(Possibly Garrick's POV) For whatever reason, Garrick is taking the lead on this one. They've managed to get Tirrus to meet with them and Ravzar, and Garrick is playing therapist, trying to sort out what the issues are.

They go back and forth for awhile, with the other Blood Mercs interjecting at times (usually humorously), but it's mostly Garrick doing the talking.

Note: The beast god is considered a "lesser" god, but the goddess of nature/the earth is one of the main goddesses. The beast god answers to her in a lot of ways, but he's bullheaded and doesn't want to. That causes a lot of their strain in their relationship.

There should be a line from Tirrus about Ravzar persisting in impregnating mortal girls with rabies babies—that is, werewolves and other abominations. And Tirrus is sick of it. Riff off of that for awhile.

Eventually, they come to an agreement, and they celebrate by starting to get frisky in front of the Blood Mercs, who promptly leave for the night with plans to come back in the morning. They don't get much sleep, though, because of the assorted animal noises coming from Ravzar and Tirrus all night.

⚙

Late that night, Nexus and Kymil make a deal. Kymil will retrieve the final stone for him and complete the spell to restore his strength if Nexus will take Kymil away from the Blood Mercs and back to Hunera Palace in Goldmoor.

⚙

The next morning, as they're finally starting to fall asleep, Ravzar and Tirrus awaken them again, this time by appearing in the middle of their camp.

They bless the merc with rewards for their service:

Ravzar gives Garrick an elixir that will permanently make him WAY stronger and even more durable. He tells him not to think about what's in it, and maybe he makes a semen joke.

Ravzar gives Wafer the ability to breathe fire and makes him stronger and bigger as well. He can carry more weight without issue now, and rings of red scales now outline his golden eyes where they all used to be teal/turquoise-colored.

Ravzar also gives Aeron a crossbow that reloads itself and shoots bolts that can slay just about any beast, fell or otherwise, in one shot. It won't kill the dragon because he's been god-touched by Fjorst, but it'll hurt him and might be useful as a distraction, anyway. It'll hurt people too, but only about as much as a normal crossbow bolt would.

The goddess Tirrus blesses Kent with a deeper understanding of magic as it pertains to almost everything natural—so his anima skills are heightened substantially, and it's a permanent change. He basically becomes an anima archmage in an instant, and his command over the elements grows by the day as he tries things out.

His skills that are permanently heightened include magic pertaining to (basically all anima magic):

- rocks/earth/gemstones/all things geology (including molten rock)
- plants
- metals (including molten metal)
- Ice
- Water
- Fire
- Air

As a result of the change, Kent no longer needs fodder for his magic. He can sense nearby elements and can summon them without having to have fuel for the magic. He is godlike in that sense, but his power still isn't even close to god-level, as the amount of magic he has within him hasn't been increased, and he still hasn't fully mastered all of it anyway.

Mehta gets his shadow-moving ability from Tirrus in the form of a deep-blue jewel. Tirrus explains that it was given to her by Xyon himself as a sort of wedding gift to her, his sister, upon her union with Ravzar. It will enable Mehta to move through shadows in an instant, and it may even serve other purposes as well. Tirrus has no need of it and never did.

They don't give anything to Kymil since he practices dark magic and they don't like him, but they do give Nexus a beast-killing sword under the condition that if he uses it, he isn't allowed to use it on any other beasts except the ice dragon and/or its babies. He's allowed to use it on any other massive threats as well, but he is not to abuse its power.

Nexus thanks them for the gift but says what he really wants to know is what happened to the rest of his people. Ravzar and Tirrus refuse to tell him because it's a dark secret held among the pantheon as to what really happened to the Aletians. They evade the topic entirely.

With that, the gods send the Blood Mercs out of the deep dark of the forest, and they are reunited with the Tribunal Lord and the members of the Red Helm, who are amazed at what the Blood Mercs describe to them.

In that moment, Kymil seizes his chance and snatches the final stone from Kent's possession, activates it, and tosses it to Nexus. (Cliffhanger)

Chapter 21

Nexus's full strength is immediately restored, and with his new beast-slaying sword in hand, and with magic on his side again, he backs the Blood Mercs up and leaps high into the air with Kymil, escaping. They try to follow, but it's fruitless. He's too powerful and quick with his full power restored.

So now they have an ice dragon rampaging in the north as well as an ancient warrior on the loose in the south. They know they can't invest time in going after Nexus, so they head north to face down the dragon.

Chapter 22

Nexus drops Kymil off at Hunera Palace, as promised. Kymil tries to get him to stay, but Nexus refuses, saying he must learn what became of his people.

Kymil convinces him to stay by offering him access to Inoth's royal library, including a secret, hidden library full of ancient Aletian texts.

Nexus agrees and he begins his search. He eventually finds what he is looking for, and then he leaves.

Chapter 23

Back in the north, the Blood Mercenaries are surprised to find that Nexus has rejoined them. Together they make a plan to fight the dragon.

Then they set out to face the dragon head-on. (Cliffhanger)

Chapter 24

The battle with the dragon ends poorly. Most of the remaining Red Helm are destroyed. Nexus manages to land several blows with his weapon, but nothing fatal. The ice dragon is wickedly smart and resilient, and it doesn't go down easy.

The Blood Mercs and Nexus end up retreating. They have failed to win.

Chapter 25

Nexus convinces them that he cannot defeat this dragon, even with their help. Not by traditional means. Instead, they must trap it and open the cratered mountain (a volcano) to destroy it. They're not trying to get it to erupt—they're just trying to get it to open enough so the eggs fall into the magma within.

They're incredulous on how to do that. Kent doesn't believe it's possible.

Nexus convinces him that it IS possible if they work together. Between his vast power and Kent's new mastery of anima magic, they can do it, thereby destroying the nest and possibly even the dragon itself.

Kent is still incredulous, so Nexus further explains that they can set him up with some scorallite to amplify his magic—if only there was some scorallite around...

Then Lord Valdis's soldier explains that there's a scorallite mine nearby Mehta's village; it's part of the reason his men kept raiding Mehta's village over the years—to feed the miners and the soldiers keeping watch over the mine. They agree to go get some.

With no army to speak of to distract the dragon, it'll primarily be up to Wafer and Aeron to distract him. They regroup and try again, but first, Mehta goes back to his village and instructs everyone to flee.

Not many remain anyway, but his family and Ferne are among those who've stayed this long. Now they don't have a choice. He tells them to head toward Sefera, and he promises to meet them there once the threat is neutralized. They agree, there's a final goodbye with Ferne, and then he heads back to battle the dragon once more.

NOTE: Faylen shows up at some point as well during this book. She helps in the last battle with the dragon but not the first one.

Chapter 26

The Blood Mercs regroup, battle some leftovers of Lord Valdis's soldiers, and Garrick hauls a massive chunk of scorallite out of the mine. Maybe they fight a mine monster of some sort, too, but maybe not.

The Blood Mercs also want to free the miners (dwarves, or whoever is enslaved to do the mining there), and Nexus says he will handle it. Instead of freeing them, he keeps them locked in there and tells them they're not safe because of the dragon, but when it has all ended, he will come and free them.

He leaves them with enough rations (from the soldiers' stores) for several days, then he meets up with the Blood Mercs again and overtly lies to them about the dwarves fleeing to the hills.

Then they go to set up to trap the dragon.

Chapter 27

With everything set up, and everything in the right positions, they spring the trap. The main goal is to destroy the eggs first, and then once the volcano has done its work, Nexus will try again to kill it with his sword.

Mehta is darting through shadows in the trees with a torch in his hands, lighting trees on fire to create a line of burning flames that will draw the dragon away from its nest. It works really well. Then, while Mehta is running for his life, Aeron and Wafer flank the dragon and load it up with fire from Wafer and bolts from Aeron's crossbow. Meanwhile, Faylen and her wyvern, Nilla, also fly past the dragon at fast speeds to aggravate and confuse it.

All of this sufficiently angers and enrages the dragon, and it is thoroughly distracted by now.

Garrick, meanwhile, is actually on the lip of the volcano, scouting for Kent and Nexus to update them on what is happening both with the dragon and with the volcano. As soon as the volcano begins to crack open, the dragon changes course and heads straight for them.

Act III

Chapter 28

The dragon attacks, and Kent and Nexus dive for cover. Its ice breath seals the volcano shut again, and it begins to try to collect its eggs as if it is aware of the danger of the volcano now. Garrick, Aeron, and Mehta try to keep it from ascending, and they knock eggs off its back and out of its talons as they are able.

Nexus abandons his post, leaving Kent alone to open the volcano.

They manage to destroy some of the eggs with Wafer's fire in the process.

✺

At some point, Aeron gets walloped by the end of the dragon's tail. The ensuing slam against a tree or some rocks or whatever results in his back cracking. At first he's worried that he's paralyzed from the waste down because his legs go numb, but he quickly regains feeling and realizes his back pain is totally gone—fixed by the freak blow from the dragon's tail.

Faylen tends to him and is there for this realization, and she makes him get up, mount Wafer again, and keep riding. They're not done yet. Maybe there's another kiss there, too?

✿

CLIMAX

Kent doesn't believe he can open the volcano on his own, but he marshals all of his concentration and takes hold of the huge scorallite crystal. It amplifies and draws his magic out of him, and he redirects his magic into the earth. It's more power than he has ever experienced before, and it is a terrifying, majestic experience to wield that much power.

He's the only one who can stop this dragon, even if it kills him. He couldn't squash its head now, but he can crush and burn it to oblivion right now if he can just concentrate hard enough. With the blessing from Tirrus and the scorallite, he can achieve the impossible.

As the dragon rises with all of its eggs, the volcano starts to open. Aeron and Wafer snag Mehta and Garrick and get them out of there, and to buy Kent (and themselves) some time, Wafer manages to knock the last dragon's egg free from the dragon's grasp, and it plummets toward the open volcano.

The dragon dives after it and gets it, and it looks like it's going to get away with the egg until Kent makes the volcano completely erupt, consuming the dragon and the egg and flinging Kent away from it.

Chapter 29

Once the volcano starts erupting, it doesn't stop. It just keeps going, and lava keeps flowing. Aeron and Wafer find Kent unconscious and grab him and fly him free of the mountain, back to Mehta's village, which may eventually get destroyed by the volcano but for the time being is safe.

✿

Two days later

(Kent's POV) The cratered mountain is no longer the tallest peak in the area as the entire top has been blown off. Kent awakens in a bed in a modest home made of pine. It looks somewhat familiar.

He realizes he's in Mehta's family's house. Garrick is sitting in a chair waiting for him to wake up, and Mehta is sitting in another chair watching him as well. Aeron is standing there, looking down at him with Faylen next to him. Nilla and Wafer are poking their heads in two different windows, staring down at Kent as well.

He's fine, they're all fine, etc. More falling action stuff and conversation.

Kent asks about Nexus, and they tell him they haven't found him yet. He disappeared at some point during the fighting, and they think he might've been killed, but they don't know. Kent insists that they go search for him again, to be sure, and they assure him that they will when Kent has fully recovered.

Kent tries to demonstrate that he is fine right then, but his magic feels wrong—weak, like a whisper of what he could once do. He tries to conjure some, but only manages to raise a faint blue glow from his hands, barely noticeable, and it hurts like hell inside his body, as if his veins themselves have been scraped from the inside.

They give him another day to recover, and physically, he's okay, but his magic just isn't the same anymore. He doesn't really make that known to anyone—he just kind of lives with it as-is.

✿

(Aeron's POV) The next day, they all go searching for Nexus. Aeron and Wafer carry Garrick and Mehta, and Faylen takes Kent on Nilla's back. They fly a few arcs over the volcano and see lava still bubbling below, but no sign of Nexus.

Then they notice something emerging from the lava below. It's a humanoid form, too small to be either the dragon or Nexus. It climbs out like it's being born, and slowly the lava oozes off of it in big chunks, leaving only a naked female form behind.

Aeron can't believe his eyes. It's Kallie.

Epilogue

Several weeks later

Nexus, still very much alive, is overseeing the uncovering of the Aletian Gate from beneath the rubble of the Cratered Mountain after it erupts, killing the dragon.

As the dwarves from earlier in the book chip away at the stone and haul boulders away, he sees the corner of a structure popping through the rock. It is glistening and unique somehow, and obviously distinct against the rubble around it.

It is the Aletian Gate, which is exactly what Nexus learned about in that book back in Inoth. And it is the answer to the question of what happened to the Aletians.

✿

Kent has taken up residence in Valdis Keep as its lord and works in harmony with the Tribunal in Xenthan to help rebuild the nation, especially Tebaryx. He may be building an army with which he can invade Muroth, specifically Etheridge, so he can finally take revenge on his brother for his father's murder.

His magic still isn't working right. He can use it some, but it hurts like hell when he tries to use it. At the end of his scene, he catches a rat skittering through Valdis Keep. He thinks back to Kymil's blood arrows and decides to try it. The rat screeches as Kent takes its essence, and Kent forges a misshapen blood arrow in his hand. But it doesn't hurt to do it, and the magic comes easily.

He flings the blood arrow, and it plunges into one of the throne room walls and lodges there until it dissipates. He sees why dark magic is so attractive, but he resolves he won't become addicted to it like Lord

Glavan, Lord Valdis, Eusephus, and Kymil. He won't do it out of a craving for power—he'll do it so he can achieve his vengeance on Fane, and then he'll be done with magic forever if he has to.

Even so, as another rat skitters past, Kent finds himself reaching for it, then he hesitates.

✿

Mehta meets up with his family in Sefera and establishes a new home there. Mehta is training Ferne in the ways of being a Xyonate, but without all the cult stuff, and she's taking to it incredibly well.

Mehta goes out at night and searches for criminals, and he delivers swift, brutal justice to them. Doing so keeps his skill sharp, keeps his thirst from driving him crazy, and also reduces crime in Sefera.

Ferne doesn't know this, exactly, but she knows he goes out at night. One night, she follows him and catches him doing it. From that point on, she insists that she comes along. Mehta reluctantly agrees, because if she's old enough to follow him and not get caught, she's old enough to be involved. They head off together toward another commission.

✿

Garrick ventures into Caclos, where he finally happens upon Noraff and Phesnos. He kills Phesnos right away, and then he kills Noraff as well, finally avenging Coburn and Irwin's deaths.

Or maybe Garrick kills Phesnos, and Noraff hears about it, so he's boarded a ship back to the mainland, thinking he's escaped from Garrick.

But Garrick is already on the ship, hidden (maybe he learns a neat hiding place on the ship while he's captured by the merchant earlier in the book, and it's definitely a ship being run by the elf healer woman and Trag, who is chumming the water for sharks for some inexplicable reason). Eventually, Garrick confronts Noraff.

Noraff is ready, and he stabs at Garrick with another blade. But instead of it piercing through Garrick's skin, which it should've done, the blade shatters against Garrick's skin. They talk a bit. Noraff asks how he was found, and Garrick tells him a bounty hunter named Ronin Shroud found them—he's a friend of a friend.

Then Garrick uses the mage steel knife that Noraff had tried to kill him with, and he kills Noraff and tosses his body over the edge of the ship, where he is promptly devoured by the sharks that are already following the ship.

Then Garrick sidles up next to the elf woman and they sail into the proverbial sunset.

✿

(Aeron's POV) Aeron is sitting in a pub in Govaliston, very much incognito, with Kallie, before he takes her and their parents down to Caclos (thanks to the MASSIVE sum of coin he earned from the Tribunal for killing the dragon, most of which came from lord Valdis's treasury in Valdis Keep).

He and Kallie talk about what happened with her and surviving the volcano blast. She's still fire-resistant or fireproof (which she demonstrates by holding her hand over a burning candle, and it doesn't harm her), and she's also cold-proof.

Furthermore, she has weird powers, too. She's strong, can hover in the air (but not really fly), can smell and sense things that normal people can't. Her right hand can loose blazing flames upon command, and her left hand can blast ice upon command. The dragon's powers have imprinted on her.

She's also really big into eating meat—more so than ever. She pretty much doesn't eat anything but meat anymore, and sometimes she even crunches through the bones, too.

Aeron encourages her to hide all of those attributes as best as she can, both now and once she settles in Caclos. They discuss the other Blood Mercs and what they're up to because Kallie is still hazy on what all went down. Aeron explains briefly, as we've just seen what each of them are doing.

Faylen isn't in Govalia—she's already in Caclos, scouting out a place for Aeron's family where they'll be safe. But she can't stay for long because her wyvern will overheat if she's not careful. She'll be coming back to help with the transport of the family down there, and then she'll be relocating to Etrijan, Urthia, or Xenthan.

She and Aeron are taking it slow, relationship-wise. They're not even sure if they'll end up in the same country, though Aeron is pretty interested in making sure they end up sharing the same airspace at all times, if possible.

As Aeron and Kallie are sitting there in the pub, talking, Aeron overhears people in the pub murmuring the rumors and legends of the four mercenaries. People are talking about how they defeated a dark lord, how they freed an ancient Aletian warrior, how they made a volcano erupt and felled an ice dragon.

Mum and Pa walk in and say that they're ready to go (Pa very obviously still has no clue how important Aeron is), and they prepare to leave. As Aeron is on his way out, he overhears the following dialogue:

"Who are these people? What are they called?"

"The Blood Mercenaries."

(Wrap up anything and everything else that needs to be wrapped up)

STORY BIBLE PART 20: BASIC THREE-ACT STRUCTURE OUTLINE

A Brief Introduction

If you aspire to write stories, books, or screenplays, there are countless resources out there that can help you learn to do it well.

Here's one more that I'm offering for free, just because you saw fit to buy this book, and also because twenty story bible chapters is better than nineteen for the sake of round numbers.

Oftentimes when I advise other authors on their projects, I routinely encounter stories that fail to deliver in at least one of two crucial ways: they either lacked a workable plot, or their plot wasn't properly "hung" on the classic three-act structure... or both. As such, these stories often didn't flow right, and that lack of a well-constructed plot and structure created a host of other issues as well.

In response, I whipped up the following graphics, which demonstrate two essential truths: First, they present the concept of the three-act structure in visual form, and second, they prove that in no iteration of our universe should I ever create my own graphics.

In addition, I created the sample outline below for you to utilize when you're plotting your next story. Feel free to copy/paste or type it into a Word document and use it as a template or a guide to construct your own story.

Or, if you've actually read this far and want your own copy, visit **www.benwolf.com/Power-Author** to download it.

Before we get into the sample itself, here's a quick breakdown of why the three-act structure is so useful to authors. Refer to the miserably designed graphics below as part of the explanation. As a side note, most of this info is explained in much more detail in this book:

Plot and Structure
by James Scott Bell - https://amzn.to/2XRH24D

In *Plot and Structure*, James Scott Bell likens the three-act structure to a suspension bridge like the one pictured below. You can see the various elements of a typical three-act structure delineated on the graphic below at approximately where they should fall in your story.

The Three-Act Structure Model

www.benwolf.com/editing-services | ben@benwolf.com

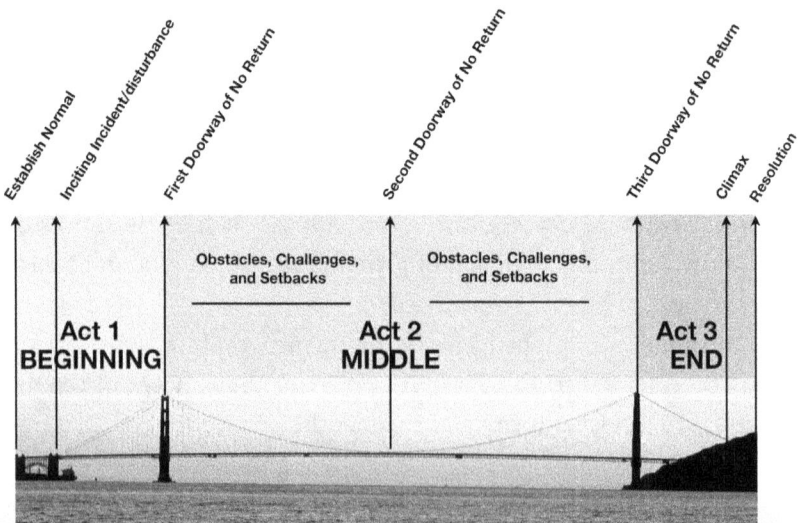

Establish Normal
Inciting Incident/disturbance
First Doorway of No Return
Second Doorway of No Return
Third Doorway of No Return
Climax
Resolution

Obstacles, Challenges, and Setbacks

Obstacles, Challenges, and Setbacks

Act 1
BEGINNING

Act 2
MIDDLE

Act 3
END

The Hero's Journey

www.benwolf.com/editing-services | ben@benwolf.com

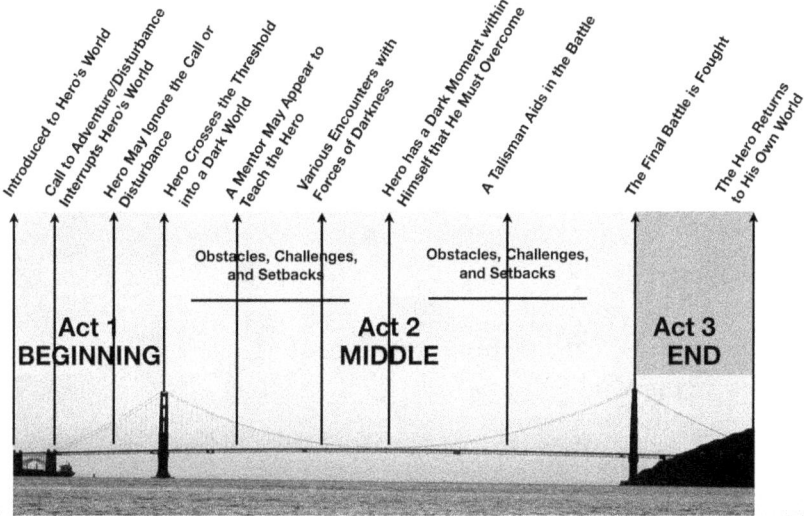

Introduced to Hero's World

Call to Adventure/Disturbance
Interrupts Hero's World

Hero May Ignore the Call or
Disturbance

Hero Crosses the Threshold
into a Dark World

A Mentor May Appear to
Teach the Hero

Various Encounters with
Forces of Darkness

Hero has a Dark Moment within
Himself that He Must Overcome

A Talisman Aids in the Battle

The Final Battle is Fought

The Hero Returns
to His Own World

Obstacles, Challenges,
and Setbacks

Obstacles, Challenges,
and Setbacks

Act 1
BEGINNING

Act 2
MIDDLE

Act 3
END

Here's the exact same image, but instead of keeping the three-act structure's pivotal moments on it, I laid out the high points of what is known as the Hero's Journey, or the "mythic structure," a classic, tried-and-true storytelling method utilized throughout literature and films for centuries.

If you compare the two, you'll note there's plenty of useful overlap between the two formats. Really, they're almost identical; it's just that the Hero's Journey doesn't always work for every genre, so the three-act structure gets utilized more universally.

In any case, understanding these two paths can open a lot of doors for your storytelling. Once you learn to tether your characters' values, ambitions, and story goals to your plot and structure, it'll be like crawling out of a dark abyss right at dawn—the future will be wide open to you as an author.

Here's the actual structure (text with short descriptions) that you can apply to your next project. Don't forget that you can download it for free at my website, **www.benwolf.com/Power-Author**.

Sample 3-Act Outline for Novels

Backstory

(Add in these details before or after—just make sure you add what is necessary for the sake of your character/their character development.)

ACT I

Prologue

(Optional; typically shares a part of the story that will come into play later on in the plot.)

Inciting Incident

This is the event that sets your story in motion. Usually occurs in the first chapter—sometimes at the end, sometimes right at the beginning.

First Disaster/Door of No Return (DNR)

This is the event that sets your character on a path that will irreversibly change their life forever. Once the character makes this choice/walks through this "door," they cannot go back to the way things were.

The entire story shifts, along with the character's perspective, once the choice is made. This moment also marks the end of Act I and the beginning of Act II.

ACT II

Second DNR

This is the second event that forces your character to make another choice that will irreversibly change their life forever. It should happen in the exact middle of your story or very close to it, right in the middle of Act II.

As with the First DNR, once the character makes this choice/walks through this "door," they cannot go back to the way things were. The entire story shifts again, along with the character's perspective, once the choice is made.

Third DNR

This is the final event that inspires your character's final, most crucial choice in the story: will they take the risk and face the challenge head-on, or will they resign themselves to failure?

This choice must *always* plunge your character into the climax, which takes place at the peak of Act III. This moment also marks the end of Act II and the beginning of Act III.

As with the previous DNRs, once the character makes this choice/walks through this "door," they cannot go back to the way things were. The entire story shifts, along with the character's perspective, once the choice is made.

Act III

Climax

The story's central conflict culminates into one final moment where a final choice (or several) is made. This can be a battle, an encounter, an event, a conversation, or any number of other happenings. It is the moment of the highest tension in the story.

Grey Moment

This is the moment when everything looks incredibly bleak for your protagonist, and it is unlikely they will succeed in meeting/achieving their personal story goal(s).

Black Moment

This is the moment when everything looks inescapably bleak for your protagonist, and it is virtually impossible that they will succeed in meeting/achieving their personal story goal(s). The protagonist is merely seconds away from failure or has, perhaps, already failed.

The Turnaround

Something happens that shifts the story again, and it enables the character to find a new solution to the story problem. This can be the interference of another character, a new piece of information, a weapon, a freak happening or moment of good luck (as long as it is set up in advance), a twist, or anything else that has the capacity to affect significant change to the situation in the climax.

(This plot aspect is optional in some story types; if the protagonist will succeed and overcome and win, then it is necessary. If the protagonist loses or fails, it is not necessary.)

Denouement/Resolution

The protagonist has overcome the challenge presented in the climax (or not), and the story moves toward its logical conclusion.

Falling Action

Tie up any and all loose story threads. If necessary or applicable, set up or tease the conflict for the next book.

✿

Remember: you can download this document for free, no strings attached, at **www.benwolf.com/Power-Author**.

✿

MAP of Aletia

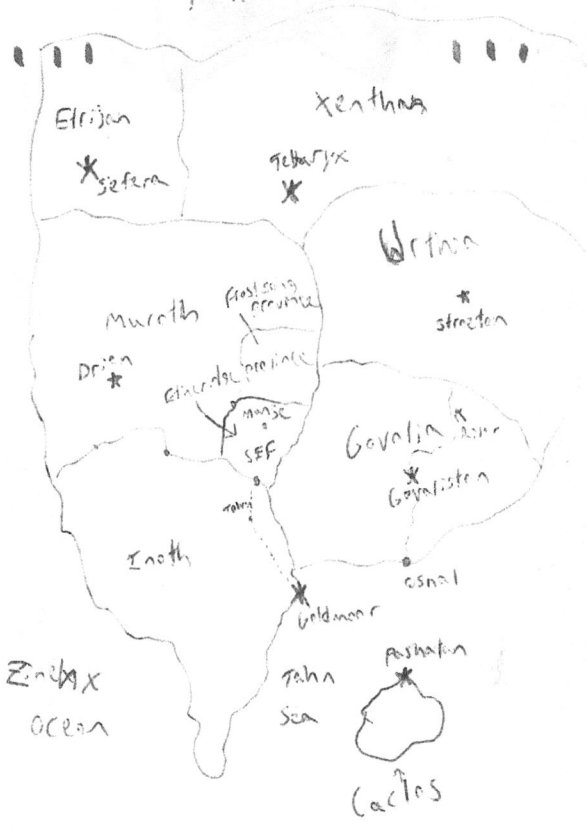

Elrijan

Xenthas

X Sefern

Gethuryx X

Urthia

Muroth

Frostsong province

★ Streeton

Drien ★

Ethurdei province

Govalia

Maase

SEF

Govaristen ★

Govaristen

Inoth

Osnal

X Goldmoor

Zinthax Ocean

Tahn Sea

Pashatin ★

Cactos

Banon Ocean

Meow.

Aletia

KUHNLEAS
OCEAN

ETRIJAN

Mirstone

THE THORNBACK MOUNTAINS

The Cratered
Mountain

★ Sefera

XENTHAN

★ Tebaryx

Valdis
Keep

URTHIA

TOSCA RIVER

LIPARULO RIVER

★ Stroeton

MUROTH

FROSTONG

ETHERIDGE

★ Drion

GOVALIA

Ranhold
Fortress

Dewmire
Fortress

★ Govaliston

● Hachéron

Telyn

INOTH

Osnal

Goldmoor

ZINEHX
OCEAN

TAHN
SEA

Pashatan ★

CACLOS

BONAN
OCEAN

178

AERON IRONGLADE AND WAFER

KENT ETHERIDGE

МЕНТА

GARRICK SHATTERSTONE

Original Path of Shadows logo

Original Frostbane Logo

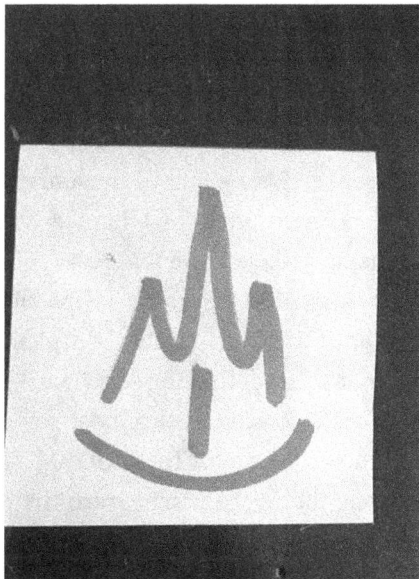

THE TECH GHOST STORY BIBLE

I f you've made it this far, I'm going to assume you're either a glutton for punishment or you skipped directly to this section because you write sci-fi. Either way, I commend you, because in order to write good sci-fi, you have to be able to withstand a lot of punishment.

You'll notice that the story bible for the Tech Ghost series is considerably shorter than the one for the Blood Mercenaries. In addition to being shorter, a couple of other key distinctions separate the two story bibles from each other.

The obvious difference is, of course, in genre. Fantasy functions differently than sci-fi. I mentioned in Chapter 8 (about Magic and Magic Systems) that magic is the engine that runs your fantasy world.

In sci-fi, it's technology that (literally) keeps the lights on—or in cases like post-apocalyptic fiction, it's the conspicuous absence of or failure of technology that helps define the story world.

As such, the story bible for the Tech Ghost series looks and functions a bit differently than the one for the Blood Mercenaries. You'll see some sections in this one that were absent from the Blood Mercenaries version, and you'll find that some sections could apply to either version or both.

The nice thing about this presentation is that you'll be able to pick and choose between the options and even add your own new sections that I haven't thought of as you see fit.

Another major difference between the two is how I went about creating them. I said earlier that I wrote a good chunk of the Blood Mercenaries story bible before I wrote even a single word of the origins novellas. That wasn't the case when I was writing *The Ghost Mine*, which is now Tech Ghost book #1.

Back in the summer of 2018, I had actually published *The Ghost Mine* as a standalone sci-fi/horror novel. When I was prepping it for publication, I had no strong inclination to make it into a series... but right around the time I published it, I came up with an idea for a sequel.

Fortunately, I had set the ending up so a sequel was a possibility, and about two years later, in March of 2020, I signed a three-book contract with Aethon Books to re-release *The Ghost Mine* and publish two new sequels as a series.

Since I had the Blood Mercenaries story bible already written, and since it was pretty good, I adapted it to function for my Tech Ghost sci-fi universe, but aside from a basic outline, I had to start completely over. I had nothing written down for the universe.

So as I did a re-edit/added a bit of new content to *The Ghost Mine*, I began building the Tech Ghost story bible, character by character, planet by planet, technology by technology. When I wrote *The Ghost Pact* (book #2) in the summer of 2020, I added more, and then, as I wrote *The Ghost Plague* (book #3) in the fall of 2020, I added even more.

The Tech Ghost story bible is pretty robust now, but I learned from my first story bible experience and managed to trim a few things out, which is another reason it's shorter.

Perhaps the main difference between my approach to these two story bibles (not to mention the stories themselves) was in how they came about and how I ended up writing each of them. I already mentioned that I had preconceived characters in mind when I wrote the Blood Mercenaries. With characters, all I had to do was figure out a mess to throw them into and let them sort it out.

With *The Ghost Mine*, it was exactly the opposite. I had the mess but no characters.

The Ghost Mine actually started as a freaky nightmare that I had sometime in the first half of 2015. The next morning, I wrote down a bunch of notes that eventually led to the formation of a concept. (The notes are dated 8/23/15, but I suspect that was after I had added to them a few times. I'll include them in an early chapter in this section.)

The dream sparked the entire story world for me, and eventually, a story universe, which is basically the same thing, only bigger.

Eventually, the characters showed up, and they took on personalities and minds of their own. I tend to be a plot-first writer, and back then, I hadn't dedicated as much of my focus to learning to create interesting, believable, and colorful characters, so it took me a lot longer to get the story and the characters to do everything I needed them to do.

In the end, it all worked out, but *The Ghost Mine* endured a lot of rewrites, revisions, and modifications before I published it... and even then, I still ended up adding more and refining it on my last round of revisions before sending it to my publisher. Now I'm really proud of it.

With that said, having written all four of the Blood Mercenaries books and two more Tech Ghost books, I can safely recommend to anyone and everyone that you nail down your characters first and then put them into your plot. (To be frank, it was actually easier to come up with viable plots for the two subsequent Tech Ghost books once I had the characters better nailed down.)

Incidentally, a story bible is a helpful way to do all of that, so I'm pleased to share the Tech Ghost story bible in the upcoming pages for you. Compare, contrast, and conscript elements from both story bibles as you see fit.

✿

WANT TO DOWNLOAD A BLANK TEMPLATE OF THIS STORY BIBLE FOR FREE? VISIT WWW.BENWOLF.COM/POWER-AUTHOR TO GRAB ONE.

✿

ORIGINAL GHOST MINE NOTES

A Brief Introduction

I mentioned in my introduction to this section that *The Ghost Mine* first came to me as a nightmare. I was locked in a dark mine on Jupiter (of all the planets in our solar system, it's probably the least feasible for a person to be physically present and mining anything there, but my subconscious doesn't care about scientific facts), and I couldn't get out.

And something was coming for me—something I couldn't see, hear, etc., but I could still somehow sense it.

I woke up that morning stunned and nearly overwhelmed by the pervading darkness I had experienced thanks to my subconscious. Everything I had experienced was so visceral, so haunting... so hopeless.

As an author, naturally, I wanted to share/inflict those exact sensations with/upon my readers. So I grabbed my phone, opened my trusty Notes app, and furiously typed everything I could remember.

In the coming days and weeks, as the dream matured into a story concept, I added more notes and refined it further. Then, eventually, I started outlining. The rest is history.

Spoilers ahead and throughout. Read with discretion!

Jupiter Dream

Genre: Sci-fi horror/paranormal (= awesome)

- Abandoned mining station on Jupiter
- Ghost workers
- Bales/barrels full of shovels, pickaxes, other tools, plus heavy machinery for excavating
- Massive fans/air processors make the air breathable (find some gravity reducers as well)
- Bully character wants to fight people/be in charge
- MC is a dude, stands up to bully
- Boxes of Kleenex on racks
- One of the ghost workers (still wearing a hard hat) saves the MC somehow by letting him out of an area that gets shut down when the atmosphere suppressors fail.
- Why is this new team there?
- What happened to the old team?
- Zombie workers? And one is a ghost? What would make this unique is the locale and the setting.
- Maybe they're deformed like the Flood from *Halo?*

Characters

A female character should be in charge.

She should be new, but confident, in spite of her team's lack of faith in her ability to lead (particularly the bully, who was passed over for the promotion).

Four main characters/POVs:

- Lead Male Protagonist (Laborer)
- Lead Female Protagonist (Foreman) (she may need to die)
- Lead Male Antagonist (Bully)
- The ghost (male, creepy, probably won't have POV scenes)

Supporting roles:

- other workers
- command
- Planetary Marines/Security forces and their officers
- an android or two? Maybe a cyborg?
- The laborer's friend(s) who will obviously die
- doctor
- cook (android--I can see him going haywire and attacking people with butcher knives, spinning the knives and killing)
- pilots
- mechanics (work on vehicles and androids, machinery)
- head of housing
- head scientist (maybe this is an android or the cyborg, would be cool to be female cyborg)

Hook

A common laborer who travels to Jupiter as part of a team encounters the ghosts of the dead laborers he is sent to replace, and he struggles to unravel the mystery behind their demise amid a variety of scary occurrences.

Inciting Incident

Freaky opening chapter where the initial workers get trapped and suffocate/get gassed when the turbines fail. Chapter ends with the doctor barely escaping. (She was in love with the worker who is now a ghost, and she isn't a cyborg until after the incident--they make her one due to her injuries.)

Act 1

Arrival at planet base, meet some characters, initial conflict with bully, etc. ends with first appearance of ghost and near accidental death of the lead male protagonist.

Act 2

End: the cyborg doctor is in on it, but we're made to think it's the bully? Maybe the lead female protagonist is in on it?

Maybe the ghost guy is actually alive?

For research: http://www.cnn.com/2015/08/21/world/jupiter-juice-mission/?iid=ob_homepage_deskrecommended_pool&iref=obnetwork

STORY BIBLE PART 1: CHARACTERS

A Brief Introduction

Already in our first chapter, you'll notice the difference between the Blood Mercenaries story bible and this one. They're arranged slightly differently, and this one feels less "cluttered" to me.

Keep in mind, I had to go back and create this after I had *The Ghost Mine* done, and while I adapted it from the Blood Mercenaries story bible, I learned from the process and managed to streamline everything.

Major Characters

Justin Barclay - Protagonist

Physical Traits
- has brown hair
- has blue eyes
- is 24 at the beginning of Ghost Mine

Personality Traits
- Has vertigo and hates space travel/flying
- Is kind of a punk

- Think Aaron Paul (Jesse from *Breaking Bad*)
- Definitely has a thing for blondes and probably Asian girls, too

History

- When Justin was a kid, he lived with his aunt and uncle for awhile, and they showed him old Marx Brothers movies for entertainment
- Also lived with his mom off and on (more on than off), and they don't get along at all.
- Been working in copalion mines for 7 years as of the time of *The Ghost Mine*: 2 years as an apprentice and 5 as a full-fledged miner
- Grew up pretty poor

Keontae Oluwelu - Supporting Protagonist

Physical Traits
- Black guy
- Based on Monét Camel (one of my best friends)

Personality Traits
- Is awesome
- Is a badass

Shannon Davis - Supporting Protagonist (Book 1)

Physical Traits
- White woman
- blonde
- nicely built

Personality Traits
- Hard-nosed/willful
- doesn't take shit from anyone
- tough
- durable
- intelligent
- independent
- has high standards

<u>Captain Enix Marlowe</u> - captain and owner of the *Viridian*

Physical Traits
- White guy
- brown hair
- strong and capable, former soldier
- Has metal mesh parts in his gut/side from war wounds

Personality Traits
- talks to himself
- answers himself
- good critical thinker and strategist
- tough but fair

<u>First Officer Arlie Bush</u> (Wife of Enix Marlowe)

Physical Traits
- white woman
- redhead
- dark eyes
- short, five-foot-two, but compact and sturdy
- has a metal shinbone with skin/muscle around it.

Personality Traits
- firecracker
- Quieter
- cutting wit
- tough
- independent
- has high standards
- Is very unhappy with her current situation aboard the rig

<u>Admiral Siroch Sever</u> - Antagonist

Physical Traits
- male
- strong but accustomed to his men doing the heavy lifting for him

- brown-skinned (think Indian)

Personality Traits
- brilliant
- cunning tactician/strategist
- brutal
- heartless
- soulless
- impatient (but displays it through immediate action rather than complaints)

Vesh (super soldier) - Antagonist

Physical Traits
- male
- genetically engineered
- ridiculously strong (augmented)
- highly trained and capable in virtually every way
- half of his face is tattooed
- wears black-and-blue armor
- black eyes like the void of space
- violet skin, translucent, can see most of his veins

Powers
- augmented eyes; can zoom up to at least 100x; can see in ultraviolet, infrared, biometric, night vision, and other types of vision
- augmented fingers/hands; can enter networks like Keontae can with his mind by touching them with his fingers; fingers and hands have circuitry in them which allows him to connect with screens and tech
- extra durability/thick skin
- Can jump really far
- crazy strong
- Occasionally senses a burning/tingling sensation behind his eyes.

Personality Traits
- smart
- good strategist

- brutal
- heartless
- effectively soulless

Dr. Hallie Hayes

Physical Traits
- white woman
- long blonde hair
- decent height—probably 5' 8"/5' 9"
- Great curves
- light-blue eyes with rings of green around the irises
- has an implant just above her collarbone near left shoulder joint

Personality Traits
- cutting wit
- brilliant
- independent
- has high standards
- has multiple Ph.D.s
- quirky and flirtatious

Valkyrie (Val)

Physical Traits
- middle-eastern/Asian/south pacific (or comparable skin tone) woman; very tan
- bald
- decent height—probably 5' 5"/5' 6"
- thinner
- dark eyes
- lots of tattoos and piercings (including some we can't see); septum pierced, one lip piercing, one eyebrow piercing, and lots of ear piercings.

Personality Traits
- matter-of-fact

- asks lots of questions; inquisitive
- independent
- marksman-level shooter/sniper/assassin
- great hand-to-hand fighter
- can be ruthless when necessary
- smart
- patient
- "flows with it"

Other Characters

The Ghost Mine

- Etya Stielbard - part cyborg, head of Science Division at ACM-1134
- Mark Brown - the original tech ghost
- Harry Skylar - Head Foreman for ACM-1134
- Stecker - Security guard who betrays everyone to side with Etya
- Carl Andridge - Owner of all of Andridge Copalion Mines
- Laithe Gerhardt - Head of Security for ACM-1134
- Garth - IT guy—brilliant but a slob
- Rodney - Head of IT—not as brilliant as Garth and insecure
- Noby - Carl Andridge's personal head of security
- Dirk Hammer - antagonist and bully; huge and strong
- Reggie - One of Dirk's friends
- Pig Nose - another of Dirk's friends
- Ofelia Dunham - Head of HR for ACM-1134
- Vanessa - Personal secretary to Bartholomew Morgan
- Bartholomew Morgan - Head/CEO of ACM-1134
- Bryce "Pinch" Pincher - the local drug dealer at ACM-1134
- Connie - one half of a lesbian duo—she's older and has red hair and talks all the time
- Candy - the other half of a lesbian duo—she's younger, has dark hair, is always silent. Bulkier.

The Ghost Pact

- Rowley Pine - The annoying supervisor who gets passed over for his promotion. Beady brown eyes.
- Lora Clayton - the wannabe girlfriend of Justin Barclay
- Dr. Hallie Hayes - the scientist in charge of the weapon; blonde with light-blue eyes with a green ring around the irises
- Bryant Sokolov- First officer/copilot of the science vessel; tall and handsome and strong
- Captain Mitch Dawes - the captain of the science vessel
- Dr. Angela Wainwright - one of the scientists; a larger girl, about ten years older than Hallie, has an MD.
- Dr. Luke Messa - the only male scientist on the trip; noble and honorable
- Dr. Cecilia Bright - one of the scientists; older by about ten years than Hallie; black woman
- Vesh - the super soldier
- Doctor Carrington - the rig's medical doctor
- Carey Hughes - the rig's science officer

Other rig workers:

- Al Paulson - older, beard, 30 years of rig experience (not all on the same rig)
- Shaneesha - middle-aged, about 15 years Justin's senior, black woman, colorful, hair in dreads, dyed red
- Bobby Carlisle - some guy
- Morse - another guy who worked a different shift from Justin and slept in Justin's bed when he wasn't there on a rotation. Always stank of body odor.

Colonist Ship Soldiers (Forest-green fatigues)

- Officer Charles Wendell - Coalition official who met with the

rig workers in the docking bay when they disembarked from the ship
- Captain Wilson James - Coalition Captain of the Nidus

Ikari Gang Members

- Quan Yazhu- a mid-level guy, but important enough that he gets listened to; is sort of Justin's rival in this book. Has obviously bleached blond hair and a prosthetic left leg.
- The Dragon's Breath - the head of the gang - a full-grown woman who looks 8-9 but has a growth disorder and is actually several years older. Rules with poise and grace; unflinching.
- Lei Bai - an older man who is respected as a storyteller and chronicler of the *Ikari's* history and present day dealings.

Avarice Crew Officers

- Captain Jacob Gable - second-in-command of the *Avarice*; charged with running the *Avarice* day-to-day.
- Commander Caustus Falstaff - the *Avarice's* third-in-command official and Admiral Sever's right hand when it comes to troop operations.

Avarice Brig Prisoners

- Jonesy (Fennimore Jones) - a former ACM fighter spacecraft mechanic who was framed for petty crimes and thrown in the brig aboard the Avarice… except he's actually a crime boss.
- Bear (Arthur Henry) - really fat and tall. Pretty much slow and useless (and also a "gentle giant"-type) when he's not in his mech suit, but when he is, he's a damned prodigy. Easy to hurt his feelings, especially if you mention his weight. Talks with a sort of southern accent/dialect.
- Zed Cavale - albino-white hair, jaundiced eyes with golden

irises, and the lower half of his face is a black breathing apparatus that hooks directly into his prosthetic lungs. He is a chemist/demolitions guy. His voice is electronically modulated. Angered easily, defensive. Generally unapologetic for being blunt.

- Ritz (Ritzveld Townsend) - has prosthetic eyes worn as goggles (glowing orange bulbs for eyes). They can move somewhat freely and independently of each other, including extending out of his skull and looking in two different directions. He's a scout-type and his crazy eyesight makes him hard to fight in hand-to-hand combat, too because he can see multiple attacks coming at once. Talks fast, is defensive of criticism.

The Ghost Plague

- The Grand Dragon - a young girl (in appearance) who is the leader of the *Ikari* gang. She actually has a genetic disorder that messes with her aging. She is dressed in fancy Asian gear and has glowing amber eyes that look reptilian (slitted pupils).
- Lei Bai - the right hand and top advisor to the Dragon's Breath. He's an older Asian man. He oversees the financials for the *Ikari*, and the Dragon's Breath acts as the executive. Lei Bai is basically a treasurer/historian CFO.
- Fu Yan - an *Ikari* captain of sorts who is with Val's group when they go to destroy the hives. Has fiery red hair (not his natural hair color).
- Bambang - an *Ikari* captain of sorts who is Indonesian in descent. Speaks very little English. Usually one- or two-word sentences endnote much more.
- Kara - the little girl Vesh rescues after her parents are killed.

✿

STORY BIBLE PART 2: CHARACTER VALUES

A Brief Introduction

I don't think I need to rehash everything we discussed last time this section rolled around. I didn't do values for everyone in this series, but I did them for the characters I feel matter the most in the long term. So for now I'll refer you to Randy's awesome book again:

```
(For more on this topic, check out
      Writing Fiction for Dummies
by Randy Ingermanson - https://amzn.to/2XvCtOa.)
```

Core Character Values

Justin
- Nothing is more important than loyalty.
- Nothing is more important than justice.
- Nothing is more important than finding my purpose in life.
- Nothing is more important than surviving.

Keontae

- Nothing is more important than loyalty.
- Nothing is more important than friendship.
- Nothing is more important than helping and protecting Justin.

Val

- Nothing is more important than avenging my parents' murder.
- Nothing is more important than loyalty.
- Nothing is more important than survival.
- Nothing is more important than growth.

✿

STORY BIBLE PART 3: GROUPS, ORGANIZATIONS, COMPANIES, & CORPORATIONS

A Brief Introduction

This one is different from the previous Chapter 3. Instead of focusing on people groups and creatures, we're shifting the focus to groups, organizations, companies, & corporations since it's more relevant to my specific story universe.

Please note that I do *not* have alien life forms in my Tech Ghost series. If you're writing sci-fi that does include aliens, or if you're writing dystopian or post-apocalyptic sci-fi that has different people groups and/or creatures, you'd want to include the original "People Groups & Creature Types" section in your story bible, and depending on your world, you may want to include this section as well.

You might even want to add this one to your fantasy story bible.

Groups & Organizations

The *Ikari*

An Asian-style gang that has "chapters" throughout the whole galaxy. They represent a mixture of multiple Asian cultures, and to join, one must be 100% Asian in ethnicity/heritage (a mixture is okay as long as it's all Asian). This tends to exclude Indian (from India), Pakistani, Afghani, and other Arab heritages.

The Ghost Mercs

This is the band of mercenaries that Justin is working with. They get their name because of Keontae and Justin's involvement and because they are pretty damned effective. Their founding members include:

- Justin/Keontae - DPS/Hacker
- Valkyrie (Val) Moon - Sniper/Leader
- Arthur Henry (Bear) - Mech suit/tank
- Zed Cavale - Demolitions/explosives
- Ritzveld Townsend (Ritz) - General Tech Wiz/Scout
- Quan Yazhu - DPS/Hand-to-hand

Companies & Corporations

MetaFlight Space Transport

Pretty self-explanatory: a space transportation company capable of anything from short jaunts between planets to longer voyages as well as local air travel as necessary.

Andridge Copalion Mines

One of the largest companies in the galaxy, it is responsible for a huge portion of the copalion mining that takes place on planets across the galaxy.

- Also responsible for multiple wars with other mining/energy companies
- Incredibly powerful and influential because of how wealthy

they are and how much of the galaxy's energy supply they control and produce.

- Their logo is an orange-and-blue ACM logo.
- ACM is fifty years old as of the time of Ghost Mine.
- "Excavating Efficient Energy for 50 years"
- Controlled by a board of directors
- Their military is controlled by the Joint Chiefs, who answer to the board/CEO

Farcoast Mining

Another of the largest copalion mining companies in the galaxy, and one of ACM's chief rivals. They've been in wars with each other and are always seeking out new planets to mine for copalion. Whoever finds the planet first usually gets to stake the claim to mine it first.

STORY BIBLE PART 4: PLANETS & SYSTEMS

A Brief Introduction

It depends on the type of sci-fi you're writing, but if it's takes place in outer space, you'll be naming planets, star systems, and possibly even entire galaxies and universes. With all these places to keep track of, it'll save a lot of time and frustration to write everything down.

In lieu of "Places & Locations," we're going with Planets & Systems for this section instead. As with the previous chapter, you can have both in your story bible if you feel you need to.

You'll notice that some of the planet descriptions don't have much there (denoted by the word "exists"). That's because these places were only mentioned, and thus I haven't developed them much beyond that point yet.

Planets & Systems

The Coalition Planets

- A huge group of systems that have formed a coalition for their mutual economic and security benefits.

- The governing body of the Coalition is centralized on one planet in particular: Moline Prime.

Moline System

- The central system of the Coalition Planets.
- Moline Prime is the seat of the Coalition's power, and it's the most heavily fortified and weaponized planet in the galaxy.
- Usurped Earth's Solar System as the seat of power because Moline Prime had more than a dozen planets capable of being terraformed, whereas only Earth, Mars, the moon, and a few of Jupiter's moons proved to be habitable in the long run.

Ketarus System

- Ketarus-4 - The site of ACM 1134 (Ghost Mine)

Yovado System

- Yovado-2 - (exists)

New Germania System

- New Germania-7 - A cosmopolitan planet that is well-populated and technologically advanced. It is a hub for travel as well and functions as a springboard into more distant systems and planets. It is also home to the New Germania Blazehawks, a professional sports Omniball team (like football, but more high-tech).

Carmelion System

- (exists)

Beskapt System

- Beskapt-12 - the site of an ACM competitor's mine. It's where Justin and Keontae met.

Bortundi System

- Keontae is from the Bortundi System.
- Keontae's mother still lives on Bortundi Prime.

Xardona System

- Keontae's grandfather was killed on one of the planets there while he was on a mission as a Christian missionary.

Ylipsin System

- Ylipsin Prime - Stecker lived there briefly.

Bizona System

- Bizona-14 has the Marauders as their professional Omniball team

O'Connor System

- O'Connor-2 has the Space Pirates for their professional Omniball team

Pinterius System

- Pinterius-3 is where Shannon is from. Nicknamed "three-pin."

Grostonia System

- Grostonia-11 - Multiple ACM mines on this planet
- Grostonia-13 - is a secret planet that is owned outright by ACM. It is well-fortified and "off the books" to some extent. This is where they perform much of their illegal/unethical research and experimentation, including Vesh's creation.
- "Kicks like a Grostonian racehorse" is an expression, I guess

Zhevalia System

- They have nasty mosquitos, known throughout the galaxy.

Jevilos System

- Jevilos-6 - the planet where Justin goes after ACM is done with him at the end of Ghost Mine. It's a neutral planet, free of ACM's influence. It's also where Justin joined up with Captain Marlowe's crew.

Rzasa System

- Rzasa Prime - Carl Andridge was supposed to give a commencement speech there at Nietz University.

The Hippie Planet

- The hippies were given their own terraformed planet on the condition that they were never allowed to leave.
- This arrangement was lauded by everyone across the galaxy.

STORY BIBLE PART 5: MILITARY & GALACTIC GOVERNMENT INFO, LAWS, & HISTORY

A Brief Introduction

I happen to love a nasty galactic empire. I like good ones, too, but what I really enjoy are the morally gray ones.

After all, it's the government, right? Corruption abounds, yet some of the folks working there are doing so to try to effect real change.

But its still a sprawling galactic government, and no one likes paying taxes.

In this section, I've blended the soldiers and colors info with my "military" section. Additionally, in the Tech Ghost universe, I have a much clearer idea of the history between the various warring corporations, the government, and other entities, so there's a good rundown of the galaxy's recent history in here as well.

Military

Interplanetary Space Marine Corps (IPMs)

- The same as your standard marines, only in space.
- Highly trained, badass, dangerous.

- Operated and controlled by the Coalition Planets.
- There has been some genetic engineering/DNA altering happening with them recently.
- The Third Copalion War happened thirty years prior to *The Ghost Mine*
- Black armor/attire
- Officers wear burgundy attire/uniforms

Farcoast Mining Corporation Soldiers

- These are soldiers under the employ of Farcoast.
- They fight and protect on behalf of the company.
- Highly trained
- Forest-green attire and armor

Andridge Copalion Mines Soldiers

- These are soldiers under the employ of ACM.
- They fight and protect on behalf of the company.
- Highly trained
- dark-blue attire and armor
- *Code Ebony*: means two or more warships are en route, and the ACM ship receiving the alert is to fall back and regroup with the nearest ACM fleet for reinforcements/protection and to minimize potential losses.

The Galactic Coalition for Governing United Planets

- AKA "GCGUP" or more often referred to as "The Coalition"
- This is the governing body for the Coalition Planets.
- Slightly (or not-so-slightly) oppressive
- Definitely corrupt and more about self-preservation and growth than actually concerned about serving/protecting people across the galaxy

Coalition Laws

- The Universal Disclosure Act: requires that any conversation or communication that is being recorded must be disclosed as such to participating parties. Coalition representatives are of course exempt from this law, and it's hard to enforce in private situations.
- Inheritance Law: If a beneficiary is not specified in a formal last will and testament, their property, finances, and bank accounts will be transferred to the nearest next-of-kin.
- "Innocent until proven guilty" is not inherent on every planet.
- Search and Quarantine Laws: when setting foot on a Coalition-controlled ship or in a Coalition-controlled base on a planet, a person is subject to a medical scan of their person for foreign pathogens or illnesses. In addition, they agree to be searched and submit to their ship and personal property being searched as well.

Galactic History

The Copalion Wars

Wars fought primarily between competing energy companies with minimal Coalition interference or involvement. These wars have been going on for the last century or so, with plenty of hot and cold periods.

First Copalion War

Records are spotty on who instigated this war, and there is no consensus on who "shot first." There were originally eighteen or nineteen different energy/mining companies involved, with shifting alliances and betrayals galore. In the end, only fourteen remained, and all of them signed treaties with each other and with the Coalition ensuring fair treatment for all of them.

Second Copalion War

This war was instigated by a group of six of the smaller energy companies in the galaxy. (Smaller, of course, is relative—they were still massive companies, but they couldn't compete in size and scope with the biggest players on their own).

Tired of the preferential treatment given to the larger companies by the Coalition, these companies banded together to try to force the Coalition to level the playing field. When that didn't happen, they attacked one of the big players and, to everyone's surprise, they actually succeeded in crippling most of their infrastructure.

The remaining large energy corporations banded together and conspired to wipe this band of rogue companies out entirely. During this war, the rogue companies wanted ACM, at that time only a medium-sized player in the energy field, to join them to help bolster their strength. ACM played neutral for much of the war and stayed out of it, but behind the scenes, they were working a different angle.

When the time came, ACM swept in and took out the majority of the six rogue companies' forces in a series of quick, coordinated attacks, fracturing the band of companies permanently and leaving them defenseless. In the aftermath, ACM quickly and hostilely took control over the devastated companies' infrastructure, resources, and mining operations by force.

That shrewd sequence of events by ACM launched them from being just a medium-sized company to ranking among the top four of the remaining eight or so energy corporations in the galaxy.

Treaties were again signed, with ACM receiving a decent amount of preferential treatment from the Coalition for having pretty much singlehandedly ended the conflict.

Third Copalion War

Disenchanted and threatened by ACM's rapid growth, the largest energy corporation in the galaxy launched a series of coordinated attacks on ACM to weaken and hopefully wipe them and their leadership out. However, ACM received intel on these attacks in advance and leveraged the Coalition to help them repel the attacks. They managed to launch a quick counterattack which resulted in the eventual downfall of the largest company.

However, to ACM's chagrin, instead of granting the largest company's assets, etc. solely to ACM, the Coalition divided them up proportionally among the remaining energy corporations. They didn't want ACM to become a monopoly, the Coalition claimed. This created a rift between ACM and the Coalition that remains, to some extent, to this day.

Fourth Copalion War

The fourth war came about as a result of ACM's unmitigated, unstoppable, and ravenous growth. They had developed better technology and processes for quickly identifying copalion-rich planets, establishing mines there, and thus exerting their control over not only planets but entire systems of planets.

At the request of the remaining energy corporations, the Coalition changed the laws and rules about how copalion was allowed to be harvested/extracted and who had claim to it when they found it. Copalion was declared a protected resource, and only Coalition-approved mining techniques were permitted in extracting it.

Rather than fighting an all-out war, ACM has chosen to pick its battles. They comply with most of the Coalitions rules, but they exploit loopholes and fight legal battles and engage in espionage, sabotage, and other heinous acts to impose their will on anyone and everyone, including the Coalition.

The Coalition has strategically responded by shutting down various ACM mines and requisitioning them by force, thus getting them directly into the energy game as well, perhaps long overdue.

ACM, however, is now nearly the same size and strength as the Coalition itself, and it has managed to "buy" several Coalition officials who now work from the inside to advance ACM's endeavors in addition to continuing to battle the Coalition publicly, privately, and sometimes violently across the galaxy. Many believe that ACM will eventually overtake the Coalition altogether, and the other energy companies, while large, are unwilling to try to attack ACM without the guaranteed support of their fellow companies and the Coalition, so thus far, no concerted effort has been made to bring ACM down.

This war is "ongoing" today.

STORY BIBLE PART 6: SPACESHIPS & TERRESTRIAL VEHICLES

A Brief Introduction

Here's another section that differs from the corresponding Blood Mercenaries story bible. I'm not going to say there is no place for a pantheon of gods in a sci-fi story—far be it from me to limit you or anyone in how creative you want to be with your story.

What I will do is replace it here because in my Tech Ghost series, there isn't an established pantheon of any significance, but there are a metric butt-ton of spaceships and neat vehicles. So we're going with that instead.

Spaceships

Nightingale-Class Transport - good for jaunts between planets. Not real comfortable. Sardine cans. No sleeping quarters to speak of. Food and drink is served, but you're basically sitting in the same spot the whole trip with minimal walk-around room. You sleep sitting up. It's meant for efficiency, not for luxury.

Galactic-Class Starships - Used by the military. They're not quite floating planets, but they come close in size and firepower.

Mine-Class Colonizer Ship - This is a massive ship that contains everything a copalion mine needs in order to set up a mine on a terraformed planet, including equipment, infrastructure, and building materials.

- It is literally a mine-in-a-box.
- It was cheaper to put it all into one ship and to construct every copalion mine the same way (or close to it), so it sort of functions like a franchise of a fast food restaurant would in that everything the company needs to set up the mine is already on the ship.
- Once the ship is unloaded and the mine construction is complete, the ship becomes the supply ship that runs back and forth, regularly exchanging refined copalion for supplies needed in the mining process.

S-Class Star Cruiser - a gigantic transport ship, sometimes used as cruiseliners and often used for mass transit between planetary systems that are far apart.

Stinger-Class Rig - a decent-sized ship designed for the extraction and storage of raw materials, specifically molten precious metals and copalion. The *Viridian* is one such ship. Typically has a crew numbering anywhere from 12 to 35 people, depending on the captain's preferences and needs.

Striker-Class Fighter - a standard, mass-produced single-man or drone-piloted fighter spacecraft.

- can be flown in space or in most planetary atmospheres but cannot reenter an atmosphere and keep flying.
- if such a ship is forced to reenter a planetary atmosphere, it can do so, but it will be reduced to a protective pod to preserve the pilot's life; everything else will burn away.
- equipped with a range of powerful weapons including a limited number of rockets and pulse rounds.
- capable of quick flying and snappy maneuvers in the hands of

capable pilots
- not super durable, but they do have some shielding

<u>Settlement-Class Colonizer Ship</u> - Gigantic colony ships that, when they land, become cities unto themselves. The *CSS Nidus* is one such ship. Can hold and sustain tens of thousands of people.

<u>Whip-Class Ship</u> - small, nimble transport ships designed to move quickly and efficiently through space. The *Persimmon* is one such ship.

- Originally designed as a type of luxury escape vehicle to be utilized during space battles.
- Capable of jumping/warping (which is unusual for a ship of this size)
- High shield integrity/defense, light on weaponry
- Can be outfitted for multiple purposes despite limited interior space.
- Often have cloaking devices
- Super fast and agile in the hands of a skilled pilot.
- There's a *lot* of money behind this ship, both in development and maintenance.

<u>Orbital Platforms</u> - Floating battle stations that orbit planets. They are titans of firepower—think Deep Space Nine in appearance but more of a military base capable of shooting down entire fleets. (So also kind of like the Death Star.)

Terrestrial Vehicles

<u>Hovercraft</u> (both singular and plural) - they come in a variety of sizes and applications (cars, trams, buses, bikes, etc.), but essentially they all hover over (mostly level) ground at high speeds.

- ideal for traveling long, flat distances quickly
- not very good over mountains and not as fast over water, but can still function.

STORY BIBLE PART 7: WEAPONS & SHIELDS, TOOLS & MINING EQUIPMENT, & MECH SUITS

A Brief Introduction

We're skipping the "objects" part that we used in the Blood Mercenaries story bible and we're replacing it with "shields" and a bunch of other cool stuff instead. Why? Because we're getting more specific without labeling. That's why!

Note: the "Tools & Mining Equipment" section is more specific to my world, but you can use it or replace it with whatever you want.

Weapons & Shields

Justin's Robot Arm Mods

- Enhanced strength (constant) (3x the strength of a normal arm)
- Reduced pain (pretty much none in the robot arm itself)
- Laser Sword - activated by squeezing his robot hand into a fist; sword color is orange
- Stun Blast from Justin's palm; three-second recharge period
- Purdonic resistance emitter (resistant against purdonic lasers)

- Has six slots overall:

1. Palm (slot is located on the back of his hand)
2. Wrist
3. Forearm
4. Just above elbow
5. Biceps
6. Shoulder

NEW MODS for Justin to get:

- Grappling hook/tension wire that pulls him up to whatever it latches onto
- Dragon's Breath hand cannon - shoots a stream of green disruptor energy. Activated by making a tiger claw motion.
- A full-blown force field
- Finger lasers?

Electric Stun Batons: powered with violet electricity, these batons are ideal because they not only pack a hefty punch but also stun the target with a powerful electric shock.

- Low-key burns may result
- Prolonged exposure to the baton when it's active and arcing with electricity is not advised, as burns and shocks can become quite severe.

Plasma Repeater: a standard-issue plasma pistol with a limited charge and limited range.

- Capable of stunning a person or blowing large holes in them, depending on which setting the user chooses.
- Has a percentage reader on the back to denote charge amount remaining.
- Lights on the sides of the barrel glow with orange light.

- Tap the orange circle on the top, and it activates a flashlight mounted to the barrel.

Pulse Rifle: a standard-issue military rifle that shoots pulses of energy rather than bullets.

- Automatic or burst-capable
- Has a percentage reader on the back to denote charge amount remaining
- Has a higher capacity of pulse shots than a plasma repeater does plasma charge
- Fully equippable with tactical attachments of all sorts
- Can come equipped with a grenade launcher attachment.

Tools & Mining Equipment

Class 4 Purdonic Laser: Yellow Light, effective in melting rock, can cut through people as well, but not as effective in cutting through some types of metal (including anti-purdonic alloy).

Compressed Energy Shield: made of green light, strong enough to pick up molten rock

Hand-Laser: a misnomer, in that the laser actually functions more like a harness with an articulated arm that can be positioned on either the right or the left side as per the user's preference.

- The laser has a charge system that starts with red lights (low charge) and goes up to blue lights when fully charged.
- It is operated by a trigger, where the harder you press, the hotter and wider the laser shoots out of the end of the arm.
- If the laser trigger is held for too long, it will need cooldown time so it doesn't overheat the apparatus.
- Usually used for mining and other labor but also used for combat with different types of lasers and weaponry.
- They weigh about 200lbs each.

Homing Flares - standard military-issue flares.

- They can be shot from small cylinders and then retrieved back into those cylinders at any point.
- They give off a bright, pinkish light.
- Probably magnetic?

Mech Suits

Working-Class Mech Suits: composed of a network of wires, hoses, and casings supported by a lightweight but durable alloy skeleton. Able to have different attachments/appendages attached to the arms but also potentially elsewhere on the suit.

Bear's Battle Mech Suit:

- Taken from ACM
- Outfitted with a plasma cannon (imagine a mini gun but pulse rounds) on its left shoulder
- Has two legs and two arms
- Larger than a man, but not gigantic
- Has green energy shields
- Has an actual physical cockpit that Bear can barely squeeze into
- Has blue thrusters/jets
- Bear pilots the thing quickly and efficiently—he's a damned prodigy with it. He's able to do things with a mech that no one has ever seen before.
- He often resembles a pissed-off bear when he's in the throes of battle, especially when the mech is thrashing about.
- The mech often shudders and wobbles under Bear's weight, but it never gives in. He actually prefers to keep it in motion as the strain is lessened on both him and the mech in the process.

✦

STORY BIBLE PART 8: ENERGY SOURCES

A Brief Introduction

R ather than focusing on magic and magic systems in this chapter, we're going to focus on the magic-like energy source that drives the Tech Ghost universe: Copalion.

No, I'm not suggesting you need to have a magic-like substance in your sci-fi world. But for me, this precious resource is the subject of galaxy-spanning wars and conflicts, so I'm giving it its fair spotlight.

Energy Sources: Copalion - a teal liquid-like substance that is used to power 100% of known space travel. It is the most essential commodity in the galaxy.

- found on planets across the galaxy
- highly volatile
- whoever finds a planet with copalion in it (whichever mining corporation) usually gets to stake their claim on the planet
- the mining company pays to terraform the planet, and once it has been terraformed to acceptable levels, they begin working on installing the mine immediately

STORY BIBLE PART 9: ASSORTED STORY WORLD INFO

A Brief Introduction

This section covers a variety of topics, including info about unique building materials, clothing, drugs, and miscellaneous facts about the ACM-1134 mine where *The Ghost Mine* takes place.

Some of it may prove useful to you in creating your own story bible, so I included it just in case.

Unique Building Materials

Plastrex - A plastic/metal alloy that is a bit heavier than normal plastic but is many, many times more durable.

- It's basically indestructible when it comes to normal wear and tear and will never fall apart or break.
- It is mainly used for furniture (think the IKEA of the future) and some cosmetic building materials (can be used in place of drywall, but it's not intended to replace support beams and pillars which are still mostly metal or wood, which is rarer).
- Stinks when it burns, and it's a distinct stench.

- Pretty ubiquitous across the galaxy.

Anti-purdonic alloy - a metal that resists purdonic lasers. Can be used in shielding and in building/construction materials.

Clothing

Shadow Suits: energy-resistant material/armor that also provides some cloaking properties.

Refraction Fabric: Basically turns the wearer invisible to most types of vision.

Items (Miscellaneous)

Drugs

Tyval: A drug that resembles burning embers in a campfire. The brighter the glow, the more potent the dose.

- Dimmer, duller rocks can still get a person high, but the high isn't as "high," and it doesn't last as long.
- Used by homeless addicts and wealthy folks alike.
- Definitely illegal.

Mine 1134-Specific Stuff

Phichaloride Gas: a lethal inhalant, has mutagenic and paralytic properties, smells like burnt rubber, is black like smoke.

⚙

STORY BIBLE PART 10: TITLE IDEAS

A Brief Introduction

For this series, the series title (Tech Ghost) was the second easiest title to come up with. (The easiest was *The Ghost Plague*, which I landed on based on the trajectory of the story as I had conceived it.)

The Ghost Mine, however, was only ever supposed to be a working title. (Un)Fortunately, I could never come up with anything better, so I stuck with it, and now I don't regret that at all. It fits the story, and the cover design looks awesome with that as its title.

The Ghost Pact was the hardest. Below you'll see the options I considered. Some of them, I still like, but the others aren't as good, so they didn't make the cut.

Title Ideas

The Ghost Raid
The Ghost Pact
The Ghost Flight
The Ghost Trek
The Ghost Breach

The Ghost Vow
The Ghost Tactic

Finalists

The Ghost Raid
The Ghost Pact
The Ghost Breach
The Ghost Vow

Final Titles

1. The Ghost Mine
2. The Ghost Pact
3. The Ghost Plague

Final Series Title

Tech Ghost

STORY BIBLE PART 11: MARKETING COPY

A Brief Introduction

T his one is pretty similar to the one from the previous story bible, so I won't go over all of it again except to recommend Brian Meek's book on writing solid marketing copy one more time:

Mastering Amazon Descriptions
by Brian D. Meeks - https://amzn.to/2XvwQiJ

What follows are my various attempts at writing copy for these books.

You'll see that some attempts turned out better than others. Though I'm satisfied with the end results that are currently present in the respective stories' Amazon descriptions, occasionally rewrite or re-envision the descriptions for the books to optimize reader interaction and experience.

After all, if you've got a solid cover and a solid book, the only thing keeping readers from buying might be your marketing copy.

If things aren't moving, maybe try rewriting your book description.

Marketing Copy

The Ghost Mine

Fatal glitches.
A corporate cover-up.
And something haunting the depths...

Three years ago, a horrific accident closed ACM-1134, the energy mine on Ketarus-4. Now the mine has reopened, and Justin Barclay has joined the first new batch of miners hired to begin harvesting the energy stored below the planet's surface.

But as he settles into his new job and home, Justin quickly discovers that the mine's polished exterior is masking a host of hidden dangers—some of them fatal. When the mine's technology begins malfunctioning, Justin's coworkers mysteriously disappear, get injured, and some even die. Justin knows something else is going on—and he's the only one willing to do something to stop it.

With his job and his life on the line, Justin works to uncover the mine's darkest secrets to save himself and his fellow workers. But the company doesn't like Justin digging where he shouldn't be, and they're determined to put a stop to his inquest once and for all—at any cost.

As Justin begins to unearth the mine's darkest secrets, he starts to realize that sometimes it's better to let the past stay buried.

The Ghost Mine is a gripping sci-fi/horror novel sure to thrill you and chill you late into the night. If you're a fan of Ridley Scott's *Aliens*, you'll love this book.

"A snappy, fun, wild ride from hell! Wolf's knockout novel brings all the sci-fi intensity of Ridley Scott's Alien *movies together with a Michael Crichton style thriller. When space colonization goes wrong in* The Ghost Mine, *it means a long, nail-biting night of sheer reading delight! Positively unputdownable!"* - Brandon Barr, USA Today Bestseller and author of the Song of the World Series

Buy *The Ghost Mine* today—and read it with the lights on.

The Ghost Pact

A scientist with a secret...
...a colonist ship under attack...
...and only one man can save them both.

After barely surviving the horrors in ACM mine 1134, Justin Barclay and his ghostly tagalong board a colonist ship bound for a new world.

As they explore the futuristic colonist city within the ship, they quickly realize all is not as it seems.

Dr. Hallie Hayes, a fugitive scientist, arrives on the colonist ship shortly after. Her charge: get her life's work to the core Coalition planets before it falls into the wrong hands.

But she's too late.

Her pursuers have tracked her to the colonist ship...

...and they've brought a literal army with them.

Lovestruck and eager to strike at Hallie's enemies for his own personal reasons, Justin fights to preserve her secret and stop her pursuers once and for all.

Can Justin save Hallie before the enemy captures her and seizes her life's work?

Or will his intervention unleash an even greater calamity in the process?

The Ghost Pact is the second book in the riveting Tech Ghost series of sci-fi thrillers set in the far-flung future. It's perfect for fans of the *Alien* film franchise, *Dead Space* video games, and *Nemesis* board games.

You'll love this action-packed thriller for its fast pace, its colorful characters, and its twisted ending.

Get it now.

The Ghost Plague

An all-consuming weapon unleashed.
A colonist ship at risk of infection.
An entire world on the brink of annihilation.

In the aftermath of the release of Dr. Hallie Hayes's weapon aboard the *Nidus*, Justin Barclay and his fellow survivors are forced to flee for their lives, but they soon realize they can't run forever.

The weapon is devouring the ship like a sentient plague, and it will consume everything and everyone in its path.

As Justin and Hallie form new alliances with old rivals, facing down monstrous foes and treacherous enemies, they work to destroy the weapon and escape the infected ship.

But the plague has other intentions—and it will not be stopped.

Faced with the decision to save themselves or save millions, Justin and Hallie risk it all to ensure the plague never gets off the ship. Will they succeed in preventing a world-ending catastrophe, or will the necessary sacrifices come at too high a cost?

The Ghost Plague is the third book in the riveting Tech Ghost series of sci-fi thrillers set in the far-flung future. It's perfect for fans of the *Alien* film franchise, *Dead Space* video games, and *Nemesis* board games. You'll love this action-packed thriller for its fast pace, its colorful characters, and its electrifying ending.

Get it now.

✿

STORY BIBLE PART 12: WRITING MUSIC

A Brief Introduction

R ather than listing a bunch of links this time, I'm going to list some of my favorite soundtracks to write sci-fi to.

- Dead Space OST (all three of them)
- Mad Max: Fury Road OST (pretty much anything by Tom Holkenborg is gold)
- Edge of Tomorrow OST
- Blade Runner 2049 OST
- Westworld Season 3 OST (and some songs from 1 & 2)
- Cyberpunk 2077 OST
- Ghost in the Shell OST (both the anime and new live action)
- John Wick OST (all three)

There are other great ones as well, but these are some of my standby picks for writing sci-fi. They aren't as iconic as something like Star Wars, so they're not distracting for me.

✿

STORY BIBLE PART 13: ORIGINAL BOOK ONE SYNOPSIS

A Brief Introduction

I somehow managed to hang on to both my synopsis for *The Ghost Mine* and also the original outline. In addition, in late 2020, I wrote a short-form outline for the book using the three-act structure document I shared earlier, so I'm including that for you as sort of a transitional piece between the synopsis and the original outline (both of which date back several years).

So you're going to get to review all of those, which is an extra bump for you since I didn't have the really short outline (which is an important step in my process) for the Blood Mercenaries books. Rather than dumping two more book outlines in here after that, we're gonna call it good and end the book after this final sequence of documents.

We'll begin with the synopsis for *The Ghost Mine*, then we'll do the short outline, then we'll do the long outline so you can better track the progression through that process. Hopefully it proves instructive.

As a side note, you don't *have* to follow this whole process every time. You may already have your own preferred method of plotting, outlining, and writing your books., so if it works, keep doing that.

Note: spoilers for the Tech Ghost series ahead. Read with discretion!

Original Synopsis

In an Andridge Copalion mine on the distant planet Ketarus-4, a major accident results in the deaths of over a hundred workers. The lone survivor, DR. ETYA STIELBARD, undergoes surgery and is made into a cyborg, but her fiancé, MARK BROWN, perishes in the incident.

Three years later, the mine reopens operations. JUSTIN BARCLAY and his friend KEONTAE OLUWELU arrive on Ketarus-4, ready to begin their new employment at the mine. While en route to the mine, Justin meets SHANNON DAVIS, the foreman of the mining sector in which he will be working. Justin develops an immediate attraction to Shannon.

Following their orientation, Justin lies awake one night and decides to head to a vending machine for a snack. He notices a mysterious green light heading into the mine, which should be secured and locked, and he follows it. Though he gives up his search the first night, the second night he follows the light into the mine, despite it being against the rules.

The light leads him to Sector 6, the site of the mine's initial accident. Justin gets trapped inside, and the same type of accident befalls him. As he struggles to get free—and can't—from Sector 6, he nearly succumbs to death. But as his vision blackens, a man in miner's clothing and outlined in green light appears. When Justin blinks, the man vanishes, and a rescue crew enters Sector 6 and extracts him.

Days later, Justin wakes up in the mine's medbay. Ultimately, Justin is placed on light work duty upon his release from the medbay due to his weakened state from the accident.

Meanwhile, CARL ANDRIDGE, the owner of the entire network of Andridge Copalion Mines and one of the wealthiest men in the galaxy, receives a message from the Ketarus-4 mine's CEO informing him of what has happened. Carl cancels his appointments for the next month and orders his ship to head directly to Ketarus-4.

When the light work duty doesn't work out, Justin is sent back to his job in the Sector 13 of the mine. Weakened from his near-death experience in Sector 6, Justin resorts to taking an adrenalite pill (a semi-legal substance) to boost his performance output. During the subsequent crash once the pill's effects wear off, Justin causes another incident in the mine that results in his friend Keontae's accidental death.

Shortly thereafter, Justin continues his work in Sector 13. A series of inexplicable machine and equipment malfunctions leads to one worker sustaining paralyzing injuries and the death of another worker. Justin again sees the ghostly figure in green light, who again serves as a harbinger for the accident. Justin attempts to intervene, and he saves many of his fellow workers, but his right arm is cut off by a piece of mining equipment.

Justin again wakes up in the medbay with a new robotic arm. As Justin begins to adjust to this new way of life, Andridge Copalion Mines owner Carl Andridge enters his recovery room along with the director of security and the mine's CEO. Assuming Justin is guilty of corporate espionage, they confine him to his recovery bed and room.

Late that night, Dr. Etya Stielbard enters Justin's room. She explains her history with the mine, manages to win Justin to her side, and frees him from his confinement. She takes him to the room of one of the mine's information technology workers, and he hides there temporarily.

There, the IT worker convinces Justin to help them lower the mining complex's network firewalls (called "shields") so Etya can both prove the ghost's existence and prove that the mine is thoroughly unsafe for those working in it. Justin agrees to help.

Disguised in the IT worker's clothing, Justin sets out to the admin building to transfer a shutdown code into the CEO's computer. On the way, he is stopped by STECKER, one of the security officers. Stecker apprehends Justin and takes him up to the CEO's office. There, Justin finds Carl Andridge, Etya, Shannon, the mine's CEO, and others in a meeting.

Justin manages to access and transfer the command to lower the network shields, and the power flickers out. Then the ghost appears in the CEO's office.

Toxic black gas pumps into the room, and everyone escapes except for two women, who mutate into wretched creatures that try to kill everyone else. The gas fills the rest of the admin building, and Justin and the survivors have to fight the mutated workers off to save themselves. They meet up with others and try to escape the mine in a variety of ways, but all of them fail.

Ultimately, the survivors end up back in Sector 6, where this all started. There, Etya betrays everyone and joins forces with the ghost. Security guard Stecker joins her betrayal, and it is revealed that he is Etya's estranged father trying to make up for lost time and bad decisions.

The ghost is identified as Mark Brown, Etya's deceased fiancé, who has no bodily form but isn't exactly a ghost either. He's more of an energy-based entity who can control technology.

Justin partners with Shannon and Carl to overcome Mark, Etya, and Stecker to escape. Then Keontae appears in energy form (he died the same way Mark did), and he saves them by seizing control of the mine's technology and providing them with a feasible escape route.

In the end, Etya and Stecker are killed, Mark is confined to the mine's systems, and Justin, Shannon, and Carl escape to the planet's surface. There, Carl betrays Justin and Shannon. He sees them as loose ends and tries to shoot them, but his weapon is out of ammunition. Instead, Justin tears out Carl's throat with his robotic arm.

Justin and Shannon escape aboard a remote-piloted transport ship that takes them to Carl's much larger ship. The mine is razed by a slew of bombs fired from Carl's ship on his orders (prior to his death), and Justin and Shannon are questioned and eventually released.

Justin and Shannon part ways, and later that night Keontae's ghost form appears to Justin in his motel room. (The end.)

✿

STORY BIBLE PART 14: ORIGINAL BOOK ONE OUTLINE - SHORT

A Brief Introduction

This chapter takes the synopsis for *The Ghost Mine* and transfers it into the next section of the process as I move toward doing a full expanded outline with chapter and scene breaks. This one focuses on utilizing the three-act structure, which I mention excessively throughout this book, at writers conferences, and to random people passing me on the street.

Remember that it's an adaptation of the synopsis, and it is reflective of a certain point in time (much more recently than either the long outline or the synopsis), so all the details between the three steps will not line up perfectly.

This version also includes what I refer to as "Building Action" sections to help show how I planned on transitioning to the next pivotal moment in the three-act structure. Everything is clearly marked, so you should have no trouble following along.

Short Outline

Backstory

Andridge Copalion Mines (ACM) has opened a new mine on Ketarus-4, a far-flung planet that is barely habitable but rich in copalion, the galaxy's most powerful, volatile, and most sought-after energy source.

Act I

Inciting Incident

Three years before the main story of *The Ghost Mine* takes place, a group of miners working in ACM-1134, the new mine on Ketarus-4, are trapped within Sector 6 of the mine and are killed by a toxic mutagenic gas that billows up from fissures in the mine's floor.

MARK BROWN, the foreman, is operating a mech suit designed for drilling through rock, but he falls into one of the fissures in the floor, into a pool of raw copalion.

The lone survivor of the incident, DR. ETYA STIELBARD, suffers catastrophic damage to the left side of her body from an explosion in her science office, which overlooks the mine. She is (or rather *was*) Mark Brown's fiancée. She is rescued by an intervention team before she is killed.

Building Action

Three years later, JUSTIN BARCLAY and his best friend, KEONTAE OLUWELU, are en route to ACM-1134, unaware of the terrible things that happened there. When they arrive, they are quickly integrated into the mine's working structure, where they deal with a hulking bully aptly named DIRK HAMMER who insists on making their lives miserable.

Additionally, Justin develops a strong attraction to the beautiful and tough SHANNON DAVIS, who ends up being their foreman rather than just another worker. He also interacts with STECKER, a member of the security team who intervenes on Justin's behalf more than once, saving him from Dirk Hammer's wrath.

Besides navigating his new female foreman, learning the new routines at the mine, and dealing with Dirk Hammer, Justin encounters several niggling glitches in the mine's system, ranging from his ID card not working to the kitchen androids relentlessly staring at him... and only at him.

First Disaster/Door of No Return (DNR)

One night, unable to sleep, Justin ventures to the mine's cafeteria/common area in search of a midnight snack. While there, he notices a strange green light emanating from within the door leading to the mine—a door that shouldn't be open.

Curious, Justin follows the light through the various antechambers, ignoring automated and computer-controlled safety protocols, none of which are functioning due to inexplicably being shut off. The light leads him to Sector 6, the site where, unbeknownst to him, dozens of miners died three years earlier.

He notices a blue resin in the floor, filling in the fissures along with boulders and stones, sealing them shut, and he notices broken and discarded machinery, tools, and other mining equipment. He quickly realizes that despite having been told that Sector 6 was closed due to a cave-in, this isn't actually the case.

As he tries to leave, the power reactivates, and the sector door seals him inside. Then the same toxic black gas that killed the miners three years ago begins pumping into the sector, threatening to kill him.

As Justin is about to succumb to the gas's deadly effects, a man glowing with green light appears before him. When the man disappears in the blink of an eye, the sector doors open, and an intervention team rescues Justin.

Act **II**

Building Action

As Justin recovers in the medbay, he realizes he has stumbled onto something far beyond just a simple cave-in in Sector 6, but he isn't sure what. From that point on, Justin resigns himself to search for answers, often risking his wellbeing, his job, and even his life to find the answers that ACM is trying to keep hidden.

Weakened from the effects of the gas, he is caught misusing a company filing system when he is supposed to be pulling science-related files while on "light duty," and he is sent back to the mine to perform his usual tasks, including operating a hand-laser which aids in the excavation process.

Worn out, he opts to take an illicit adrenaline-boosting pill that he received for free from a shady character who operates as the mine's drug pusher. The pill temporarily boosts his adrenaline output, but then he crashes hard as the back end of the pill results in depleted adrenaline throughout his system. That, coupled with his already-fatigued state leads to Justin collapsing.

His laser activates and fires a short, overpowered blast that cracks open the floor. A fissure opens up, and a pool of raw, glowing copalion looms below. Justin is mere inches from falling in and far too weak to save himself. Just when he is about to fall in, Keontae reaches him, wearing a full mining mech suit, and he pulls Justin away from the fissure.

But then the floor opens up under the mech's feet. Keontae, Justin's best (and only) friend, falls into the pool of copalion below, and is gone.

Following Keontae's funeral, Justin is more determined than ever to discover what ACM is trying to cover up. Driven by his guilt over Keontae's death and his desire for it to mean something, Justin redoubles his efforts to uncover the truth.

As glitches and issues with the mine's technology persist, Justin's belief that something is horribly wrong is further reinforced. Now back at work, Justin witnesses a slew of catastrophes slung together all in a span of several moments, including a mech suit that has gone haywire and is shooting lasers at random.

He even sees the glowing green man he'd seen before, which also reinforces his belief that there may actually be a ghost in the mine. And when Justin tries to intervene, one of the mech's errant lasers cuts through his shoulder, severing his entire right arm from his body.

Justin awakens in the medbay with a robotic prosthetic arm made of advanced metal alloys, courtesy of ACM. He is also interrogated by CARL ANDRIDGE, the young hotshot owner of ACM, who canceled his forthcoming appointments and appearances to visit the mine because of its troubled past.

Following that conversation, Justin is placed under "house arrest" in the medbay until late one night when Dr. Etya Stielbard, who is now a cyborg with 40% of her body being prosthetic and robotic, visits him. They both want answers, and they both agree to work together to get them, so she sets him free.

Together with a disgruntled IT employee, Justin and Etya hatch a plan to break into the mine's corporate subnetwork via a computer virus that will lower the subnetwork's shields to provide them access. Justin disguises himself and makes his way into the corporate offices with the virus uploaded into his new prosthetic arm, which he intends to use to distribute the virus.

Stecker, the security guard, catches Justin en route but escorts him to a meeting of the mine's brass, including Carl Andridge, who is still on the planet to sort out what's been happening and how the mine should deal with it.

Second DNR

While there, Justin manages to touch the mine director's computer, and the virus transfers into the corporate subnetwork. The result is that the ghost who visited Justin appears atop the mine director's table, and he condemns the mine's leadership to death.

Then the same toxic black gas from within the mines begins pouring into the office as the office door tries to seal itself shut.

Building Action

Justin and the others manage to flee the office, but two women are trapped inside. They succumb to the black gas, which transforms them into wretched, mutated monsters that are both living yet also dead. These twisted, merciless mutations promptly escape the office and attack, and the security members present shoot them down.

As they try to escape the mine's corporate offices, more black gas pours in through the ventilation system, and more officer workers mutate into monsters, all of which attack the fleeing people with brutality and extreme violence.

Though Justin and an ever-shrinking slate of survivors manage to escape, the mutations relentlessly pursue them. More gas pumps in, this time in the cafeteria where the majority of the mine's workers have gathered in light of the alarms now going off throughout the mining complex. The gas corrupts them all, and they are released into the rest of the mine thanks to the ghost, which now has control of two of the three subnetworks within the mine.

Justin and the survivors, including Carl Andridge, Etya Stielbard, Stecker, Shannon Davis, and others, meet up with Dirk Hammer and some of his friends who also survived the initial onslaught.

Additionally, we learn that the ghost is, in fact, Mark Brown, who fell into the copalion pool three years earlier. More shockingly, Mark Brown is revealed to be Carl Andridge's half-brother, which casts Carl in a suspicious light. Etya accuses Carl of having Mark murdered to protect his inheritance after the passing of their father, the previous owner of ACM, and Carl denies everything.

Together with Dirk, Shannon, Carl, Stecker, Etya, and the others, Justin makes multiple attempts to escape the mine, but they are thoroughly rebuffed and completely locked inside.

Eventually, they are joined by a group of Interplanetary Marines (IPMs) who greatly supplement their numbers and firepower, but ultimately it makes little difference, as the mutations prove effective and especially deadly.

Third DNR

Following their second-to-last failed escape attempt, they decide to face the ghost once and for all. They return to the mine, to Sector 6 where this all began, with the hope of destroying the mine's subnetwork, crippling the ghost's power, and then escaping through the mine's ventilation system to the planet's surface.

Act III

Climax

As the few remaining survivors battle their way through the hordes of mutations thirsting for their blood and flesh, they manage to ascend to the upper levels of Sector 6's caverns. There, they fight off mutations while Etya attempts to crush the ghost's power once and for all.

Grey Moment

But instead of crushing the ghost's power, she allows the ghost to join with her prosthesis. Etya and Mark are finally reunited; they have finally become one. She uses her newfound power to start killing the survivors.

Then she is backed up by none other than Stecker, who reveals that he is Etya's estranged father (and yes, this twist is properly set up throughout the actual story). He betrays the other survivors and sides with her in trying to kill them.

Black Moment

While Stecker, a former soldier and skilled fighter, duels Justin and Dirk Hammer at the same time, Shannon and Carl Andridge (the only other two survivors) try to take on Etya/Mark.

Stecker has Dirk in a choke from behind, and Justin can't save him. Etya is primed to kill Shannon.

The Turnaround

Then Keontae shows up as another ghost. Since he died exactly the same way as Mark Brown did, he emerges from the ether as a second ghost in the mine, and he intervenes. He battles Mark Brown in their tech ghost realm, sometimes within Etya's prosthesis, and sometimes within the mine's subnetwork.

Denouement/Resolution

Dirk manages to rally the last remnant of his formidable strength. With Stecker still on his back, he hurls them both into a huge whirring turbine, which shreds them both to pieces. In doing so, he saves Justin.

While Etya tries to resist Keontae's influence within her prosthesis, she is unable to properly defend herself, and Carl Andridge blows her head clean off with a pulse pistol.

Falling Action

As the three survivors (Justin, Shannon, and Carl) climb through the ventilation system up to the planet's surface, Mark Brown, now impotent and unable to use the mine's technology to finish them off, follows them to the surface. He berates Carl, who destroys the lone computer terminal on the surface level with the remaining shots from his plasma pistol.

Having previously touched the terminal, Justin had felt a tingling sensation at the time, but he didn't register it as anything important.

Then Carl Andridge points his pistol at Justin, determined to bury him and Shannon with the mine, which he is about to nuke out of existence as soon as his transport ship rescues him.

When he tries to fire the empty plasma pistol, nothing happens. With his prosthetic arm, Justin seizes Carl by the throat and contemplates killing him, but he doesn't... except that his robotic arm has other plans. Acting seemingly of its own free will, the arm tears out Carl Andridge's throat, and he dies.

Horrified, Shannon doesn't believe Justin when he says he isn't responsible for killing Carl but that his arm is. She refuses to even speak with him from that point on.

The transport rescues them and returns them to Carl's ship high above the planet, and then nukes rain down and totally destroy the mine, erasing all evidence that anything ever happened. Interrogations follow, and Justin tells as much of the truth as he can, omitting the part about how Carl Andridge died. To his great relief, Shannon doesn't rat him out for it, either.

Eventually, the ACM officials agree to send Shannon and Justin away, to the planets of their choice. Before they depart, Justin thanks Shannon for her discretion, but she doesn't respond to him.

Shannon returns to her home planet, and Justin heads to Jevilos-6, where he is hoping to start anew. He never sees Shannon again.

Epilogue

While on Jevilos-6, Justin is resting in a cheap rented room. A green light emerges from his robotic arm and materializes into the shape of a man.

It is Keontae.

✿

STORY BIBLE PART 15: ORIGINAL BOOK ONE OUTLINE - LONG

A Brief Introduction

You just got through the short outline (which was actually pretty long). Now you'll get to see how an earlier version of that short outline can get expanded into a chapter-by-chapter outline.

As before, some things won't line up. This outline is the oldest one I have for this book.

For example, this one is missing a lot of character names (including those of the main character and the main supporting protagonist), but that's okay. It's all part of the process, and as long as the story is great in the end, you're good to go.

Long Outline

ACT I

Chapter 1

Normal day-to-day mining operations. What are they mining? Make the characters rough around the edges, but likable and relatable. Then kill them all, brutally.

Write this from the perspective of the female scientist (who becomes a cyborg).

Mining is happening. Alert happens—the turbines that were venting and purifying their air go down, one by one. (We will later learn that the owner brother made this happen and then covered it up.) Workers casually move to address it. The guy who becomes the ghost goes down to help clear it out. Then the complex begins to shake.

The lady scientist warns the man to get out (she's detecting radiation or something) and she says that the androids can handle the repairs. He counters by saying they haven't yet gotten it right yet. Their programming needs adjusting, and if they don't lock this down, they could lose the whole sector for weeks, and that'll kill their productivity.

The man continues to try to fix it, but something happens and the sector seals off. The workers are all trapped, and the lady scientist is trapped in her observational room watching as things go down. She's trying to override it, but the system won't respond to her commands. It's quarantined the area, it says.

As the man works, fissures rip through the floor, but no one falls in. Toxic/radioactive gas begins to pour out from the fissures, but no one falls in. They head to the blast door(s) and try to get through, but fail. Many of them put on gas masks, but their work clothing won't help shield them from the radiation poisoning they're inevitably going to get.

As they use all the machinery and tools at their disposal to try to break through the doors and even dig their way out of the sector by going deeper into the mine, the man continues to work on bringing up the turbines. A fissure opens underneath his feet, and he falls in. He grabs the edge, but as workers try to assist him, the edge crumbles and he falls in and disappears with a yell.

The lady scientist screams and is horribly upset, but she keeps trying to save the other workers nonetheless. She fails. She can't get out of her observation room at first, but she tries to force her way out with a weapon or something, and something explodes. Maybe the computers malfunction so hard that they blow up.

Pain seizes her body on her left side. Her face. Her left leg hurts. And when she looks at her left arm, all she sees is a cauterized stump just above her elbow on her left arm.

Chapter 2

Three years later...

The repairs on the mine are done, and it is operational again. The sector from the opening is, of course, closed off, and we'll learn about that later.

The protag comes in with the first group of workers to replace the old workers who died. They're on a freighter that is loaded with supplies. It docks on the planet near the mine. We see galactic marines and local planet security (they don't typically like each other much). We see that the docking station, while small and old-fashioned, is the primary "hangout" spot and the only place where anyone can get a drink or most other normal supplies.

The MC meets the bully, the woman worker who will become the foreman, and he's there with his friend, the only person he knows. They experience this location together, but we only get it through the MC's POV.

This all doesn't last terribly long. They eventually board another transport to head to the mine itself. While they're riding, the bully takes notice of the woman worker and starts to hit on her, and when it gets out of hand, the MC steps in.

The bully threatens to beat him up or whatever, and they prepare to fight.

Chapter 3

The woman pushes between them and tells them both to go to hell. She doesn't want the bully's advances and she certainly doesn't need a man to stand up for her. They go their separate ways, but the bully eyes the MC and then sits down with his pals.

They arrive at the mine a half-hour later or so. They're given a brief orientation and a tour. Maybe.

They pass the closed sector and someone asks what's behind those doors, and the person giving the tour says, "Nothing anymore. We had a cave-in, and that sector is no longer operational."

They're shown to the science wing where they briefly meet the cyborg doctor, who is cold and curt with them and barely even recognizes that they're there. Then the tour guide shows them to their dorms. There's a mess hall in there with a kitchen. Two android cooks operate shifts 10 days a week. Each of them gets a small room (think college dorm room size) to share with one other roommate.

Naturally, the MC and his friend bunk together. He spies the female worker who has a room across the hall, and the bully and his roommate have a room at the far end of the hallway nearest the exit. The female worker locks eyes with him before she shuts her door.

The friend sets up his plant and explains its importance.

Bathrooms are communal—men and women share. The scientists get their own wing, and the woman worker doesn't have a roommate. The MC doesn't get a good look into her room (but it'll turn out she's got a bathroom in there), and there are no other women on the floor, so it's not a big deal.

✿

Dinner that night is tense and quiet, and the men begin to murmur about what they heard regarding the closed-off sector. The MC and his friend listen, but they don't let it get to them. The woman worker is nowhere to be found at dinner time, despite the MC purposely looking for her. Work begins the next morning, so the MC and his roommate/friend call it an early night.

✿

Breakfast. The workday begins. The person giving the tour introduces the worker woman as the new foreman.

Chapter 4

Everyone is shocked at first—you'd think that hundreds of years after women first got the right to vote that men would finally accept women in authority, but the workers remain skeptical. She is quite convincing and demanding, though. A real taskmaster.

She explains what the different safety equipment is, including the massive turbines above that replenish their air supply and help keep the mine a few degrees cooler.

Work begins. Lunch. More work. While they're working, the bully is joking with his friends how he's not concerned about the boss being a chick. He's confident that his dick will earn him some special treatment with her.

The MC wants to go over and bash him in his head with something, but his worker friend holds him back.

Quitting time. Group showers. More jokes. Perhaps a bit of humor. Definitely some borderline abuse, but the MC and his friend get out in time. (Possibly a chapter break here? Maybe the woman foreman enters just in time to break it up, and the bully stands there, ripped and huge, dick swaying in the open, and she doesn't care at all?)

The MC and his friend grab towels with soapsuds still in their hair and on their bodies, then they leave.

Dinner time. The MC and his friend are among the first to arrive and are scratching their heads because of the lingering suds in their hair. The androids serve them what looks to be an edible meal, albeit something obviously prepared by a machine.

The woman foreman is eating at a table with the other foremen of the other mining sectors along with the head of security, and the scientists and administrative types have their own table. It's all very segregated.

The cyborg scientist lady is sitting alone at her own table with her back to everyone. She only eats half of her food, then she leaves before anyone else does.

Dinner ends. Back to the rooms.

When they get there, they find their door open, and their room is both ransacked and tossed and covered in what appears to be wet toilet paper with shampoo and soap.

Chapter 5

The MC storms out of his room and sees the bully and his cohorts laughing their heads off. He marches toward the bully against the wishes of his friend with his fists clenched. An older security guy steps out of a perpendicular hallway and stops the MC from even reaching the bully.

He manages to calm the MC down, even as the bully continues to taunt him. They head back to the MC's room and the three of them work to clean it up amid discussion. We get to know the security guard, here—he's older and will become sort of a mentor character to the MC. (Later he can teach the MC some fighting moves after he loses his first fight—badly—to the bully.)

With their linens replaced and clothes sent to the androids who wash the clothes/fabrics, the MC and his friend go to sleep. The friend falls asleep quickly, but the MC doesn't. His mattress is still quite damp, and it's keeping him from sleeping. So he gets up.

He walks down the hallway toward the bully's room, contemplating whether or not he should try to get payback now. It's dark, and there can be limited orange track lighting on the floor. He tries to access the bully's door, but it says, "ACCESS DENIED" in far too loud of a computerized voice. It repeats it twice (3x total) as he's looking around, trying to find somewhere to hide. He dives out the exit door and shuts it, and as he does, the bully's door opens.

Chapter 6

The bully steps into the hallway and rubs his eyes. He looks around, and the MC watches him squint at the exit door. He then goes back into his room, only to emerge wearing tiny spectacles. Bad vision. He must wear contact lenses during the day. Probably too cheap to have the surgery done.

He takes a step toward the exit, but he turns around and heads toward the bathroom. The MC breathes a sigh of relief, then notices a light coming from the kitchen. It's very late. It's at least 0300, and he's supposed to be up in two more hours to get ready and be at the mines by 0600, but he's curious. Barefooted, he creeps toward the kitchen/cafeteria.

The light is faint—almost like a glow. Yada yada, scary approach. Inside the kitchen, he finds the androids at their stations, powered down. Their eyes glow with an eerie light. They're charging or in sleep mode or something. Still creepy.

A knife is laying on the counter in front of them.

One of them flares to life and snatches the knife in his hand.

Chapter 7

It begins chopping carrots—the knifeblade spins like a fan and the android inserts a carrot into it, all while staring blankly at the MC. The other one awakens behind the MC and questions why he's in the kitchen.

"I saw a light…" etc.

The android who is not cutting asks the MC to leave so he and his partner can resume preparations for breakfast and lunch that day. They have a schedule to keep, and understandably, preparing to feed hundreds of workers will take a significant amount of time, so they prefer not to be interrupted.

The MC gladly leaves, his heart pounding.

As he leaves the kitchen, a faint light at the end of the hallway catches his eye. It's the hall that leads to the mines. They've already made it clear that the mine is only operating one shift at the moment, so he knows it's not a worker. He knows that no one without proper clearance is authorized in the mines during off-work hours, and the nature of the light and the way it's moving suggests that it's not an android. But it's 3:30AM… who would be going to the mines at that time even if they did have clearance? And why?

The door to the mines is definitely open, and the light definitely vanishes deeper into the mine.

He wants to follow, but the android incident has him spooked, and he needs to get some rest or tomorrow will be hell. He heads back to his room and goes to sleep. His heart keeps pounding, though.

⚙

The next morning at breakfast, the MC is super sluggish. He asks his friend if he knows anything about how early the foreman and the other folks with clearance head into the mines to prep for the day. The friend has no idea—he's only been there for a day. He asks why.

They're interrupted by a greasy, oily dude who introduces himself. He's snake-like, and he remarks how tired the MC looks. Yada yada, he offers the MC some adrenaline shots (adrenalites?) to sustain him throughout the day. First one's free, he says. MC declines and says he'll stick to the coffee, bland and tasteless as it is.

The drug dealer offers them to the friend, and the friend declines, as well, but he's slower about it. The drug dealer mentions that he's got recreational stuff too, like heroin, weed, pills—then he stops and wishes them a good day and that he hopes to see them around later.

The older security guy from the night before sits down next to them, and the MC realizes why the drug dealer went away. The security guy warns them to watch out for the drug dealer and his like. He's known his fair share of workers, blue collar and white collar alike, who blew their careers by abusing substances.

The MC assures him that he won't have to worry about that with him.

The security guy tells him that's good. The MC asks if he knows how early folks get going around here. The security guy says there are regular security patrols at night by roving bots with motion-sensor-activated guns mounted on them in the mines, and there's usually a security guy at the desk in the office watching the cameras, but that's about it. The mine doors cannot and will not open for access until 0500 at the earliest.

The security guy asks why, and the MC brushes it off. He was just curious.

Breakfast ends, but the MC catches sight of the android who was cutting the carrots early that morning. It appears as though he is staring at the MC as he leaves the room, but he's not sure. Their eyes are weird, and it's not easy to decipher where they're looking. The head doesn't move, but the eyes seem to follow the MC.

Chapter 8

Work day. Lunch.

They hit a gas pocket while mining. An unmistakable scent fills the immediate area for a moment, then it is quickly disbursed by the turbines.

Accident happens. A worker's arm gets caught in some machinery or something. It's not a terrible wound, but it'll put him out of commission for a few days. The lady foreman orders the MC to take the guy to the infirmary to see the doctor.

They go. We get introduced to the doctor's character here. Routine dressing. Writes an order mandating that the worker take the rest of the week off and be remanded to light work on a provisional basis starting next week. Gives him painkiller pills and gives him a local painkiller.

MC offers to take him back to the dorms, but the worker declines. The doctor tries to get them to stay longer, but the MC insists that he needs to get back to work.

On his way back, he sees a maintenance dude working on one of the androids—the creepy one who kept staring at him. It isn't staring now. It's totally powered down.

He reports back to the lady foreman who is disinterested in what he says about the other worker. She reads the doctor's report and curses, then she sends the MC back to work.

The bully takes notice and says something about him staying away from his girl, and the MC ignores him.

Workday ends. Instead of showering before dinner, the MC and his friend wait until after dinner, and then they shower. That way they avoid any potential conflict with the bully and his crew.

The MC notices his roommate tending to his plant and asks why, if his friend really wants to see the plant bloom, he doesn't just use an impulse accelerator on it? They're cheap, after all, and the energy would make it blossom right then and there.

The friend shakes his head and says he prefers it to be a natural occurrence, as nature intended. The MC shrugs.

That night, despite being exhausted and having a dry mattress, the MC still can't sleep. He puts on his work boots this time along with his jeans and his shirt, and he creeps out into the hallway again. It's 0300 again. He stalks past the bully's room, out the exit, into the common area, and past the kitchen. He sees the glowing light inside again but this time he doesn't go in to investigate. He learned his lesson the first time.

He sees the light again. It's faint, like last time, but he sees that the mine door is open again, even though the security guy said it definitely should be sealed shut. With trepidation, he goes inside.

The MC more or less knows where he's going, but he doesn't know what or whom he's following. He spots one of the sentry robots and sees that it is unmoving. He sits there, waiting for it to advance or turn around or do anything, but it doesn't. He finally works up the courage to throw a rock at it. It clanks off the robot's "head" and bounces away. Still no movement.

He tenuously steps out from his hiding spot, and when he doesn't get shot, he advances up to the robot, and then past it. He also notices that the security cameras aren't moving, but during the day they swivel and stuff. All of the sector doors are closed, including the one he works at.

As he approaches the sector that's supposedly sealed off, he sees the light disappear into the sector. It's not sealed off after all.

The MC ventures inside the supposedly sealed off sector, but there's no sign of the light anymore. There's no light at all. He takes out a tiny flashlight from his jeans pocket and shines it around. He sees huge cracks in the floor that have been filled in with some sort of cement or resin. He also sees a lot of machinery, some of it mangled, some of it looking normal. He also sees an observation room made of glass but not occupied. He also sees a few random tools lying around.

The room smells off. It feels off, too. Something is wrong.

Why leave perfectly good machinery inside the sector? Why leave the door open in the middle of the night? And where did the light go? There's nowhere it could have gone in the sector without the MC seeing it, especially for how dark it was.

Overhead, the turbines aren't blowing. That's not normal either. They're always supposed to be blowing everywhere to keep the air fresh. But at least there's some circulation. The door to the sector is open.

The MC notices that the smell gets stronger the closer he gets to the cracks in the floor. Upon closer inspection, he sees a small wavering of the air around the edges of where they filled in the cracks with the cement.

Gas of some sort. Toxic. He can tell by the smell. It's the same as the gas that sprayed out of their mine earlier that day, though the turbines handled it quickly. Here, though, without the turbines on, it could be fatal. He backs away from the gas and heads toward the door.

It slams shut before he can get out, and an alarm sounds. Lights flash inside. He's sealed inside the sector, and the turbines, which aren't on, won't disburse the gas.

Chapter 9

The MC panics. He calls for help, tries to get the door to open, but it won't. The gas is horrifically toxic, and he doesn't have a gas mask, nor does he find any laying around at first. Frantic, as he shouts for help, he looks around the room in more depth. Things are easier to see now that the alert lights are on.

He finds an old gas mask inside the cab of one of the machines, but the cab is bent shut. He grabs an old pickax and tries to pry the door open. He also tries to break the glass with it, but it doesn't work. In desperation, he hammers on the latch with the pickax until it finally breaks and he can wedge his arm into the opening. His fingers graze the gas mask, then he manages to grab it.

As he pulls it out, the tubing catches on the bent metal of the cab and tears. He swears, but it's better than no gas mask at all, so he puts it on and grips the spot where the tear is. Fresher, though mustier, air fills his nostrils, and he resumes his search for a way out.

He finds none.

He spies the observation room. It's encased in glass. If he can climb up there, then perhaps he could break the glass and get out that way. He hurls a rock at the glass, but the rock just bounces off. He's likely not going to get out that way.

He truly is trapped.

The air in his gas mask is starting to become more and more tainted with the smell of the toxic gas, and the MC is getting lightheaded. He heads back toward the sealed door, but as he does, his vision blurs. His knees buckle, and he collapses.

There, before him, the source of the light appears. It's a man, dressed in workers' clothes, and his whole body is casting off the glow.

"Help… me…" the MC begs.

The ghost waves his hand in front of the door and then over his head. The door opens, and the mechanical grinding whir of the turbines starts. The MC loses consciousness as the man vanishes behind some machinery (along with the light). The last thing he sees is a security guy rush in wearing full hazmat protocol garb, accompanied by two medical androids.

Act II

Chapter 10

The MC wakes up in the infirmary. He's laying in a bed with a myriad of tubes stuck to him, including some in places where he never knew tubes could go (like a catheter). The first face he sees is chrome and has those same haunting eyes as the android in the kitchen, only a big white cross subdivides its face into four quadrants. (Note that when the androids go haywire, there should be some very red human blood streaked on or dripping from the white crosses on the androids' faces. It will make for a good ironic moment.)

His reflexes try to jolt him away, but it doesn't work. His body refuses to respond.

The android notes his elevated heartbeat and apologizes for alarming him. He summons the doctor, and the doctor comes in.

"You're awake! It's a miracle." They thought the MC was a goner. He was out cold for three days. The toxicity in his lungs went into his bloodstream, but they managed to attack it with a targeted treatment because they got to him in time. His limbs are probably fatigued because of the lingering effects of the toxins, but he should eventually make a full recovery.

Meanwhile the doctor can read him poetry or something miserable.

To his relief, the MC gets a visitor. His friend/roommate. The daily shift just ended, and he's stopping by to visit. They catch up. It's the weekend by now, and the friend is going into "town" to the transport station to have a drink or two and try to meet some of the local ladies who work in the greenhouse. Maybe he can convince one of them to give him a job.

The MC asks about the female foreman, and the friend says she's pissed, but she'll get over it. How you even got inside that sector is a mystery, and how security got in to rescue you is another mystery.

The MC explains that a glowing man saved him, etc. The friend nods. "If you say so."

"I know it must sound crazy."

"Not as crazy as I'm gonna get tonight. We finished our first week of work. Well, I did, anyway."

The friend eases his way out of the conversation right when the older security guy comes in along with the head of security. He asks the doctor to leave. The doctor is hesitant, at first, but he complies. The older security guy tries to set the MC at ease, but the head of security is the "bad cop" and accuses him of criminal actions.

The MC explains the whole thing from the beginning. (Followed the light, saw the disabled robots and cameras, wandered inside the sector, saw/smelled the gas, ghost guy who saved him, etc.) MC also describes the ghost's appearance.

The head of security thinks it's all BS, but the older security guy really vouches for the MC and suggests that whether he's telling the truth or not he wouldn't have any reason to go to that sector or disable cameras or sentry robots, etc., nor would he have the means to do it. He didn't have anything more advanced than a flashlight with him that night (they found it on him) and after dissecting the flashlight, they determined it was just a flashlight.

And no, the MC wouldn't be getting it back.

The head of security threatens him that if he's caught in there again, he's not only getting locked up in the security room, he'll be sent back to the transport hub to face extradition back to the colonies for trial for trespassing. He'd also likely face a civil suit for violating company policy repeatedly.

The MC backpedals quickly. He reassures them that he doesn't want that to happen, and that it was a simple mistake. He has no idea what really happened. Perhaps the effects of the toxins were messing with him at the time.

The head of security insists (a bit too obviously) that the MC is right —he WAS hallucinating and he didn't see anything. He'd also better never see anything again.

✿

Mine Owner's POV—he receives a call from the head of security regarding the incident. Details how the MC couldn't have opened the door on his own, even if he had managed to somehow disable the cameras and the sentry bots. What's more, he gives the description of the glowing man to the Mine Owner, whose eyes widen. He says that he'll arrive at the mine within the month, and that he's leaving imme-diately.

Chapter 11

The MC recovers about a week later and is eager to get out of the doctor's office. He is cleared to go back to work on a provisional basis. He will be allowed to do light work, and his actions are all to be heavily scrutinized from that point on.

Prior to his release, an HR representative debriefs him on what the rules are and what the consequences of those rules are as well. He hates the meeting because the older HR lady is rude and clearly either doesn't like him, her job, or both. Anyway, she lets him go and sends him back to his room.

One of the medical androids escorts him, but once they get to his room, the android won't leave right away. The MC tries to close the door, but the android very forcefully blocks it from shutting, so much so that it bends the door slightly, and from that point on, he and his roommate have to give the door an extra shove to get it to latch and lock.

The android finishes its explanation of proper care and use of medication, and then a compartment opens in its side, and it extends an arm with a small bottle of pills. They're to combat any lingering nausea or other symptoms of the toxins leaving his body. The MC thanks the android and it leaves.

The friend/roommate is happy to have the MC back. They catch up a bit more and decide that, since it's the next Friday night, they should go out for the night. The MC is hesitant at first, and he says he's supposed to take it easy, but the friend insists. The MC gives in, and they go catch a ride to the transport hub. Before they leave, the MC notices that the friend's plant has grown bigger.

✺

We see a person reading the report of the MC's encounter. (It's the cyborg scientist. Whether you reveal this or not in this scene, we will see.) The person captures images of the report and stores them in a safe place for reference.

Chapter 12

At the hub, they drink, dance with girls (most of whom work at the greenhouse complex nearby), and generally have a good time. Since the MC's first paycheck is only good for two days of work, his friend happily buys the drinks and the entertainment. He offers to get them some holographic strippers, but the MC declines.

Into the bar/club walks the lady foreman. She's not wearing her work clothes, but she's wearing tight jeans and a dark coat over a low-cut top. The MC is captivated, and he wants to approach, and the friend encourages him to do so. Meanwhile, the friend heads back into the holographic stripper area.

The MC sidles up next to the woman foreman and offers to buy her a drink. He jokes, saying it has to be a cheap one since his paycheck is only worth two days of work. She's not amused and replies flatly, "No thanks."

The MC tries to initiate some conversation with her but generally fails. She continues to give him flat, curt responses. Finally, he gets frustrated and reams her out a bit, saying things like, "You know, I'm just trying to be friendly, and you keep being cold to me." Etc. "Why don't you loosen up a bit?"

As he finishes, he realizes he's about to get fired. Instead, she looks at him, nods, and apologizes. She rationalizes that it's not wise for her to get involved with co-workers, but that doesn't mean they can't at least talk.

The MC is taken aback, but he manages to converse with her. She mentions his seeing a ghost (perhaps this is the first time the glowing guy is referred to as a ghost in the story?) and the MC can respond to that. They chat a bit, and things are progressing well, when the bully shows up and interrupts. Of course.

The woman tries to convince the bully to leave, and when he persists (clearly somewhat drunk), the MC asserts himself. The bully doesn't like that. He throws what remains of his beverage on the woman when she denies him for a third time, and the MC launches at him, fists flying.

Chapter 13

The MC lands a couple of good punches, but fatigue sets into his muscles early (a lingering effect from the toxins), and he slows down considerably.

The bully fights back and is beating him savagely while the woman foreman tries to pull them apart and the bully's friends just laugh instead of helping. He shoves the woman away and throws a few more punches.

Soon after, the older security guy shows up and intervenes. He pulls the bully off of the MC and tells him to back off. The bully, now more sober, doesn't care. He threatens the old security guard and calls him a rent-a-cop. The security guy warns him not to try anything, saying that even though he's off-duty, he'll still kick the bully's ass if he has to, and he'd gladly do it for free.

The bully advances. The security guy takes him down easily. The bully gets up and tries again. The security guard puts him down again. On the third try, the security guard stops going easy. He clocks the bully in his jaw and lays him out.

A couple of the bully's friends try to jump him next, but he grabs one, clinches him MMA-style, and knees him while keeping the other guys away. He downs the guy he's holding, elbows another in the face, takes a shot to his jaw, and then retaliates with a spinning kick to the dude's face that lays him out (this is the guy who hit him, btw). The security guy dabs at his bloody lip, then beckons the other three guys in the group to come at him, but they back up.

He tells them to get their friends out of there, and they do. Then he orders himself a whiskey, helps the MC up, and downs his drink in one shot, then orders another.

The woman foreman also helps the MC up, and the MC asks a ton of questions. The woman foreman says she needs to go file a harassment report, even though it happened off the worksite and off hours. The MC thinks it's an excuse to just get out of there, but he doesn't blame her. (*NOTE: At some point in this sequence, the MC needs to notice that the android bartender, while the same model as the ones at the mine, doesn't seem to be staring at him all creepy-like.)*

The MC keeps asking questions. "How'd you do that? Where'd you learn that?" etc. The security guard just says, "Experience." (Background: he's highly trained and has a lot of fighting/weapons/combat experience. He's just old and semi-retired.)

The friend returns from his holo-strip and sees the MC. He gawks at the MC's busted lip/eyebrow, bruised face, black eye, etc. "Looks like she didn't take to your advances, huh?"

Chapter 14

The light duty the MC is assigned to is assisting with menial tasks in the science lab. He works under a scientist, a young, plump girl fresh out of grad school. The cyborg scientist lady is her boss. The girl refers to her as "Dr. Steelheart" for her cold demeanor and her heart allegedly having been replaced by some sort of machine heart—probably an alloy and not actual steel, she emphasizes, but still, it's catchy.

Things progress. Eventually he starts getting the hang of their scientific procedures, and he comes to appreciate their work. He asks what happened to Dr. Steelheart, and the girl replies that she's not sure, but she heard rumors that Dr. Steelheart was here for the accident.

"What accident?"

"In Sector X."

She assumes he knows about it, but he doesn't. She isn't really supposed to say anything since she isn't sure what is and isn't true, but she heard that Dr. Steelheart was in an explosion that took out half of her body in an accident that also left dozens of workers dead in Sector X.

"From the explosion?"

"No. From the gas and the radiation."

"Radiation?"

Dr. Steelheart interrupts them.

Chapter 15

Dr. Steelheart asks for something mundane, though she eyes the MC something fierce, then she sends the MC on an errand to the admin offices.

✿

Curious as to whether the ghost is somehow connected to the accident at Sector X, the MC heads to the admin department to fulfill the cyborg's request. While he's there, he rationalizes that this is probably his only chance to look for info on what happened.

He gains temporary access to the files on the sector—the person who escorts him to the file room leaves briefly for some reason, and he finds and reads a bunch of info on what happened.

Then he gets busted for it.

Chapter 16

Subsequently, the MC gets taken into the HR office and reprimanded by the same woman who visited him in the infirmary. She reams him out, and threatens to fire him, stating that this is his second "strike" of their 3-strike policy. She orders him sent back to the mines early, before he is totally healthy, and they make him work.

As a result of him being not fully recovered, something gets screwed up, and something goes terribly wrong. His black friend is flung into the radiation (same as the ghost) and is no more.

Chapter 17

The MC blames himself at the memorial service and afterward. The old security guard and the woman foreman try to comfort him, but he doesn't take to it. Rationally, it is sort of his fault, because him being unwell leads to the accident, but at the same time, the HR woman sent him back early.

Note: There can be some minor conflict with the bully and his friends here as well, and perhaps the mine's resident drug dealer can approach the MC again with drugs that will help him forget (temporarily) what happened.

He can lash out at the HR woman somehow. In doing so, he doesn't earn his third strike, but the old security guard lets him know he's just eaten up any advantage/leverage over the HR department that he may have had.

Afterward, the MC has his moment back in his rooms where he sees the plant bloom and blossom, something his friend/roommate was waiting for, but he didn't live to see it. Another shoot has broken through the soil as well, and it looks like it could eventually bloom too. The MC decides to continue caring for the plant in his friend's stead.

Later, the old security guard comforts the MC with wise words, etc.

�֯

Later that night, one of the old workers (now zombie-like and deformed) emerges from the mines. The scene is written from the perspective of one of the security guards (possibly) and the thing kills the security guard horribly while other guards try to take it down with their weapons. They finally do, but it's too late for the POV security guard. He dies.

Chapter 18

In light of the friend's recent death, the mine briefly shuts down that sector for examination as well (which allows the ghost virus to get into that sector). The mine furloughs the workers for two days leading into the weekend, plus they use the weekend to explore what happened. Perhaps during this time we have a scene from the cyborg scientist's POV as she is called in to help examine what is happening.

She can report that the mine is causing the entire planet to become unstable, but especially here at the site of the mine. She will send in her report, and it will largely get ignored by the person who runs the mine, as the decision will be passed down to open up the sector once the radiation gap has been filled, or whatever.

✦

Later on, things have somewhat returned to normal, and they open the sector back up. They immediately begin to have problems again, and the MC sees the ghost while at work. When he blinks again, the ghost is gone.

Then something bad happens. The result is another death or two, plus the MC's arm (one or the other) gets crushed.

Chapter 19

Meanwhile, the owner receives an update on what has been happening. He orders that all mining operations in that sector and in the other dangerous sector are stopped indefinitely, or at least until he arrives.

✦

The MC recovering in the medbay again, but he is treated as having experienced significant brain trauma because of his experience with getting his arm crushed. They think he's making stuff up again. He threatens legal action against the mine, and they send the same HR person to him. He gives her an earful and doesn't stand for her BS this time. He's learned from the old security guard's previous words that this time he actually does have the leverage he needs.

In the end, she leaves with a quiet warning that the mine is handling the expenses for his cyborg arm and medical care, and that he'd be wise to not be an idiot and sue them, because they can bury him faster in the mine than he could call a lawyer. He gawks at her and wishes he had a recording device, but he doesn't.

As she is threatening him, the owner of the mine comes in and introduces himself. (Revelation-based chapter ending.)

Chapter 20

The owner of the mine sends the HR person away and talks with the MC privately. (He also brings in the plant from the MC's room and sets it next to the bed on a table.) He urges the MC to explain the ghost experiences and describe what happened.

The MC recounts them, and the owner assures him that the experiences were most likely mental issues associated with the trauma (which is what the doctors said). The MC can also mention how he knows about what happened in the first accident.

The owner will just note how much of a tragedy it was and deny any wrongdoing on the company's part. Their conversation will be tense and the owner will continue to deny any wrongdoing, and then the conversation ends with the MC getting told that he is being terminated from his employment as soon as he is cleared by the medical team.

What about his three strikes? The MC asks. The owner will reply that that's indeed the standard metric they use, but given his recent troubles, they feel it's better to just terminate his employment now. Arguments, etc., but in the end, the MC is going to get fired, and that's it.

From that point on, the MC resolves that his only goal is to prove that he's not crazy and not wrong.

Chapter 21

The MC gets his cyborg arm. It hurts, but it functions.

He can't really leave the medbay for awhile, but then Dr. Steelheart comes to visit him late at night. At first he thinks it's an android come to kill him, but it's not.

She talks with him about how she got her cyborg parts (she's still very cold as she describes it) and she gives him a ton of information. She also tells him about the ghost's effect on the computer systems and how she doesn't think he's a ghost at all, but one of the workers who died.

She tells him that if he can find a way to link up the admin center to the mine over the network, then the ghost will likely appear in the admin center as well and be able to prove the MC isn't lying. Her stated motivation is that she knows the mine needs to be shut down, and despite all of her efforts to make that happen, it hasn't worked (corporate greed, etc.). So now she needs help to make sure it happens.

They plan to make it happen during a board meeting sometime in the next day or so. The cyborg says she can help remotely, but not physically. She can help him get access to the admin area and there's a former tech guy who is loyal to her cause as well who can help with the setup, and together they set up a way to tether the two locations together on the same network. At the end of the scene, she asks if the MC is in or not.

Chapter 22

The MC trims the new shoot of the plant at its base, sticks it in his coat pocket, and then leaves the medbay early. He and the tech work to set up the uplink while the cyborg heads into the admin center for the meeting.

After helping the tech guy get setup, the MC leaves for the admin building. On his way there, he runs into the old security guard, who stops him and tries to prevent him from going up to the admin area.

Chapter 23

The MC reasons with the old security guard and tells him the cyborg is involved and that the mine is unsafe. They're all going to die, etc. The old security guard finally gives in, stating that he's never known the MC to lie, so he believes him. He allows the MC to pass.

⚙

The MC will burst into the board room during the meeting where he forces his way in using a copy of the Cyborg's pass. (As head of the Science division, she's already in the meeting, along with the owner, the HR lady, the head of security, the lady foreman, and others.) The MC radios to the tech guy to activate the uplink, and the lights in the room (and all the screens) shut off. Emergency lights switch on.

The MC feels something in his coat moving. He pulls out the plant and watches the flower bloom. He knows it's far too early, but it blooms nonetheless. He realizes it's blooming because of extra energy in the room.

Then the ghost appears on the screens.

Chapter 24

The ghost's appearance is muddled at first, but eventually he reveals his true appearance. The ghost leaves.

Confronted with the truth, the owner clears the room except for the security guard, his number one bodyguard, and the MC, and he reveals that the ghost is his brother.

MIDPOINT

Chapter 25

The ghost, because of the MC's intrusion into the admin meeting, now has access to more of the complex. Once the ghost leaves, the flower's bloom recedes.

The ghost shuts down all the life support in the admin area and launches all the alerts/alarms. They escape the admin area because the head of the technical department has master override codes that work even against the ghost, but only temporarily.

The HR lady (and others) get caught in the admin area as the gases from the mine filter in. The survivors watch through blast-proof glass as the gas chokes them, then begins to mutate them. (Here it's revealed that the gas doesn't kill so much as it mutates and dulls people's minds to primal, murderous versions of their own actual brains.)

The door then begins to open again.

Chapter 26

Everyone backs away from the doors, and everyone is wearing gas masks, but as they try to run away, the mutated people emerge. The security forces and the bodyguards shoot at them, but it takes a lot to kill them.

Carnage ensues, etc., and the lead tech guy is killed. Before he dies, he shares the codes with the cyborg, who stores them in her database, thus making her essential to the group's survival in the long run.

Note: by this time the old security guard and the former tech guy have also shown up. They arrive and try to help. Backstory: the lead tech guy despises the former tech guy because the former tech guy was better and more tech-talented than him, but the lead tech guy got the former tech guy fired by blaming the virus on him (or something).

Here we get explanations as to how the ghost works. Now that he has an uplink to the admin center, he can begin breaking through the network's firewalls that separate the various parts of the mine from each other. If he gains control of the entire mine, he can destroy it—and everyone in it.

They have to reach the mainframe (or whatever you want to call it)—which of course is deep within the mine and difficult to get to—and shut it down before the ghost breaks through the rest of the firewalls and gets to the heart of the mine's system. If the ghost reaches it first, or if they can't escape the mine complex in time, they're all dead.

Chapter 27

The owner has already called an emergency meeting in the cafeteria to detail how the evacuation is set to take place, and he sent the guy who runs the mine (from the admin area) over to run the meeting (the biggest room). The ghost breaks through the first firewall and heads to the residential area, specifically to the cafeteria. Those who are dumb enough to go into the cafeteria during an alert are gassed and mutate, creating a small army of monsters that need to be dealt with later.

✿

The bully and his friends survive because they show up late and can't get in, and they see the gassing happening. They (wisely) run the other way when the doors open, but at least one of them (not the bully himself) is killed.

Chapter 28

The planetary marine force receives word that all hell is breaking loose at the mine, and they suit up and head out to intervene.

✿

The MC, the woman foreman, the owner, his guards, the old security guard, and everyone else who is with them escape the admin center and the cyborg manages to temporarily lock it down to buy them time to head back to the residence area. They meet up with the remaining scientists who survived as well as the bully/his friends eventually, and the monsters are right behind them.

Chapter 29

Instead of trying to get out through the residence area (which is now blocked by the mutants), they head back into the mines. There's an alternate exit there that leads outside of the mine.

When they get there (amid dark, scary environments), they find the doors are sealed shut, and no matter how they try, they can't unseal the doors.

From deep within the mines, the original workers, now mutated, emerge and attack. This time there's nowhere to run.

Chapter 30

They fight off the mutants (and more people die, of course), but things look especially bleak. The mutants are about to overrun them.

Chapter 31

Gunshots reverberate through the particular area of the mine that they're in. The planetary marines intervene. How they got inside—the doors opened easily from the outside. There's a small contingent of them (plus their vehicles) still outside the mine.

The marines vanquish the remaining mutants (people die, of course), and the group from the mine brings them up to speed.

The marines lead the people back to the doors (and fight off several terrors along the way), but right when they arrive, the doors shut again, separating them from the other marines outside. Their firepower is insufficient to blow the doors, despite trying with explosives, etc., and they fail.

What's more, the whole thing with the doors ended up being an ambush, complete with more mutants (or possibly the androids, though I think you can work that up a different way and make it scarier).

There's only one thing to do now: head toward the mainframe and deactivate it before the ghost can get to it and access the entire mine.

Act III

Chapter 32 (and so on)

1. While they're moving along, the cyborg manages to keep them alive by accessing local computer terminals (a la R2D2) to keep the gases and other dangers from getting to them as they move from sector to sector toward the central processing unit. They encounter haywire androids, more mutants, doors that won't open, haywire mining equipment, a bridge that extends but stops functioning, and other perils along

the way. It's a sci-fi horror story about a dark mine—lots of fodder for creative weirdness.

Every time the cyborg uses the code to open a door or make a piece of tech work, something good happens, but it also unlocks that new piece of tech for the ghost to access. Therefore, not every piece of tech and not every door will need master access, or the ghost would become too powerful too quickly.

This also applies to androids. Some of them have been overtaken by the ghost and they attack the people, and they're REALLY hard to kill. Agile, resilient, built to last. They act as sort of a hive mind.

2. At one point, the cyborg gets injured and can't help, so she relays the master code to the MC so he can access the terminals as well via his cyborg arm. They eventually reach the medbay and they patch her up, and she's ready to go again.

3. The cyborg helps to get them to the mainframe, and then when she arrives, she betrays them. So she keeps them alive in order to keep herself alive to get the master access code to the ghost.

(Note: once the ghost has the master access code, he verifies that, in fact, the owner caused the initial incident. This confirms both the ghost's and the cyborg's suspicions that that's what had happened all along. They were brothers, but the owner had him killed in order to keep full control/ownership over the mine, despite it not being totally safe.)

4. Then the head of security betrays them to support the cyborg. It turns out that he's the father or something of the cyborg, and when his daughter was injured, he knew he had to come and watch over her. He's doing it because he was absent all her life. She knows it's him, but she doesn't care until that moment because he had to prove his dedication to her.

Then the old security guard likely kills or severely wounds the owner and takes out his bodyguards, probably kills the bully, and beats the daylights out of the MC.

The other flower on the plant, now clipped to the MC's lapel, blooms. (Energy makes it bloom faster, and the setup to this is that it blooms earlier when the ghost appears in the conference room, and it can bloom again when the androids show up, or when the ghost is taking over equipment.)

As the old security guy is advancing toward the MC, the black friend (who was also turned into an energy ghost) appears and switches on the turbine in cooperation with the MC and possibly the female foreman. The turbine sucks the old security guard into it and shreds him.

Then we establish that the black friend is a ghost and how it happened (briefly), and then, together with whoever is left, they go to confront the cyborg who is processing the uplink to the mainframe.

5. At the end of the book, the ghost joins with the cyborg, and they fight together as one. She is "possessed" by the ghost, and as such, he can affect and enhance the cyborg's mechanical parts. They go into overdrive, and the two of them together become of one mind—one really brilliant, dangerous mind. And they try to kill everyone. They succeed in killing almost everyone.

6. When the human part of the cyborg is injured, perhaps the ghost can use his powers to shock/defibrillate her back to life. Perhaps the MC uses his cyborg arm to trick the ghost into locking itself within his arm, and then he can destroy the arm and dissipate the ghost's energy?

7. The story ends... somehow. It'll become clearer as you write it what should happen. Either the mine blows up, or they save everything and defeat the ghost/cyborg, or something. The mine probably has to get blown up because of all the mutated folks running around. I guess we'll see.

The friend who is also an energy ghost will also need to be involved, especially if he turns on the turbines. He can possibly operate in the background and deactivate the mainframe using the master code, which he can get from the MC if they join up at any point (as in, if the friend jumps into the MC's cyborg arm—he could extract the info from the arm directly).

Perhaps: both ghosts enter cyborg's body. Good ghost begins shutting it down, while bad ghost tries to keep her active. They fight each other from within. He disconnects her leg first, then her arm, then her heart. She still manages to get to the computer terminal to destroy the mine, but the good ghost buys enough time to save his friends.

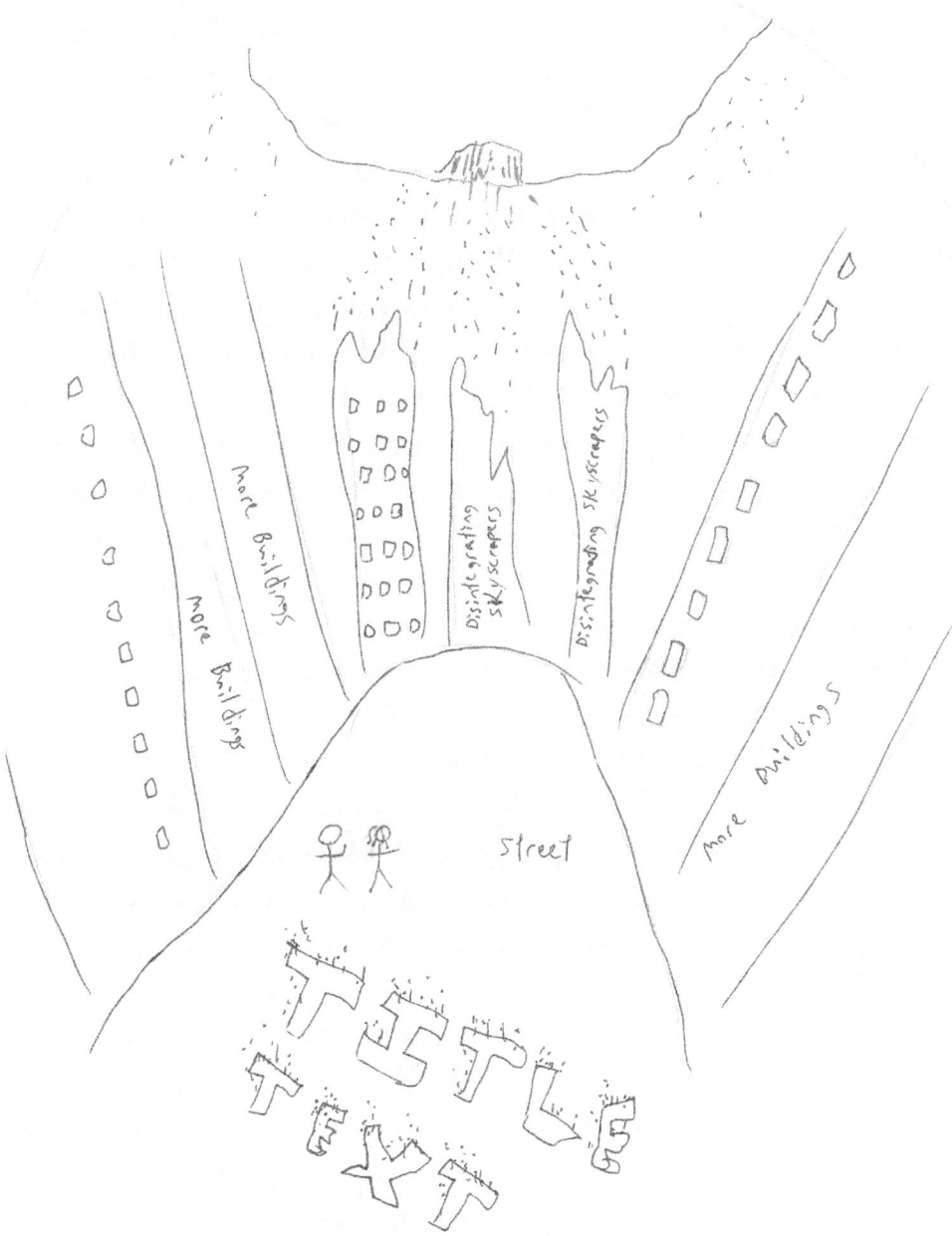

More Buildings

More Buildings

More Buildings

Disintegrating skyscrapers

Disintegrating skyscrapers

street

TITLE TEXT

CONCLUSION

Well, that was an adventure.

If you haven't drowned in information yet, then congrats! That means you probably have what it takes to write great stories and succeed as an author. Or, at the very least, you have a wicked backstroke.

Now that you've got a better sense of how to create a functional story bible, it's time for you to get started.

If you're a plot-first writer, start with your plot.

If you're a character-first author, start with your character(s).

If you're drawn into stories by colorful story worlds, start building yours, and then figure out the rest.

REMEMBER:
Your story bible doesn't have to be perfect,
but it does have to be *functional.*

If you're still struggling with how to get going, even after reading all of this, here's an easy five-point checklist you can follow to rev your writer engine and start your story bible out right:

STORY BIBLE SETUP CHECKLIST

1. **Decide on your high concept (in other words, decide which story you're going to write).** Make sure you pick a good one that will keep you engaged as you write, and that will make readers gasp and say, "that's a great idea!"

2. **Pick out your "method" for how you're going to try to create your story bible.** Are you going to open a new spreadsheet and start filling in all those miserable little boxes with crucial information? Maybe you'll open Notes like I do and brain-dump whatever comes to mind. Or if handwriting is your thing, write it in a journal or on a napkin—and watch out for my lipstick print on there—just transfer it to the computer later on so it's easier to search and maintain.

3. **Set up your story bible.** Obviously, you should download a free template story bible at **www.benwolf.com/Power-Author**. As I've said all along, there are no strings attached, and you can access the templates I use for my own writing absolutely free. Alternatively, if you think another format or breakdown will work better, then use that instead.

4. **Pick a starting point for your story bible.** What is the most vivid aspect or element of your story right now? Start by filling in details about that section first. If you've got the same writer's curse as I do, that will spiral you into a half dozen other sections, and you'll start making notes in each of those as well. This process can last as long as you can stand to write your ideas and details down. Once the well runs dry, either take a break or dig a new well.

5. **Don't forget this crucial factor:** Your story bible isn't done until your book or your book series concludes. As such, I don't want you getting discouraged at first when you see way more blank pages and sections than what details you've filled in. You're *building* a story bible after all, not blasting one into existence like the Death Star blowing up Alderaan in reverse.

Whatever you do, start writing. Start writing now, in fact.

Don't sit there wasting time thinking about how handsome I am and how great this book was.

Get up, go to your computer or journal or feather and inkwell and parchment, and start logging every detail you can think of about your story world.

Claim your rightful power as the god/goddess of your story world.

Get busy. Get creative.
Make the magic happen.

✿

One last thing.

If this is daunting to you, and you'd like some help, contact me. My direct email is ben@benwolf.com.

Yes, I'm serious.

I do my best to reply to every email I receive, and I'd like to answer any questions you may have about this book, my creative process, or the principles contained within.

If you want to get super serious about your writing and want help making it your career, I also offer amazing author coaching services for exorbitant fees (we're talking firstborn child-level rates) and high-end editing services (in exchange for your immortal soul).

You can find my breathtaking qualifications for both of these offerings (and more) on my website at www.benwolf.com/editing-services.

✿

And don't forget to claim your freebies at
WWW.BENWOLF.COM/POWER-AUTHOR.

✿

Happy writing!

ACKNOWLEDGEMENTS

Every published book is the culmination of a lot of hard work, dedication, and support. The author writes the book, but everything that comes after is equally as essential to the success of the book.

First of all, thank YOU for reading this book. I had a blast putting it together, but it was by no means a solo effort.

Second, thanks to my parents for believing in me from an early age and for helping to support my dreams and my growth. I love you both.

Thank you to Jesus Christ for changing my life (and the world).

Thanks to my all-star beta readers, Daniel Kuhnley, Luke Messa, and Paige Guido, for your excellent feedback and encouragement.

Thanks also to my mastermind group. It's a secret group, but you all know who you are. (insert evil laugh)

Jenneth Dyck, you really knocked this cover out of the park! Brilliant work. The covers for this series are phenomenal, especially since so many nonfiction covers are mind-numbingly boring. This one totally stands out! Thank you for your incredible work (and patience with me).

Dirty Mike Hueser and the BJJ boys, thanks for keeping me frosty.

And thanks to all my readers! Without you, I wouldn't be doing this.

Last of all, thank you especially to my intelligent, beautiful, thoughtful, and ultra-supportive wife, Charis Crowe. Your flexibility with my weird writing schedule for this series made all the difference in me getting everything done.

I love you.

About Ben Wolf

In 7th grade, I saw the movie *Congo*. It was so bad, I wrote a parody of it that was set in Australia (instead of Africa) and featured killer kangaroos instead of gorillas. So began my writing career.

I've spoken at 50+ writers conferences and multiple comic cons nationwide. When not writing, I like to choke my friends in Brazilian jiujitsu. I live in the Midwest with my gorgeous wife and our cat, Marco.

Check out my other books on amazon.com/author/benwolf:

If you enjoyed this book and want updates on future projects, join my author email newsletter for occasional updates on forthcoming stories.

Sign up now!

WWW.SUBSCRIBEPAGE.COM/FANTASY-READERS

Want to connect with me directly? Find me on Social Media!

facebook.com/1benwolf

instagram.com/1benwolf

amazon.com/author/benwolf

www.ingramcontent.com/pod-product-compliance
Lightning Source LLC
Chambersburg PA
CBHW070744270326
41927CB00010B/2089